# Project
# Management
## FOR

# DUMMIES®
### UK EDITION

# Project Management

## FOR

# DUMMIES®

## UK EDITION

# by Nick Graham and Stanley E. Portny

A John Wiley and Sons, Ltd, Publication

**Project Management For Dummies®, UK Edition**

Published by
**John Wiley & Sons, Ltd**
The Atrium
Southern Gate
Chichester
West Sussex
PO19 8SQ
England

E-mail (for orders and customer service enquires): cs-books@wiley.co.uk

Visit our Home Page on www.wiley.com

For general information on our other products and services, please contact our Customer Care Department within the U.S. at 877-762-2974, outside the U.S. at 317-572-3993, or fax 317-572-4002.

For technical support, please visit www.wiley.com/techsupport.

Wiley also publishes its books in a variety of electronic formats. Some content that appears in print may not be available in electronic books.

British Library Cataloguing in Publication Data: A catalogue record for this book is available from the British Library

ISBN: 978-0-470-71119-4 (paperback), 978-0-470-97219-9 (ebk), 978-0-470-97299-1 (ebk), 978-0-470-97298-4 (ebk)

Printed and bound in Great Britain by Bell & Bain, Ltd., Glasgow

10  9  8  7  6  5  4  3  2

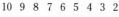

# *About the Authors*

**Nick Graham** is the founder and Managing Director of Inspirandum Ltd, a small and specialised company focused on achieving excellence in project management. In his company he has set very clear objectives to teach all project approaches and methods in a practical way so that they can be applied intelligently and productively.

With a career that has covered both the public sector and the private sector, Nick is able to communicate readily with managers in both communities and he's been involved in project consultancy and training for more than 17 years. Nick's experience with structured methods in projects goes back much further where he has specialised in the PRINCE2™ method and is the author of another fine book, *PRINCE2 For Dummies*. More recently he has been involved as joint author of the new, simple-to-use and business-based project management method, PRIME.

Nick is an experienced project practitioner, trainer and author, and he's also a qualified teacher. He runs project management and project risk training events worldwide for companies both large and small, public sector organisations and charities. Those attending his training events have described his style as energetic, lively, fun, very practical and very informative. Nick's consultancy work has ranged from helping to plan individual projects to advising senior managers on how to implement a project method throughout their organisation.

When not away on consultancy or training assignments, Nick lives in Weymouth in Dorset, UK. His wife Kath also works for Inspirandum.

Nick is a member of the Association for Project Management (APM) and the Institute of Directors (IoD).

www.inspirandum.com

**Stan Portny,** president of Stanley E. Portny and Associates, LLC, is an internationally recognised expert in project management and project leadership. During the past 30 years, he's provided training and consultation to more than 150 public and private organisations in consumer products, insurance, pharmaceuticals, finance, information technology, telecommunications, defence and healthcare. He has developed and conducted training programmes for more than 50,000 management and staff personnel in engineering, sales and marketing, research and development, information systems, manufacturing, operations and support areas.

Stan combines an analyst's eye with an innate sense of order and balance and a deep respect for personal potential. He helps people understand how to control chaotic environments and produce dramatic results while still achieving personal and professional satisfaction. Widely acclaimed for his dynamic presentations and unusual ability to establish a close rapport with seminar participants, Stan specialises in tailoring his training programmes to meet the unique needs of individual organisations. His clients have included ADP, ADT, American International Group, Burlington Northern Railroad, Hewlett Packard, Nabisco, Novartis Pharmaceuticals, Pitney Bowes, UPS, Vanguard Investment Companies and the United States Navy and Air Force.

A Project Management Institute-certified Project Management Professional (PMP), Stan received his bachelor's degree in electrical engineering from the Polytechnic Institute of Brooklyn. He holds a master's degree in electrical engineering and the degree of electrical engineer from the Massachusetts Institute of Technology. Stan has also studied at the Alfred P. Sloan School of Management and the George Washington University National Law Center.

Stan provides on-site training in all aspects of project management, project team building and project leadership. Web site www.StanPortny.com.

# Dedication

**From Nick:** This UK edition of *Project Management For Dummies* is dedicated to Max, one of my grandsons, who with his bright outlook on life, awesome bilingual capability at age 7 and infectious laugh, is an inspiration.

**From Stan:** To my wife, Donna; my son, Brian; and my son and daughter-in-law, Jonathan and Marci. May we continue to share life's joys together.

# Authors' Acknowledgements

**From Nick:** Writing a book, even when partly based on an existing text, is a long and hard job. I want to thank David Palmer at John Wiley for his vision, support and encouragement which was such a boost to me. Also Simon Bell at John Wiley whose support and input as editor is always so valuable. I have learned to listen very carefully to Simon because though he doesn't say much, when he does he's invariably right.

At home I have, as always, to thank my wife Kath. Running a small business is usually demanding and Kath takes so much of the pressure to leave me in peace while I work away at the keyboard having fun.

Finally I must thank my friend Philipp Straehl from whom I have learned so much in project management, and also those who have attended Inspirandum's project training events. Even when delivering training I am constantly learning more and more about projects as course members share their own insights even while learning material from me. It's very much a two-way street and I am privileged indeed to have worked with so many kind and intelligent people.

**From Stan:** Writing and publishing this book was a team effort, and I would like to thank the many people who helped to make it possible. First, I want to thank Tracy Boggier, my acquisitions editor, who first contacted me to discuss the possibility of my writing the latest edition of my book. Thanks to her for making that phone call, for helping me prepare the proposal, for helping to get the project off to a smooth and timely start, for coordinating the publicity and sales, and for helping to bring all the pieces to a successful conclusion. Thanks to Georgette Beatty, my project editor, and Amanda Langferman, my copy editor, for their guidance, support, and the many hours they spent polishing the text into a smooth, finished product. And thanks to Anita Griner, my technical reviewer, for her many insightful observations and suggestions. Finally, thanks to my family for their continued help and inspiration. Thanks to Donna, who never doubted that this book would become a reality and who shared personal and stylistic comments as she reviewed the text countless times while always making it seem like she found it enjoyable and enlightening. Thanks to Brian, Jonathan, and Marci, whose interest and excitement helped motivate me to see the book through to completion.

## Publisher's Acknowledgements

We're proud of this book; please send us your comments through our Dummies online registration form located at www.dummies.com/register/.

Some of the people who helped bring this book to market include the following:

*Commissioning, Editorial, and Media Development*

**Project Editor:** Simon Bell

*(Previous Edition: Georgette Beatty)*

**Commissioning Editor:** David Palmer

*(Previous Edition: Tracy Boggier)*

**Assistant Editor:** Ben Kemble

**Copy Editor:** Charlie Wilson

**Technical Editor:** Anita Griner

**Publisher:** David Palmer

**Production Manager:** Daniel Mersey

**Cover Photos:** © Imagebroker/Alamy

**Cartoons:** Ed McLachlan

*Composition Services*

**Project Coordinator:** Kristie Rees

**Layout and Graphics:** Vida Noffsinger

**Indexer:** Ty Koontz

# Contents at a Glance

# Table of Contents

# Introduction

**P**rojects have been around since ancient times. Noah building the ark, Leonardo da Vinci painting the *Mona Lisa*, Edward Gibbon writing *The Decline and Fall of the Roman Empire*, Jonas Salk developing the polio vaccine – all projects. And, as you know, these projects were all masterful successes. (Well, the products were a spectacular success, even if schedules and resource budgets were sometimes overrun!)

Why, then, is the topic of project management of such great interest today? The answer is simple: the audience has changed and the stakes are higher.

Historically, projects were large, complex undertakings. The first project to use modern project management techniques – the development of the Polaris weapons system in the early 1950s – was a technical and administrative nightmare. Teams of specialists planned and tracked the myriad of research, development and production activities. They produced mountains of paper to document the intricate work. As a result, people started to view project management as a highly technical discipline with confusing charts and graphs; they saw it as inordinately time consuming, specialist driven and definitely off limits for the common man or woman!

Because of the ever-growing array of huge, complex and technically challenging projects in today's world, people who want to devote their careers to planning and managing them are still vital to the projects' success. Over the past 25–30 years, however, the number of projects in the regular workplace has skyrocketed. Projects of all types and sizes are now *the* way that organisations accomplish work involving development and change.

At the same time, a new breed of Project Manager has emerged. This new breed may not have set career goals to become Project Managers – many among them don't even consider themselves to be Project Managers. But they do know that they must successfully manage projects to move ahead in their careers. Clearly, project management has become a critical management skill for many, not just a career choice for a few.

Even though these Project Managers realise they need special tools, techniques and knowledge to handle their new types of assignments, they may not be able to devote large amounts of time to acquiring them, which is where this book comes in. This book is devoted to that vast majority of Project Managers.

# About This Book

This book helps you recognise that the basic tenets of successful project management are simple. The book provides information and explains powerful techniques that help you plan and manage projects successfully. Here, you discover that the real challenge to a successful project is dealing with the multitude of people whom a project may affect or need for support. You find plenty of tips, hints and guidelines for identifying key people and then involving them.

But knowledge alone won't make you a successful Project Manager – you need to apply it. This book's theme is that project management skills and techniques aren't burdensome tasks you perform because some process requires it. Rather, they're a way of thinking, communicating and behaving to help you achieve successful delivery. They're an integral part of how people approach all aspects of their work every day.

We've written the book to be direct and easy to understand. But don't be misled – the simple text still navigates all the critical tools and techniques you'll need to support your project planning, scheduling, budgeting, organising and controlling.

You'll find that we present the information in a logical and modular progression. Examples and illustrations are plentiful – so are the tips and hints. And there's some humour from time to time to keep the writing down to earth. The idea is that you finish this book feeling that good project management is a necessity and that you're determined to practise it!

# Conventions Used in This Book

To help you navigate through this book, we use the following conventions:

- *Italics* point out new words and alert you to their definitions, which are always close by. On occasion, italics also add emphasis.
- **Bold** text indicates keywords in bulleted lists or highlights action parts in numbered lists.

We avoid web addresses because they change and the information so quickly goes out of date. However, the text gives enough information for you to search for a particular site or reference.

# What You're Not to Read

Of course, we want you to read every single word, but we understand that your life is busy and you may have time to read only what's relevant to your experience. In that case, feel free to skip the sidebars. Although the sidebars offer interesting supplementary information and real-life stories, they're not vital to grasping the concepts.

# Foolish Assumptions

When writing this book, we assumed that a widely diverse group of people will read it, including the following:

- Senior managers and junior managers (tomorrow's senior managers)
- Experienced Project Managers and people who've never been on a project team
- People who've had significant project management training and want to catch up on the latest ideas, and people who've had none
- People who've had years of real-world business and government experience, and people who've just started work

We assume that you have a desire to take control of your environment. After reading this book, we hope you wonder (and rightfully so) why all projects aren't well managed – because you'll think these techniques are so logical, straightforward and easy to use. But we also assume you recognise that a big difference exists between *knowing* what to do and *doing* it. You'll have to work hard to overcome pressures that conspire to prevent you from using these tools and techniques. Pressures include any people senior to you who think that if you don't plan and control a project properly, it all works out fine just the same, only you'll have saved time and so deliver faster. Interestingly, the same people don't take that view when organising their family holidays.

Finally, you'll find that you can read this book repeatedly and find out something new each time. Think of this book as a comfortable resource that has more to share as you experience new situations.

# How This Book Is Organised

Each chapter is self-contained, so you can read the chapters that interest you the most first, without feeling lost because you haven't read the book from front to back. The book is divided into the following six parts.

# Part I: Understanding Projects and What You Want to Achieve

The first part discusses the unique characteristics of projects and the key issues you may encounter in a project-oriented organisation. We look at the life of a project and then focus on its justification – the Business Case – before looking at identifying and managing stakeholders in the project.

# Part II: Building the Plans

Part II is fun and practical because it covers the various dimensions of planning, including the very powerful front end to planning, *product led* or *product based* planning. We go on to show you how to develop the project schedule and estimate the resources (both the people and physical resources such as equipment) you need. Then we turn to the essential areas of financial planning and risk management.

# Part III: Putting Your Management Team Together

You won't have much success in projects unless you get the people side right. All the plans in the world won't help if your people aren't functioning well. This part covers roles and responsibilities in the project, and then goes on to discuss leadership within the project and how to motivate your team members for success.

# Part IV: Steering the Project to Success

Planning is vital, but after the project is running, you must keep it on track. This part explains how to monitor, track, analyse and report on your project's progress and what to do if it goes off track. We also cover the vital area of communications to help you avoid the communications problems that are one of the highest causes of project failure. The part finishes by looking at the end of the project: how to shut down and determine its success.

## Part V: Taking Your Project Management to the Next Level

This section gives you a bit more in your toolbox to take your project management forward. It covers the powerful Earned Value Management technique and also takes a look at programmes (groups of projects) and portfolios and gives you some hints on where to find useful software to help you with your project management – and the good news is that if you are short of funds, you can get a lot of really good software (and that really does mean good) for free.

## Part VI: The Part of Tens

Every *For Dummies* book has this fun part that gives you tidbits of information in an easy-to-chew format. In this part you'll find tips on project planning, writing a convincing Business Case and how to be a better Project Manager.

# Icons Used in This Book

The small icons in the left margins of the book are to alert you to special information in the text. Here's what they mean:

This icon gives a real or hypothetical situation to illustrate a particular point we make in the main text.

We use this icon to point out terms or issues that are a bit more technical, or at least that sound more technical.

This icon to points out important information you want to keep in mind as you apply the techniques and approaches.

The Tip icon highlights something you can use to improve your project management practices.

This icon highlights potential pitfalls and dangers.

# *Where to Go from Here*

You can read this book in many ways, depending on your own project management knowledge and experience and your current needs. However, it's worth starting out by taking a minute to scan the table of contents and thumb through the sections of the book to get a feeling for the topics.

If you're new to project management and are just beginning to form a plan for a project, first read Parts I and II, which explain how to plan outcomes, activities, schedules and resources. If you want to find out how to identify and organise your project's team and other key people, start with Chapter 11 and Part III. If you're ready to begin work or you're already in the midst of your project, you may want to start with Part IV to look for advice on keeping things on track. Or feel free to jump back and forth, hitting the chapters that contain the topics that interest you the most.

No matter how you make your way through this book, plan on reading all the chapters more than once – the more you read a chapter, the more sense its approaches and techniques will make. And who knows? A change in your job responsibilities may create a need for certain techniques you've never used before. Have fun!

# Part I
# Understanding Projects and What You Want to Achieve

'And now, to tell you about micromanagement, we have an expert to talk to us.'

Part I

Understanding
Projects and What
Key You Want to
Achieve

# In this part . . .

**P**rojects are different from ordinary 'business as usual' work. This first part helps you understand more about the nature of projects, how they are structured and why they are needed. It also helps you answer the question 'Is this really a project?'.

# Chapter 1

# Project Management: The Key to Achieving Results

*O*rganisations are constantly changing, and ever faster, as they adapt to new market conditions, new financial conditions, new business practices, new legal requirements and new technology. Running projects often creates the change, and as a result businesses are increasingly driven to find individuals who can excel in this project-oriented environment.

## Taking on a Project

Because you're reading this book, the chances are that you've been asked to manage a project for the first time or that you're already running projects and are looking to see whether you can find easier and better ways of doing things. If the project is indeed your first one, that's a challenge and may well give you the chance to excel in something you haven't done before; for many, managing a project even opens a door to a new career. Try not to think of project management as a career death threat, even if others do and they now avoid looking you in the eye when passing you in the corridor. The really good news here, whether you're completely new or have some experience, is that project management has been around for a very long time. In that time, Project Managers have come up with highly effective strategies and a range of very practical techniques. You can benefit from all that experience, and this book takes you through all you need to know.

So, hang on tight – you're going to need an effective set of skills and techniques to steer your projects to successful completion. This chapter gets you off to a great start by showing you what projects and project management really are and by helping you separate projects from non-project assignments. The chapter also offers some insight on why projects succeed or fail and starts to get you into the project management mindset.

# Avoiding the Pitfalls

By following a sound approach to the project, you automatically avoid many of the pitfalls that continue to contribute to, or cause, project failure on a mind-boggling scale. You may ask why, if good ways of doing things exist, people ignore them and then have their projects fail. Good question. People make the same project mistakes repeatedly, and they're largely avoidable. You may have come across the joke by comedian Tommy Cooper:

> *I went to the doctor and said 'Every time I do this, it hurts.'*
> *The doctor said, 'Well, don't do it then.'*

A national public project run in the UK to create a database of offenders for use by the Prison Service, Probation Service and others has attracted heavy criticism for poor management. The National Audit Office, which checks up on government departments, investigated and reported that the project was delayed by three years, and the budget was double the original, but the scope had been radically cut back. Edward Leigh MP, chairman of the powerful Public Accounts Committee in Parliament described the scheme as a 'spectacular failure' and 'a master-class in sloppy project management'.

The following list takes a quick look at the main causes of project failure (we address each of these causes in later chapters in the book). The list makes for depressing reading, particularly if you recognise some elements in parts of your own organisation. Nevertheless, the list gives a good background against which to contrast successful project management and the approach and techniques that we set down in this book.

- **Lack of clear objectives:** Nobody's really sure what the project is about, much less are people agreed on it.

- **Lack of risk management:** Things go wrong that someone could easily have foreseen and then controlled to some degree or even prevented.

- **No senior management 'buy in':** Senior managers were never convinced and so never supported the project, leading to problems such as lack of resource. Neither did those managers exercise normal management supervision as they routinely do in their other areas of responsibility.

- **Poor planning:** Actually, that's being kind, because often the problem is that no planning was done at all. It's not surprising, then, when things run out of control, and not least because nobody knows where the project should be at this point anyway.

✔ **No clear progress milestones:** This follows on from poor planning. The lack of milestones means nobody sees when things are off track, and problems go unnoticed for a long time.

✔ **Understated scope:** The scope and the Project Plan are superficial and understate both what the project needs to deliver and the resource needed to deliver it. Project staff (often team members) then discover the hidden but essential components later in the project. The additional work that is necessary then takes the project out of control, causing delay to the original schedule and overspending against the original budget.

✔ **Poor communications:** So many projects fail because of communication breakdown, which can stem from unclear roles and responsibilities and from poor senior management attitudes, such as not wanting to hear bad news.

✔ **Unrealistic resource levels:** It just isn't possible to do a project of the required scope with such a small amount of resource – staff, money or both.

✔ **Unrealistic timescales:** The project just can't deliver by the required time, so it's doomed to failure.

✔ **No change control:** People add in things bit by bit – scope creep. Then it dawns on everyone that the project's grown so big that it can't be delivered within the fixed budget or by the set deadline.

That's ten reasons for failure, but you can probably think of a few more. The interesting thing about these problems is that avoiding them is, for the most part, actually not that difficult.

# Deciding Whether the Job Is Really a Project

Before you start to think too deeply about how to set up the project, the first thing to do is check whether it really is one. No matter what your job is, you handle a myriad of assignments every day: prepare a memo, hold a meeting, design a sales campaign or move to new offices. Not all these assignments are projects. So what makes something a project?

You can consider three easy areas to determine whether a job is a project:

✔ Is it a one-off job or something that's ongoing? If the job is ongoing, like producing bars of soap on a production line or taking customer orders, then it's business as usual, not a project.

✔ Does the job justify project controls? Project management means incurring some overheads, although in this book we offer advice on how to keep overheads to the minimum. But the fact remains that overheads exist and some jobs are so small or straightforward that they just don't justify that degree of control.

✔ This last one may sound a little weird, and it certainly doesn't fit with the formal definitions; it's the question, 'Do you want to handle the job as a project?' You may choose to deal with a block of work as a project, but I wouldn't – so, in some instances, you have a choice.

## Understanding the four control areas

Different project approaches have slightly different definitions of a project; here's one:

A *project* is a temporary undertaking performed to produce a unique product, service or result.

The 'unique product' is true, but don't let that put you off setting up projects that are effectively repeated, such as organising the annual company conference. Although, strictly speaking, the task is unique each time, you will nevertheless find large areas of commonality with previous projects, and you don't need to go and reinvent the wheel. For example, you can probably adapt last year's plans rather than starting from scratch.

Large or small, projects involve the following four areas of control:

✔ **Scope:** What the project will deliver

✔ **Time:** When the project will deliver

✔ **Quality:** So often forgotten, but an essential dimension

✔ **Resource:** Necessary amounts of people, funds and other resources such as equipment and accommodation that the project needs

You need to balance these areas for each project, and you can see immediately why so many projects get into difficulties. You look at a project, think about the four control factors and say to yourself, 'They want that scope, to that quality level, with just that resource and by then? They've got to be joking!' Strangely, organisational managers often commit projects to failure by insisting on unachievable deadlines or unrealistic resources. What's even stranger is that those same managers are surprised and even angry when the projects inevitably get into difficulties and fail.

Getting the balance right in the early part of the project when you do the main scoping and planning is, obviously enough, essential. Jerry Madden of NASA, the American space agency, produced a great document called 'One Hundred Rules for NASA Project Managers'. Rule 15 is:

> *The seeds of problems are laid down early. Initial planning is the most vital part of a project. The review of most failed projects or project problems indicate the disasters were well planned to happen from the start.*

It's also useful to think about the four areas of control when dealing with change in the project. Chapter 14 includes a 'four dog' model to help you think about the interdependences. Although many other considerations may affect a project's performance, these four components are the basis of a project's definition for the following reasons:

- ✔ The only reason a project exists is to produce the results specified in its scope.

- ✔ The project's end date is usually an essential part of defining what constitutes successful performance – in many cases, the project must provide the desired result by a certain time to meet its intended need.

- ✔ The quality requirement is a vital part of the balance and may be the most important element, even though many organisational managers are preoccupied with time and cost. But what's the point of delivering an unusable heap of garbage on time and within budget?

- ✔ The availability of resources can affect which products the project can produce and the timescale in which it can produce them.

Quality can be a very important factor, and is sometimes the most important, so do think about it carefully. A project to build and install a new air traffic control system for the south of the UK was criticised for being over budget and late on delivery. As a number of people have pointed out, though, if you're sitting in an aeroplane circling while waiting to land at London Heathrow Airport – one of the world's busiest – would you rather that they'd got the air traffic control system in on time and to budget or that they'd got it right?

## Recognising the diversity of projects

Projects come in a wide assortment of shapes and sizes. For example, projects can:

- ✔ **Be large or small:**
    - Building a new railway link across London, which will cost around £16 billion and take seven years to complete, is a project, perhaps linked to other projects to form a programme.
    - Preparing the annual report for the department, which may take you six days to complete, may also be a project.

- ✔ **Involve many people or just you:**
    - Training all 10,000 of your organisation's sales staff worldwide in the working of a new product is a project.

• Redecorating an office and rearranging the furniture and equipment is also a project.

✔ **Be defined by a legal contract or by an informal agreement:**

• A signed contract between you and a customer that requires you to build a house defines a project.

• An informal agreement by the IT department to install a new software package in a business area defines a project.

✔ **Be business related or personal:**

• Conducting your organisation's five-yearly strategy review is a project.

• Preparing for a family wedding is also a project – and a much more pleasant one than the five-yearly strategy review.

No matter what the individual characteristics of your project are, you can use the same four elements of scope, time, quality and resource to think it through.

---

# A project by any other name – just isn't a project

People often confuse the following two terms with *project*:

✔ **Process:** A *process* is a series of routine steps to perform a particular function, such as a procurement process or a budget process. A process isn't a one-time activity that achieves a specific result; instead, it defines *how* you do a particular function every time. Processes such as the activities that go into buying materials are often parts of projects.

✔ **Programme:** This term can describe two different situations. First, a *programme* can be a set of goals that gives rise to specific projects, but, unlike a project, you can never accomplish this sort of programme completely. For example, a health-awareness programme can never completely achieve its goal (the public will never be totally aware of all health issues as a result of a health-awareness programme). More commonly, though, a *programme* (sometimes controlled with programme management) is a set of projects that need to be coordinated in some way. Perhaps it's a strategic programme to change the whole way the organisation works, or perhaps it's a group of projects with significant interdependencies that all need to be managed to finish at the same time. See Chapter 17 for more on programmes.

# *Understanding the four stages of a project*

Every project, whether large or small, passes through four stages:

- ✔ **Starting the Project:** This stage involves generating, evaluating and framing the business need for the project and the general approach to performing it, and agreeing to prepare a detailed Project Plan. Outputs from this stage may include approval to proceed to the next stage, documentation of the need for the project, and rough estimates of time and resources to perform it, and an initial list of people who may be interested in, involved with or affected by the project.

- ✔ **Organising and Preparing:** This stage involves developing a plan that specifies the desired results: the work to do; the time, the cost and other resources required; and a plan for how to address key project risks. Outputs from this stage include a Project Plan documenting the intended project results and the time, resources and supporting processes to help create them, along with all the other controls that the project needs, such as for risk management.

- ✔ **Carrying Out the Work:** This stage involves performing the planned work, monitoring and controlling performance to ensure adherence to the current plan, and doing the more detailed planning of successive phases as the project continues. Outputs from this stage may include project progress reports, financial reports and further detailed plans.

- ✔ **Closing the Project:** This stage involves assessing the project results, obtaining customer approvals, assigning project team members to new work, closing financial accounts and conducting a post-project evaluation. Outputs from this stage may include final, accepted and approved project results and recommendations and suggestions for applying lessons learned from this project to similar efforts in the future.

For small projects, this entire life-cycle can take a few days. For larger projects, it can take years! Chapter 2 goes though these stages – the life of your project – in more detail so you can see exactly what you need to be doing and when.

In a perfect world, projects run smoothly and always go exactly to plan. However, because you don't live in a perfect world and because your project certainly won't be running in one, you need to be flexible. When starting to think about your project, you need to allow for:

- ✔ **The unknown and uncertain:** Projects are rarely 100 per cent predictable. The normal territory of projects is that, to some extent at least, you're going into the unknown. Therefore, your plans need to allow for things going off track. Sometimes the uncertain areas are predictable, which falls partly into the area of risk management (see Chapter 10 for how to assess and manage risks). Sometimes the areas aren't at all predictable, and that comes into the area of contingency. You need contingency; remember Murphy's Law – 'If it can go wrong, it will go wrong.' We talk about contingency in Chapter 10.

✔ **Learning by doing:** Despite doing your best to assess feasibility and develop good plans at the front end of the project, you may find later on that you can't achieve what you thought you could or in the way you thought you could. When this situation happens, you need to rethink in the light of the new information you've acquired. Sometimes you can see up front that you won't know how a particular part of the project is going to work out until you get nearer to that point and better information is to hand. Don't worry about that; just point it out clearly at the beginning.

✔ **Unexpected change:** Your initial feasibility and benefits assessments are sound, and your plan is detailed and realistic. However, certain key project team members leave the organisation without warning during the project. Or a new technology emerges, and it's more appropriate to use than the one in your original plans. Perhaps the business environment changes and with it your organisation's whole market strategy. Because ignoring these occurrences may seriously jeopardise your project's success, you need to rethink and re-plan in light of these new realities.

# Defining the Project Manager's Role

The Project Manager's job is to manage the project on a day-to-day basis to bring it to a successful conclusion. He'll usually be accountable to a senior manager who's the project sponsor, or to a small group of managers who form a project steering committee or project board. The Project Manager's job is challenging. For instance, he often coordinates technically specialised professionals – who may have limited experience working together – to achieve a common goal.

It's important to understand that the Project Manager's position is indeed a role; it's not about status. That's true of all roles in the project and there may, for example, be very senior people working as team members (such as chief engineers and legal advisers) who are accountable to the Project Manager even though in the normal business they're very much his senior. Both team members and the Project Manager himself must understand that he has responsibility and authority in the project that comes with the role, independent of his organisational grade or rank. When the Project Manager has a clear accountability to a sponsor or steering committee, life is much easier because everyone can see that his authority comes from them. It's the same mechanism that allows a corporal on the gate of a military camp to refuse entry to a general until he's satisfied that the general's security pass is valid.

The Project Manager doesn't do any of the technical work of the project in his role as Project Manager. If he's involved in technical work it's with a different hat on – that of a team member. The distinction is important because if you're doing teamwork as well as project managing, you must be clear about both roles and only wear one hat at a time. It's all too easy to neglect the management and let the project run out of control because you're so engrossed in the detail and challenges of your part of the technical work.

The Project Manager's role requires hard skills such as planning and costing, but also soft people skills, and his success requires a keen ability to identify and resolve sensitive organisational and interpersonal issues. The next section covers the main tasks that a Project Manager handles and notes potential challenges that he may encounter.

## *Looking at the Project Manager's tasks*

Your role as the Project Manager is one of day-to-day responsibility for the project, and that might involve so much work that your job must necessarily be a full-time one. Or it may be that the project is smaller and less complicated and project management is just part of your job. Either way, the responsibilities are the same; it's just the scale and complexity that are different.

Here's a summary of the main tasks. Some things on the list involve consultation with others:

- ✔ Sketch out initial ideas for the project, with the justification, outline costs and timescales.
- ✔ Plan the project, including mapping out the controls that will be put in place, defining what quality the project needs and how it will be achieved, analysing risk and planning control actions.
- ✔ Control the flow of work to teams (or perhaps just team members in a smaller project).
- ✔ Motivate and support teams and team members.
- ✔ Liaise with external suppliers.
- ✔ Liaise with Project Managers of interfacing projects.
- ✔ Liaise with programme management staff if the project is one of a group of projects being coordinated as a programme.
- ✔ Ensure that the project deliverables are developed to the right level of quality.
- ✔ Keep track of progress and adjust to correct any minor drifts off the plan.
- ✔ Keep track of spending.
- ✔ Go to others, such as the steering committee, if things go more significantly off track (for example, the whole project is threatened).
- ✔ Report progress, such as to the sponsor or steering committee.
- ✔ Keep track of risks and make sure that control actions are taken.
- ✔ Deal with any problems, involving others as necessary.

- Decide on changes, getting approval from others where the Project Manager doesn't have personal authority to make a decision (for example, when changes involve very high cost).
- Plan successive delivery stages in more detail.
- Close the project down in an orderly way when everything's done.

So, the tasks will keep you very busy but also be very enjoyable if you're a Project Manager at heart.

A key to project success is being proactive. Get out in front of the project and direct where it's going. Don't follow on behind the project being reactive and having to fire-fight countless problems because you didn't see them coming.

## *Staving off potential excuses for not following a structured project management approach*

Be prepared for other people to oppose your attempts to use proven project management approaches. The following list provides a few examples of excuses you may encounter as a Project Manager and the appropriate responses you can give:

- **Excuse:** Our projects are all to short deadlines; we have no time to plan.

  **Response:** Unfortunately for the excuse giver, this logic is illogical! With a short deadline, you can't afford to make many mistakes. If it doesn't matter too much when the project delivers, you don't need as good a plan as if it matters very much and time is short.

- **Excuse:** Structured project management is only for large projects.

  **Response:** No matter what size the project is, the information you need to perform it is the same. What do you need to produce? What work has to be done? Who's going to do it? When will the project end? Have you met expectations?

- **Excuse:** Project management just means more overheads.

  **Response:** So does corporate management, and that's essential too! But in any case, if you don't manage a project properly and it fails, how much will that cost you in wasted time, money and lost benefits?

- **Excuse:** These projects require creativity and new development. You can't predict their outcomes with any certainty.

  **Response:** You can predict some projects' outcomes better than others. However, people awaiting the outcomes of any project still have expectations for what they'll get and when. Therefore, a project with many uncertainties needs a manager to develop and share initial plans and then to assess and communicate the effects of unexpected occurrences.

## Avoiding 'shortcuts'

The short-term pressures of your job, particularly if you're fitting in project management alongside other work, may tempt you to cut corners and miss things out. That's not the same as adjusting the project management needs to the project, but rather missing stuff out altogether that in an ideal world you would have done. Resist the temptation to cut corners, because usually doing so comes back and bites you later.

Don't be seduced into seemingly easier shortcuts such as:

- **Jumping directly from Starting the Project to Carrying Out the Work:** Sounds good, but you haven't defined the work to be done! A variation on this shortcut is: 'This project's been done before, so why plan it out again?' Even though projects can be similar to past ones, some elements will be different. Always check the plan thoroughly.

- **Failing to check progress at frequent intervals:** After all, everyone's working hard and things seem to be going okay. But just as when you're walking somewhere you need to check the map from time to time, so you need to check the project. Otherwise you won't see warning signs and may be a long way off track by the time you do eventually notice that something is wrong.

- **Not keeping the plan up to date:** That includes logging *actuals* such as the time actually taken to do things and the expense actually incurred. Yes, it takes discipline to stay up to date, but you'll never be able to control the project if you don't know where you are at the moment.

- **Not completing the closing stage:** At the end of one project, you can face pressure to move right on to the next. Scarce resources and short deadlines encourage this rapid movement, and starting a new project is always more challenging than wrapping up an old one. But you must make sure that everything is properly finished and, if necessary, handed over. You also need to check that the project has achieved what it's supposed to have done and that you and your organisation take on board any lessons, good and bad, for the future.

# Do You Have What It Takes?

You're reading this book because you want to be a good Project Manager, right? Well, try a quick quiz to see what your strengths and weaknesses are.

## Questions

1. Do you prefer to be everyone's friend or get the job done?

2. Do you prefer to do technical work or manage technical work?

3. Do you think the best way to get a tough task done is to do it yourself?

4. Do you prefer your work to be predictable or constantly changing?

5. Do you get immersed in the detail or can you hold on to the big picture?

6. Do you handle pressure well?

7. Do you like to plan and organise the work of others?

8. Do you think you shouldn't have to monitor people after they've said they'll do a job for you?

9. Do you see a need to motivate people, or do you leave them to get on with it because they should be self-motivated to perform their jobs?

10. Are you comfortable dealing with people at all organisational levels?

## Answers

1. Good working relations are vital, but you must also deliver the goods.

2. Management is exactly that, and you move away from hands-on stuff.

3. Your role is to manage, and that includes letting others develop.

4. No project ever goes exactly to plan and, anyway, things change. That's part of the challenge and also the buzz of project management.

5. You may need to deal with fine detail, but not at the expense of losing the big picture.

6. The Project Manager needs a cool head; some times will be pressured.

7. Being an organiser and planner goes with the territory.

8. Just like with general management, you have to know that work is getting done.

9. You need soft people skills too. Projects are about people.

10. The Project Manager must deal with people at all levels – from upper management to support staff – who perform project-related activities.

# Chapter 2

# Thinking Through the Life of Your Project

*T*his chapter covers the lifespan of the project from the initial idea through to closure. Sometimes seeing how things like business justification, planning and risk management fit into a project can be difficult until you have the big picture, so this chapter provides that big picture. It covers what you need to do and at what points, and it also mentions a couple of key project documents that you may find helpful.

# Being Methodical

Projects have a sequence from the first idea through to closure, and this chapter provides you with a clear structure, although it is simple. If, after reading this book, you want to move on to a more detailed approach, you can use a project methodology. A number of methodologies exist, such as:

✔ **PRINCE2® (PRojects IN a Controlled Environment):** Owned by the UK Government

✔ **PRIME (PRoject IMplementation Method):** A powerful but straightforward business-focused project method that Nick Graham, co-author of this book, has helped produce

Other methodologies include those associated with tools like Microsoft Project and those developed by most major consultancies for use with their clients. In all cases, methodologies offer a structure that takes you through your project. PRINCE2 is rather more complicated than most because it has processes that don't run in a straight sequence, and it uses rather obscure terminology that takes some study and, usually, training to understand. (Find out more in Nick's book *PRINCE2 For Dummies*, published by Wiley.) In contrast, this book sets out the work of project planning and management in a simple and linear way.

## Breaking the Project Down into Stages or Phases

Just about all project management approaches break projects into stages, or you may know them as *phases*. Chapter 1 set out the four main stages in any project:

- ✔ Starting the Project
- ✔ Organising and Preparing
- ✔ Carrying Out the Work
- ✔ Closing the Project

Of these stages, the third one – Carrying Out the Work – can repeat, so you can have more than one delivery stage. In a small project, you may decide on a single delivery stage, but in most projects you have several. You can see a project example with two delivery stages in Figure 2-1.

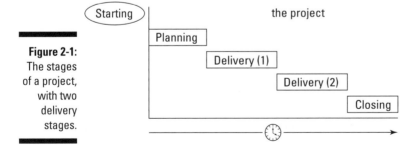

**Figure 2-1:**
The stages of a project, with two delivery stages.

Some say that the first stage, Starting the Project, isn't part of the project but is rather preparation beforehand to include things such as checking to make sure that the project really is a project. That's a logical argument, and Figure 2-1 reflects that view.

---

# The unofficial stages of a project

We're not sure who came up with these unofficial stages, but we like them!

✔ Enthusiasm

✔ Disillusionment

✔ Panic

✔ Search for the guilty

✔ Punishment of the innocent

✔ Praise and honour for the non-participants

---

If you go with the idea of Starting the Project not actually being part of the project, then the project starts for real with the full planning in the second stage. In a small project, starting with planning may not matter too much, unless the project has its own budget codes or, despite its size, different management responsibilities exist for the first two stages. Where you do have strict budgets to deal with, the work in starting a project is often financed out of a general fund, and if a project looks to be worthwhile, the budget code is opened for use from the beginning of the second stage.

## Appreciating the advantages of stages

Breaking the project into stages has many advantages. Take these four, for example:

✔ While not taking away from the big picture of the project, it allows everyone to concentrate on one part of the work at a time. One person described it as 'looking at one stair instead of the whole staircase'.

✔ It breaks up the detailed planning into convenient blocks, and you plan each delivery stage in detail just before that stage starts with the benefit of the very latest information available.

✔ It allows the sponsor or steering committee to stay in firm control of money and staff resource by authorising one stage at a time.

✔ It provides a clear point when each stage ends, usually called a *stage gate*, for checking that the project is still in control, is heading in the right direction, and remains viable and worth continuing.

## Deciding on the number of delivery stages

How many delivery stages should you have? Well, how long is a piece of string? Actually, you can answer the question about the string: it's exactly twice as long as half a piece. As for the delivery stages, it all depends.

The first thing to say about delivery stages is that they're not all the same length. They're not timed units of, say, one month long. Rather, delivery stages reflect two main criteria:

- Blocks of work that are cohesive and where things belong together
- Amounts of work that the sponsor or steering committee is willing to authorise at a time – the amount may vary at different points in the project according to, for example, the degree of risk in that part of the project

The end of each stage is marked by a stage gate meeting with the sponsor or steering committee. The stage gate is a useful control point to take stock and check that the project is still on track.

As to the number of stages overall, that's a control decision taken by the sponsor and it's very like supervision in general management. How much does your boss supervise you and how much do you supervise your staff? The level of supervision depends on a range of factors, including human factors, and it's exactly the same with a project. Partly because of human factors, no-one can say how many delivery stages there must be in a particular type of project. A more controlling steering committee may decide on four stages in a project. A more laid-back steering committee might have decided on just two stages for exactly the same project.

---

# A few stage decision factors

Some factors to bear in mind when deciding on stages:

- Stages should consist of sensible, cohesive blocks of work
- Set a maximum spend; for example no stage is to be more than £1 million, and you need a stage break just before that major investment in equipment to be sure the project is still okay
- Set a maximum time; for example no stage is to be longer than two months
- Consider breaks for important business events; for example financial year end or the publication of a major strategy review for the company that may trigger a substantial change to the project
- Consider how business critical the project is and the degree of risk involved
- Know who the Project Manager is: if the Project Manager is very experienced, then the sponsor may be happy with quite long stages and few of them, but if the Project Manager is inexperienced, then you need shorter stages and more of them

# *Understanding the Four Main Stages*

The rest of this chapter focuses on each of the stages in turn, looking at what you need to do at each stage and the main project management documents you deal with.

## *Starting the Project*

Three good reasons for having the Starting the Project stage:

- ✔ **You need to know whether the project is worth pursuing.** Lots of people have lots of ideas for projects, but unfortunately not all ideas are good ideas. Far too many projects start that simply shouldn't have. A common problem is that over-enthusiastic managers really want the project, have become emotionally attached to it (it's their 'baby'), have underestimated the cost and time, and have overestimated the business benefits. Rather than rushing into full planning, having a quick look at the idea makes sense before committing more time and resource to it.

- ✔ **You need to get basic information together.** You won't find it easy to go into stage two to plan the project if you haven't established, at least in outline, what the project is, what resource is available and any constraints such as on the delivery date.

- ✔ **You're best sketching out the idea for the project and getting everyone with an interest to agree to the idea before going on to full planning.** If you leap straight in to full planning because you think doing so saves time, you often discover that great disagreement exists when people check the plans, because they have very different ideas about the project even though they're using the same words.

  Habit 2 set out by Stephen Covey in his book *The 7 Habits of Highly Effective People* (Simon & Schuster) is: 'Begin with the end in mind'. To use Covey's illustration, before you climb a ladder, make sure that you've leaned it against the right wall. Starting the Project is leaning the ladder against the wall. If everyone agrees that the ladder's in the right place, you can climb the ladder and do the detailed planning. That's much better than climbing to the top and then finding out that you have to change a mass of detail, which takes much longer than the Starting the Project stage would have taken.

### *Understanding the characteristics*

The main thing to remember about Starting the Project is that you need to go fast. A common mistake is confusing Starting the Project with the next stage of Organising and Preparing, which takes a while. Conversely, the work in the Starting the Project stage may take a couple of weeks but it's more likely to be a couple of days and may just be a couple of hours, even for a fairly substantial project.

Imagine that you're a rich and successful Project Manager (or perhaps you don't have to imagine it) and you want a huge house built for you. You go to an architect and say, 'I'd like you to build a house for me please.' What does the architect reply – 'That's fine, I'll come back to you in eight weeks with some scaled drawings'? No, the architect says, 'That's fine. Please take a seat and let's talk about what you have in mind, and we'll do a sketch plan.' The architect starts with a sketch, not a beautifully finished scale drawing. So it is with Starting the Project. You do a sketch 'on the back of an envelope' to check whether the project idea is a good one and whether it's worth going on to full planning.

## Knowing what to do

In Starting the Project, you think roughly what the project is and whether it's worth continuing to the next stage to do the full planning. You look at six key areas:

- ✔ **Objective:** What exactly is the objective of the project? To save money perhaps, or speed up the ordering procedures? You need to discuss the objective with people who have an interest in the project to make sure everyone's clear on the objective(s), has thought things through and is then agreed.

- ✔ **Scope:** What's the project intended to cover and, usefully, what won't it cover if some areas are unclear? What will the project finally deliver? Scope is different from the objective. The objective may be to simplify your accounts procedure, but the scope shows that invoicing won't be included in this review, and the project will cover only offices in the European Union because those outside are subject to different types of financial regulation.

- ✔ **Resource:** How much do you expect the project to cost? Be realistic here. How much staff resource will the project likely need, and will it need particular skills? For example, if the project needs significant input from engineers and your engineers are already hard pressed, that's a major consideration when deciding whether to go ahead. The resource figures are very much ballpark ones at the moment because the planning has yet to be done.

- ✔ **Time:** How long is the project likely to take, on the assumption that resource can be provided when it's needed? This is a ballpark estimate.

- ✔ **Justification:** Why do you want to run the project? Perhaps this is a no-brainer because the project is mandatory – head office has instructed that each regional office runs a project to review its local client base. Normally, though, the project is justified because of benefits such as greater market penetration, lower costs or faster customer service.

- ✔ **Constraints:** Will anything influence the way that the project is run, or even what it delivers and when? For example, it might be time critical – if this project can't be delivered by the end of the financial year, then don't do it. You should also think about the required quality level of the project, such as whether it's 'quick and dirty', safety critical or, usually, somewhere in between.

### Thinking about management documents

Unless you have a very small project for which you can keep the full detail in your head, and nobody else needs to read anything about it, you're going to have to write some things down. The trick here is to keep documents to the minimum and to 'think wide' about how you communicate information. You can find more on documents in 'Organising and Preparing', later in the chapter.

Projects seem to attract paper (and the electronic equivalent) like doctors' surgeries do. The PRINCE2 method (see the earlier section 'Being Methodical') hasn't helped by using a large number of management documents, many of which are very detailed. This has contributed to a view that the method is bureaucratic to the point of actually working against projects by slowing them down unnecessarily. Remember that other people need to read and check everything you write down, so think very carefully about what you really need. The PRIME method has a catchphrase in its business-focused approach that's worth repeating here: 'If there's little to say, say little.' Keep your project documentation trimmed down or you'll drive up project costs and push out the delivery date.

For the Starting the Project stage, in nearly every project, you need to write down the information you find out in the form of a document that others, such as steering committee members, can read and then approve or reject. Different approaches call this document different things, and you may have heard of one or two. The terms include Project Terms of Reference, Project Outline, Project Blueprint and Project Brief.

Whatever label you attach to it, the Project Outline is exactly that – an outline. Don't get too detailed. The Project Outline covers enough to support the decision as to whether to go on to the next stage and full project planning or to stop right here. Although the information is in a document, you may well discuss the content in a meeting or give a short illustrated presentation to the decision makers and give out the document as a written backup.

## Organising and Preparing

Ah, so the members of the steering committee loved the idea, did they? Well done on your presentation of the Project Outline. Okay, on with the next stage then: roll your sleeves up and get down to the real work of project planning.

### Understanding the characteristics

The Organising and Preparing stage gets you ready for the delivery stages of the project. It covers the overall planning of the project, and also the detailed planning of the first delivery stage. If the sponsor or steering committee says 'go' at the end of the Organising and Preparing stage, the first delivery stage can start immediately, because the detailed plan for it is already in place.

When thinking through this stage, balance the work very carefully. A major cause of project failure is poor plans or a complete lack of plans. The answer to that problem isn't to go to the other extreme of developing excessively detailed plans for everything. Over-planning brings with it three problems:

- ✔ You spend longer producing the plan than you should.

- ✔ You need to maintain these over-complicated plans throughout the project, and that takes up even more time.

- ✔ Unless the project is very short and clear, things will change and you'll be faced with a lot of work later to adjust all the fine detail you set down at the start.

The approach of developing a high-level Project Plan now and then more detailed stage plans as you approach each delivery stage, gives you good control. As with most work, use the KISS principle for planning: **K**eep **I**t **S**imple, **S**tupid! Start simple and only get complicated where really necessary in order to exercise sufficient control over the project.

### Knowing what to do

For the detailed planning work, you need to investigate a number of areas, and usually that means consulting other people. You may be a subject expert and need little advice, but Project Managers don't necessarily have to be subject experts and so often need to get input from the people who are.

Some of the areas will be familiar from the Project Outline you produced in Starting the Project. That shouldn't come as a surprise, though, because the outline was a sketch plan and now you're working those same areas into more detail and with greater precision to form the 'scale drawing' for the project. Be careful here to strike a good balance: you don't want unnecessary overheads, but you do want the project to be properly defined and effectively controlled.

The following items reflect the main areas of project management. In this section we just touch on each, but we cross-reference later chapters of the book where you can find the full information when you're ready.

- ✔ **Scope:** You sketched this out in the Project Outline, but now it's time to finalise the scope. Say exactly what the project will cover and deliver and also, if you identify areas that could otherwise be misunderstood, what it won't cover. Chapter 3 has more on this.

✔ **Business Case:** This is an extension of the justification in the Project Outline. The Business Case sets out the full justification of the project, including its costs, and also defines the business benefits that the project will deliver and the way in which those benefits will be measured. Please see Chapter 3 for much more on the Business Case.

✔ **Project Plan:** The Project Plan is a high-level plan of the delivery stages and closure stage, although the closure stage may be particularly tentative at the moment. The Project Plan sets down what the project will deliver, the activities, and the staff resource and finance involved. Part II of this book gives lots of practical advice on planning and some really powerful techniques to help you.

✔ **Risk:** You should look at the risk involved in the project and also the means of controlling it. Chapter 10 helps here with some useful techniques. Some people question whether you really need risk management in every project, even the very small ones. Yes, you do.

✔ **Quality:** In the Project Outline you've already indicated the quality level needed for this project. Now is the time to establish exactly how you'll carry the quality through into the deliverables, what degree of control you need to exercise, and how you'll audit to make sure that the required quality exists. Your thinking about quality includes listing any standards that you need to comply with. Those might be organisational standards or even legal ones such as financial, security, and health and safety. Chapter 5 covers quality.

✔ **Roles and responsibilities:** Who needs to do what in the project? You probably decided this back in the first stage, but it's worth setting down roles and responsibilities now, with any adjustments. In that way, everyone involved knows what they should be doing on the project and, importantly, what everyone else should be doing as well. That helps avoid communications problems where things fall down the gaps. You can read much more on roles and project organisation in Chapter 11.

---

# Everybody, Somebody, Anybody and Nobody

This is a story about four people named Everybody, Somebody, Anybody and Nobody.

There was an important job to be done and Everybody was sure that Somebody would do it. Anybody could have done it, but Nobody did. Somebody got angry about that, because it was Everybody's job. Everybody thought Anybody could do it, but Nobody realised that Everybody wouldn't do it. It ended up that Everybody blamed Somebody when Nobody did what Anybody could've done.

*Author unknown*

---

## Control areas to consider

Some areas to bear in mind when considering controls include:

✔ **Project Manager authorities,** such as spending limits and decision-making limits on things like change and adjustment of the project

✔ **Reporting,** covering the frequency and content of reports such as those for progress, finance and risk

✔ **Flexibility,** including whether the Project Manager can proceed with a certain amount of a following delivery stage (percentage, value or time) if a short delay occurs in getting the steering committee together for a stage gate

---

✔ **Communications:** Hard on the heels of roles and responsibilities comes communications. That's no coincidence, because a lot of comms problems start with people being unclear about who's doing what. You need to think through the communications carefully, because this area is a major cause of project failure. In fact, if you look at surveys of project failure factors, communications is almost always in the top five listed causes, and frequently occupies the number one slot. Chapter 15 goes into full detail.

✔ **Controls:** For this section, you need to consider what controls the project needs. For a very small project don't get carried away, because you probably won't need many controls at all. In a larger project, though, you need to think through controls carefully.

### Thinking about management documents

You should document all planning and control areas, albeit simply on small projects. On larger projects, expect the documentation to be more substantial. Remember the balance of having sufficient information to define and control the project but not more than that.

The name given to the Organising and Preparing stage document is often *Project Charter*, but other terms are in use that you might recognise, such as Project Framework, Project Definition Document (PDD) or Project Initiation Documentation (PID).

The Project Charter has three uses:

✔ **As a definition** to say exactly what the project is and how it will be controlled

✔ **As decision support** to provide the sponsor or steering committee with the information needed to decide to go on to the delivery stages

> ✔ **As an ongoing reference** for those coming into the project later on and those who need to know what the procedures and controls are, for example to submit a change request or report a new risk

So, the Project Charter is good value for money, and it is worth a bit of effort to get the Project Charter right. The headings of the Project Charter mostly reflect the areas we list in the previous section, 'Knowing what to do'. You can always add to the headings if you need to, but you'll probably find that you can't leave any out.

---

# A Project Charter

Some of the areas in the Project Charter develop those you sketched out in the Project Outline, and others are new. In all cases, though, adjust the content of the Charter to meet the needs of the project. Excessively big Charters aren't impressive; they just make work for everyone. Inadequate Charters are a waste of time because they don't define the project or its controls adequately to run the project.

The Project Management Institute (PMI), in its *Guide to the Project Management Body of Knowledge (PMBoK)*, defines a Project Charter and project management approach. But although the institute is very big, it still only represents a small minority of Project Managers – and mostly career ones. The Charter as defined here is for more general use and for less complex projects. The PMBoK is available from bookshops and is an excellent reference if you'd like more detail.

✔ **Objectives:** The agreed objectives for the project.

✔ **Scope:** What's included in the project, and what's excluded where confusion may exist.

✔ **Business Case:** The justification of why the project is being run, together with a list of benefits and how benefits will be measured.

✔ **Roles and responsibilities:** Who's doing what in this project? This section can also list the stakeholders – those with an interest in the project.

✔ **Communications Management Plan:** What information will be moving about and how it will be communicated, including reports within the project (which may be verbal).

✔ **Quality Plan:** The level of quality that's needed, how the project will achieve the quality, and how the project will be audited to be sure that the quality has indeed been achieved.

✔ **Risk Plan:** How risk will be controlled in the project and who's responsible for it.

✔ **Project Plan:** Information on what will be produced, the activities needed, and the required resource, notably in terms of finance and staff time.

✔ **Control procedures:** In anything other than a small project, people need a clear statement of procedures such as for problem reporting. This section also can set down the Project Manager's authority limits and the procedures for referring anything beyond the Project Manager.

✔ **Constraints:** Anything that affects how the project is run and delivered, such as security, a fixed delivery date for the project, or limitation on the type of equipment used.

Along with the Project Charter, you also need the stage plan for the first delivery stage, so that you can proceed without undue delay.

# Carrying Out the Work – delivery stages

This is the stage that usually repeats; you can have multiple stages.

### Understanding the characteristics

This stage is simple in concept, as its title suggests – Carrying Out the Work. But the delivery stage is where all the teamwork builds project products and tests them, so it's the main part of the project.

### Knowing what to do

In the delivery stage or stages, you give work out to teams, get progress information back in, and generally keep track of where the stage is. Is the stage going to plan? If the stage is going off the plan, you need to establish why that is and take any necessary action to get it back on track. That adjustment is part of the routine 'steering' that you need to do throughout.

If things go off track by more than an amount set by the sponsor or steering committee, then, just like in general management, you need to refer the matter back for discussion and a decision.

You also need to make allowances for unplanned stuff. If you've used any time management approach, you know that you should always make a time allowance for unexpected things, or your schedule falls apart pretty quickly. The same holds true for projects, so, to use the words of *The Hitchhiker's Guide to the Galaxy*, expect the unexpected.

In particular, people working on the project need to pass to the Project Manager information such as details of problems, changes or new risks. You must allow time, and perhaps the time of other people, to deal with these things.

Then, towards the end of each delivery stage, you need to do the more detailed planning of the following stage and update the Project Charter as necessary. For example, some of the projections of benefits in the Business Case may now be different because the business environment has changed, and almost certainly some of the risk factors will have changed.

### Thinking about management documents

During the stages, you produce regular progress information for the sponsor or steering committee, and towards the end of each stage, you also produce a stage plan for the following stage.

### *Progress*

It's important for a number of people, both inside and outside the project, to be kept up to date on the project's progress. The Communications Management Plan, part of the Project Charter, can include quite a list of people who need to get a copy of progress reports:

- ✔ Team leaders – to keep track of the big picture

- ✔ The sponsor or members of the steering committee

- ✔ Programme manager – if the project is part of a programme

- ✔ Business managers of areas that the project affects

- ✔ Stakeholders – perhaps people in other departments and organisations who have an interest, even customers

- ✔ Project Managers of interfacing projects – to know how progress on this project affects theirs

### *Stage Report*

Depending on what the sponsor or steering committee wanted and on how formal the project is, you may need to produce a note or report at the end of the stage to record how it went and what the final figures are on cost and time. You may need to include more information such as about the delivery of quality and productivity of the teams – you'll have established the exact detail when thinking about the communications and writing the Communications Management Plan for the Charter. Flick to Chapter 15 for more on the Communications Management Plan.

# *Closing the Project*

The final stage of a project is to shut it down. Normally, things don't just stop dead when you complete the final delivery stage, but rather you have work to do on the project management side to close down the project and release resource, and on the technical side to deal with any teething problems with and adjustments to the things that the project delivered. This section is a summary because we include a whole chapter on closure later in the book, Chapter 16.

## *Understanding the characteristics*

In most cases it makes sense to have a separate stage for closure, because of the change in the nature and pace of the project. In closure, things are going to be a bit unpredictable, and that's the reason that the view of closure in the Project Plan is tentative. As you approach the end of the final delivery stage, everything is much clearer and you can plan the closure work with confidence.

### Knowing what to do

In closure, you need to evaluate the work required to sort out any teething problems and then decide how to wind down the work and hand over to operational support. You may have already agreed some of the handover, and it may even be subject to legal arrangements such as on the handing over of a new building.

Then, on the project management side, you need to think through what documentation will be required in the future, and store it. You should also check for things to pass back into the organisation, such as ongoing maintenance schedules and even information about things like risk management which are to carry on into the working life of the project deliverables.

Finally, you report the outcome of the project (unless you're in a very informal environment). Frequently, you produce a Project Report to give final costs and the level of any business benefits that you can already see and measure at the end of the project. You should also pass on any lessons you learned in the project – both good and bad – so that future projects can benefit from your knowledge.

### Thinking about documentation

You need to break the documentation down into two groups: information to be kept about the project itself, and information to be sent to others for action:

- **Project information:** Information about the project may include
  - A Project Report
  - Product information – for future reference in the event of problems, or for maintenance
  - Control information – such as about the risks and 'actuals' of the time and cost of the project, which may be useful for future estimating of similar projects
- **Outbound information:** This information can include
  - Lessons learned – to help other projects
  - Benefits realisation – plans for any measurement of benefits after the end of the project
  - Ongoing actions – outstanding actions and ongoing controls such as continuing risk management of dangerous machinery

# Chapter 3

# Defining the Project and Producing a Business Case

*In This Chapter*

▶ Setting down clearly what your project will cover, but also what it won't

▶ Writing a Business Case – the justification for the project

▶ Understanding the different types of benefit

▶ Avoiding the pitfalls of Business Cases

*A*ll projects are created for a reason – you identify a need and devise a project to address that need. You then determine the success or failure of the project by how well it meets that need and whether it delivers the business benefit that justified expending all the effort on the project in the first place. This chapter helps you develop clear boundaries for the project – the *scope* – and then set down the justification, or *Business Case*, for running the project.

The scope and Business Case go hand in hand. Each affects the other, so thinking about them together is helpful. The Business Case lists the business benefits of running the project; it may be worth adjusting the scope in order to get better business benefits. Equally, it may be advantageous to chop another part of the project out because it isn't absolutely necessary and very few benefits exist in that part to offset the work involved – it just isn't worth it. The scope, then, is the 'What?' and the Business Case is the justification, the 'Why?'

Although you may need to adjust the degree of formality from project to project, you shouldn't ever leave out the work of defining the scope and justifying the work. You always need to be clear about what you are covering in the project, and you should always be very clear about why you want to do that work – well, unless you're intent on wasting your effort and that of other people and then delivering the wrong thing as a crowning glory.

For the Business Case in particular, you sometimes need to be more formal than at other times. But you always need to write things down in an ordered way if someone other than you has to approve the project. You may even have to work to a set format if you'll have to go through some organisational approval process such as getting the go-ahead from a finance committee.

This chapter shows you what's involved, helps you think about the Business Case clearly, outlines a few techniques, and even helps you side-step some Business Case bear traps.

# Defining the Scope

The *Scope Statement* is a written statement that sets down exactly what the project will cover, and usually also what it won't. Both the people who requested the project and those managing it (including the sponsor or steering committee) should agree to the Scope Statement before actual project work begins.

Although, obviously, stating clearly what the project will cover is important, additionally setting down what it won't (*negative scope*) is often really helpful. The negative scope isn't the whole world outside the intended project, but rather things that people involved in the project could confuse.

## Managing expectations and avoiding disappointment

Misunderstanding the scope when agreeing it is so very easy, and this isn't necessarily because the Scope Statement is imprecise or careless. Rather, misunderstanding comes from the age-old problem of people seeing what they expect to see, even if it isn't there, and making unconscious assumptions. Even worse is when busy managers sign off the Scope Statement having only skim-read the headings while grabbing some water from the cooler between meetings. What's that? Oh no, not in your organisation, of course. Your managers are always very thorough and read important documents with great care, but in *other* companies . . .!

At the end of the project, a common problem is that people look at the deliverable, such as a new computer system for accounting, and a conversation develops with the development team along these lines . . .

'I can't see the invoicing function on the main menu.'

'Err. The system doesn't do invoicing. We never set out to include invoicing.'

'What? You can't have an accounts system without invoicing!'

'Well, actually you can. This is one.'

'But we need invoicing.'

'Look, here's the Scope Statement from the Project Charter listing all the functions we were going to include, and here's your signature on the bottom where you signed the statement off to agree it, and it doesn't mention invoicing . . . does it?'

'Oh no, you're right. It doesn't . . . but we need invoicing!'

How simple would it have been to say in the Scope Statement right at the beginning of the Starting the Project stage (see Chapter 2 for more on stages), that the planned system will include this, this and this, but exclude that, that and invoicing? Defining the scope properly is about managing expectations. People are clear about what they'll be getting when the project is delivered, but are also clear on what they won't be getting.

## Challenging the scope

The negative scope could well lead to a challenge. Continuing with the invoicing example from the last section, if the scope says that the new accounts system won't include invoicing, this may then be challenged by those asking for the system, who say that actually they need it included. Indeed, if time and funds are limited, they say, they'd rather have invoicing than a couple of the other functions listed. That leads to a change of scope, and the project will be all the better for it.

You're better off discussing and changing the scope when developing the Project Charter (see Chapter 2 for more on this document) than in the depths of the project when it slowly starts to dawn on those receiving the project deliverables that they aren't getting quite what they wanted. Better still, however, is discussing the scope when producing a Project Outline in the Starting the Project stage. When you discuss and adjust the project boundary while the plan is still a sketch, making changes requires relatively little work. Clearly, though, making changes after you're into more detailed planning is a much bigger job.

## Understanding the dimensions of scope

A dictionary definition of scope is 'the extent of the area or subject matter that something deals with'. In your case, the 'something' is the project. So what's the extent of your project? You can define the scope in one or more of the following ways:

- ✔ **Deliverables, or products:** In many projects, setting down scope in terms of what the project will deliver is helpful. Yes, the end product, but also any significant products along the way.
- ✔ **Functions:** This is useful for new or revised systems (whether they're computer ones or procedural ones). Which functions will the project cover and which won't it cover?

> ✔ **Geography:** Which areas of the organisation will the project cover, for example just your offices in Scotland or just three departments at your corporate headquarters?
>
> ✔ **Time:** A more unusual scope definition, but valid and helpful for some projects. The project will cover all work on this subject area between now, when nothing's been done, up to the end of the financial year, when the project must deliver a management review document.

## Being clear

When thinking through the dimensions of scope and writing it all down, think about who'll be reading the Scope Statement in order to approve it. It's no good filling the Scope Statement with all sorts of technical detail if it must be agreed by people in the business area who don't understand such things. The scope must communicate, and must do so particularly to the sponsor or steering committee: they must be able to sign off the Scope Statement to say, 'Yes, that's the project we want, and that's what we're willing to pay for.'

On the other hand, the Scope Statement must be specific, so don't shy away from detail where you need to spell things out. If that does include some technical stuff, then put in a plain-language explanation. Those reading it know that they may need to get some technical confirmation that the information is correct. Sponsors don't necessarily need to struggle with the fine detail that the equipment will be covering amplitude-modulated signals on frequencies up to 8.8 gigahertz, but attenuated to avoid excessive output on the fifth and seventh harmonics and especially, of course, the seventh.

Put simply, if you're asking people to sign off a Scope Statement, make sure it's one they can understand and so confirm. It's in nobody's best interests, including yours, for sponsors to sign off documents that they don't understand and are having to take on trust.

## Prioritising

When you first think about the scope of the project and talk about it with others, you often find that not everything is essential. In your new car project, wheels are pretty important, but lights on the mirrors on the sun visors, while nice, probably aren't essential. It can be a real help, then, to prioritise the requirements.

Some use the MoSCoW approach to help with prioritising:

> ✔ **Must have:** The essentials; the project must address all these elements.
>
> ✔ **Should have:** High priority, but not absolutely essential.

- ✔ **Could have**: Useful and worthwhile, but lower priority.

- ✔ **Won't have:** Something suggested but now not considered worthwhile, or that will be held over, perhaps for a later enhancement project.

# Producing a Business Case

Having got the scope clear, although you may go back and adjust it, it's time to look at the justification for the project – why your organisation should do the project. This is the Business Case.

## Getting to grips with the basic contents

You can adjust the contents of the Business Case to suit the project and also any organisational standard or methodology you're using. Here are the basic contents that you'll need as a minimum for any project:

- ✔ **Benefits:** Information on the benefits, but usually also when they'll come on stream, when they'll be measured, buy whom and how.

- ✔ **Context:** For example, the fit with the organisational five-year strategy or just to say it's a small stand-alone project to improve performance in a particular area of the business.

- ✔ **Cost:** Ballpark at first, but kept up to date as better information comes to hand.

- ✔ **Justification:** Is the project solely benefits driven, or does it have any element of compliance, such as there being a legal requirement to run the project?

- ✔ **Timescale:** A rough estimate at first, but updated from better information later.

## Keeping the Business Case up to date

The Business Case is one of the most important documents you'll have in your project. It shows the justification for doing the project in the first place, but it's then important when monitoring the ongoing viability of the project. If, for example, part way through the project, circumstances change and the benefits projections now fall through the floor, you probably want to shut the project down; but don't forget that the project may be justified on more than benefits. It follows that you're going to have to keep the Business Case up to date throughout the project if it's to remain helpful in monitoring the viability of the project and as an aid to decision-making.

In UK government departments, a common misunderstanding over Business Cases was that they were something you did at the start of projects in order to secure the funding and then quietly forgot all about. In a study on IT project problems in government, the McCartney Report mentioned this misunderstanding and used a great phrase.

> *The business case needs to be seen as a living document that will run for the lifetime of the project, not just as a mechanism to obtain funding. It is only by using the case as a tool for monitoring progress that it is possible to make sure the intended benefits of the project or programme are realised.*
>
> The McCartney Report
>
> *– Successful IT: Modernising Government in Action*

So then, a 'living document'.

Keep a copy of the Business Case when it's approved at the start of the project and again at every approval point such as a stage gate (the end of a stage; see Chapter 2 for more). But keep the Business Case up to date and so immediately usable to help check the impact of changes to the project and changes in the environment in which the project is running.

## Figuring out why you're doing the project

When you take on a project, *why* you're doing it may seem obvious at one level – because your boss told you to. The deeper question, though, is why the organisation wants the project. If you're down the line a bit from where the project idea started out, you may need to go and talk to a few people to help you get the justification clear.

### Identifying the initiator

Your first task in examining your project's underlying justification is to find out who had the original idea that led to your project. Project success often requires that, at a minimum, you meet this person's needs and expectations.

### Talking to end users

The people who'll use what the project delivers ultimately generate the benefits of the project. Getting their assessment of the advantages of the project and what benefits it will deliver is helpful.

### Checking documents

You may also find information in documents such as:

- ✔ Correspondence and emails referring to the project
- ✔ Minutes from division, department and organisation-wide planning and budget sessions
- ✔ Reports of planning or feasibility studies

### *Recognising others who may benefit from your project*

Although they may not have initiated the idea, other people may benefit from your completed project. They may also be able to contribute information to help with the Business Case. Think about people including:

- ✔ Business partners (or other agencies if you're in the public sector)
- ✔ Clients and customers
- ✔ Operational staff who'll use what your project will deliver
- ✔ Suppliers

Identify these other people as soon as possible to determine what their particular needs and interests are and how you may need to address them. These additional audiences may include people who:

- ✔ Know the project exists and have expressed an interest in it
- ✔ Know the project exists but don't realise it can benefit them
- ✔ Are unaware of your project

To help identify these additional audiences you can:

- ✔ Review written materials related to your project.
- ✔ Consult with your project's supporters.
- ✔ Encourage everyone you speak to about the project to identify others who may benefit from it.

As you identify and note down people who can benefit from your project, you can also note down those who'll oppose it. This helps with your stakeholder analysis, which we cover in detail in Chapter 4.

## *Understanding project justification*

There's a tendency for senior managers to think that all projects must have business benefits to be viable. That's not right thinking, though, and other perfectly valid reasons exist for justifying projects. Having said that, business benefit is the most common justification. Project justifications may include:

- **Business benefits:** Things such as cost savings, better customer service, improved profits, better market penetration.

- **Compliance:** Relates to projects that are compulsory, even if they bring no business benefits. This includes legal and organisational compliance.

- **Enabling:** The project doesn't provide any business benefit in the normal sense, but does something that allows other projects to run, and those projects will deliver business benefit.

You can, and often do, have a hybrid Business Case that has more than one type of justification. For example, your organisation may have to run a project for legal compliance, but the project will nevertheless deliver some business benefits. Although those benefits won't completely pay for the project, they'll at least offset some of the costs.

## Understanding benefits

Within the justification, three types of benefits exist, and it's important to appreciate the differences between them:

- **Direct saving:** A direct saving is where the organisation will save real money. If you change an old machine for a new one, the maintenance costs of the new one will be substantially less. The saved money will be in the maintenance budget, and it's real; you're going to get that cash saving.

- **Quantifiable benefit:** This is a saving that you can measure in money terms, so it's *quantifiable*. However, you probably won't see the actual money. For example, a new procedure that will reduce sales admin means that salespeople will save an hour a day. It's unlikely that the sales force will be reduced, it's just that they have an hour more each day to be doing what you employ them to do – sell – and that's a benefit that you can express in money terms.

- **Non-quantifiable benefit:** As the name suggests, you can't express this benefit in money terms, at least not meaningfully. The benefit may be very worthwhile, though. An example is staff working conditions. If the project improves the factory or office environment, then that's worthwhile. But what's it worth in money terms? Can you prove that people who may otherwise have left will now stay, for example? Sometimes you can measure a part of this, such as productivity, but it's a tricky area, and generally you accept the benefit as important but non-quantifiable.

Don't ignore non-quantifiable benefits. Things like quality improvements can be hard or impossible to quantify, but they may be extremely important. If documents are going out to clients with spelling errors, that may lose future business because of the negative impact on the company image. If the project reviews all documents and produces a new set, all carefully checked, that will eliminate the bad impression. What's that worth though? Can you prove that some customers didn't re-order because of the poor impression created by the spelling errors, and exactly how many didn't re-order for this reason?

 Now for a warning in the other direction. Be careful with non-quantifiable benefits and try hard to be realistic about them. Because you can never prove them, you need to be all the more careful that you're not fooling yourself about the existence and significance of non-quantifiable benefits.

### Being prudent with benefit projections

A well-established accounting principle is that of being prudent. Being cautious and erring on the safe side is a well known trait of most accountants and the source of a lot of accountant jokes. You'd do well to follow the accountants' example when considering project benefits, though. Two very strong reasons exist to err on the safe side and, if anything, slightly understate the benefits rather than overstate them:

- **Perceptions of success and failure:** If your project delivers slightly more benefit than projected, everyone will think it's a particular success. If the project delivers less than projected, then people may see even a great project as a failure.

- **Incorrect strategy decisions:** If you overstate the benefits, the project may be run when it shouldn't be. That will have a double impact. The first is that the project won't be the good investment everyone thought it would be; second, it may well mean that the organisation didn't run, or delayed, another project that would have delivered worthwhile benefit.

### Understanding benefits realisation

*Benefits realisation* is one of those terms that's caught on as management speak, and it's the one to use at important meetings to make it sound like you're at the very forefront of current management thinking. However, like many, but not quite all, management catchphrases, some value is tucked away inside the phrase. Put simply, benefits realisation is saying when you're going to see the benefits and how you're going to measure the benefits that you can quantify to demonstrate that they were forthcoming.

A common misunderstanding is that you see benefits only after the end of the project. Although it's true that you may see some of the benefits after the end, you may also see some before then. In fact, you can see benefits at three places in the process, and you need to put plans in place to measure and report benefits at those points:

- **During the project:** In some projects, particularly but not solely business projects, deliverables are taken into operational use right through the project, and there isn't just one big delivery at the end. If things are being taken into operational use during the project, it's likely that you'll start to see benefits during the project too. You can and should measure these benefits and report them straight away to give confidence that the project is on track to deliver the benefits that justified running it.

✔ **At the end of the project:** You may see some benefits at the end of the project after the final delivery. For example, as soon you commission a the new machine at the end of a project, an immediate drop in maintenance costs follows over an old machine that needed daily attention.

✔ **After the end of the project:** Where you introduce something new, it's often the case that it takes a while for everything to settle down so that you can make an accurate measurement of the benefits. For example, with a new business procedure, staff work more slowly than usual when it's first introduced because they're still learning the procedure and it's unfamiliar. After a few weeks, performance picks up to what's now a normal level, so you can accurately measure and report the cost savings over the old procedure.

You can include your plans for measuring benefits in the Business Case itself or, particularly in larger projects where benefits realisation is often more complex, in a separate plan.

### Avoiding benefits contamination

*Benefits contamination* is a term coined by Inspirandum when giving guidance on benefits realisation and, in particular, deciding how the benefits should be measured. The danger is that benefits are claimed for the project which are really due to something else. If you weren't quite the good Project Manager that you are, you might have been tempted to think that extra benefits are quite good and will make your project seem better. However, being both intelligent and thoroughly professional, as *For Dummies* readers are, you'll be quick to realise that such contamination is dangerous. It means that measures of what the project has actually achieved are inaccurate; worse still, contamination may lead to the organisation running more similar projects on the assumption that they'll also show this imaginary benefit.

In setting up benefits measures, you need mechanisms that will isolate benefits and directly link them to the project. That's harder than it sounds and sometimes needs very careful thought. It does no harm at all to get some help when thinking this through, and indeed it's a mark of professionalism to call in some help if you need it to get the Business Case right. In the case of benefits measures and avoiding benefits contamination, some input from a finance manager can be particularly helpful.

# *Writing the Business Case*

When you are actually producing the Business Case, the format depends on who it's aimed at and your plan for the content. You can keep the Business Case very short and factual. However, if others have got to look at it for information or perhaps to approve it, then you may need to add some explanation. If you do include more information, keep your target audience in mind:

- ✔ **Keep it simple.** However, don't talk down to your readers. You need to assess where they're at and then write at that level.

- ✔ **Consider appendices.** You may have some detailed financial information, for example. If the fine detail isn't of interest to the bulk of your readers, consider putting an outline in the main part of the Business Case and having an appendix with the full data.

- ✔ **Spell out the benefits.** You're familiar with the project idea and perhaps with the organisational area in which the project is running. But what may seem obvious to you may not be so obvious to people outside that area or to senior managers at the top of the organisation.

## A membership example

A professional organisation in the UK has a membership and runs exams that are recognised worldwide. It wants to grow, because a bigger membership means a more secure future – it has competitors – and also that it can offer better services to its members. So it ran a project with the objective of increasing membership. So how do you know whether the project was successful? What was the measurable benefit?

- ✔ **Increased membership:** Ah, so membership has increased has it, but at what cost?

- ✔ **Increased membership at a reasonable cost:** That's better, after you define *reasonable*. However, what if membership increased but no more than that of competitive organisations that didn't run any membership projects at all – it was just natural growth in the market, and the project made no difference at all?

- ✔ **Increased membership 5 per cent above the market norm:** So, better still. But what if people are joining for other reasons, such as word-of-mouth recommendations, that have nothing whatever to do with the project?

- ✔ **Increased membership linked to a project action:** The application form could include a 'why are you joining' question with options that relate directly and specifically to project activity.

## Complying with organisational standards

If you don't already know, check whether your organisation has a standard for project Business Cases. If so, comply with it. If you need more information in the project's Business Case than the organisational standard covers, you can always add an appendix that contains that extra information.

If you have to put information forward in a set format for financial approval, try not to separate that work out from the project's Business Case and so end up doing the work twice. Instead, adjust the Business Case format to fit the approval submission, put any extra information needed for the project into appendices, and then don't include the appendices in the copy that goes to the finance committee.

# Going Back to the Scope

Having set down the justification and benefits, it's time to revisit the scope to check it in two ways:

✔ To challenge the scope
✔ To see whether you need to add anything

In both cases, you work within any set constraints unless you think that you need to challenge such constraints and you're in a position to do that. You won't be able to challenge things like changes in the VAT rate, but you may well be in a position to challenge a constraint that you must use a particular brand of equipment, if new equipment has come onto the market from a different manufacturer that's cheaper to buy, technically more advanced and much easier to maintain.

### Challenging the existing scope

For each area of the project, systematically check whether it's really worth doing or whether you could cut it out. For some things, the considerable project effort needed to include something simply isn't worthwhile given the very limited benefits that will result.

Vilfredo Pareto, an Italian economist, came up with the 80:20 principle that 20 per cent of the population controlled 80 per cent of the wealth. Since then, people have applied the *Pareto Principle* to many areas, and commonly to effort. The rule is that 20 per cent of your effort brings about 80 per cent of the benefits, and the remaining 80 per cent of your effort gets that last 20 per cent of benefit. It's a bit like wringing water out of a soaked towel. A relatively small effort at the start gets a large amount of water out, but you end up putting in a huge effort and going red in the face to squeeze out those last few drips.

When challenging the scope, do bear in mind that some things are necessary even though they won't directly produce benefits (see the earlier section 'Understanding project justification' for examples).

### *Going the second mile*

Keeping within the main thrust of the project, could you add anything usefully to the project to deliver extra benefit? It may be that you're already doing a substantial amount of work and by adding just a very small amount of additional functionality you could get considerably better benefits. This step isn't to encourage scope creep but rather to get the maximum possible value from the project.

In the UK, a stationery supply company put in a system to deal with customer orders. That system, obviously enough, had to hold information on what the customers had ordered. The company wondered whether the system could serve any other purpose. The company realised that the data gave it valuable information, so extended its system to print personalised front pages to stick onto the front of mailed catalogues. So, if a customer buys a laminator for covering card and paper with plastic, but not the plastic pockets, on its next catalogue the customer sees on the front page: 'You haven't yet ordered laminating pouches from us. On page 5 you'll see that the A4 pouches are £5 a pack, but quote code XXX for your special price of £4.50.' The added functionality for the system led to significant extra sales based on a small amount of processing of data that the company had to hold in any case.

# *Getting to Grips with Techniques*

A few techniques can help with Business Cases. The remainder of this chapter explains two, including a particularly important one: cost–benefit analysis. For more detail on project techniques, you can look on the Internet or in specialised publications such as *The Project Techniques Toolbox*, written by Nick Graham andpublished by Inspirandum.

## *Calculating return on investment*

The *return on investment* (ROI) is a simple division of the quantifiable benefits by the project cost in a stated period. Perhaps the project will cost £1 million but will lead to £5 million of benefits.

5,000,000/1,000,000 = ROI of 5

This ROI figure is useful but it's not everything. Remember that the project may have important non-quantifiable benefits (see the earlier section 'Understanding benefits'), and the benefits projections may not be 100 per cent accurate in any case. To make the ROI figure meaningful, you should also state the time needed before the return; this has been called *the dollar day* – for how many days is each dollar invested? Investing £1 million and getting a return of £5 million within one year is very different from having to wait ten years for the same return.

## Understanding cost–benefit analysis

Cost–benefit analysis is the most widely used technique for project Business Cases. The technique may sound complicated, but really it's very simple. You set down the costs of the project and compare them with the savings or benefits. However, because all the project costs are incurred during the project, and because the savings or benefits will continue year on year, it makes sense to look at a period of five years or so to get the overall picture and to see when the project will pay back or break even.

From Figure 3-1 you can see that the project is run in Year 0 and will pay back during Year 2. It will have offset the costs of the project and in fact will show a slight gain of £10,000 by the end of that year. Great: by the end of Year 2 we're already making money.

| £ '000s | Year 0 | Year 1 | Year 2 | Year 3 |
|---|---|---|---|---|
| **Costs** | | | | |
| Equipment | 105 | | | |
| Project teams | 135 | | | |
| Maintenance | 0 | 5 | 5 | 5 |
| **Total costs** | 240 | 5 | 5 | 5 |
| **Benefits** | | | | |
| Saved maintenance | | 15 | 15 | 20 |
| Higher productivity | | 35 | 35 | 35 |
| Increased order value | | 80 | 80 | 80 |
| **Total costs** | 0 | 130 | 130 | 135 |
| **Balance** | −240 | 125 | 125 | 130 |
| **Cash flow** | −240 | −115 | 10 | 140 |

**Figure 3-1:** The direct payback model.

### Allowing for inflation

The *direct payback* or *break-even model* is useful but it leaves out an important factor: future money isn't as valuable as today's money. If (and please note carefully the *if*) I offered you £5,000 and asked whether you'd like it today or whether you'd prefer the £5,000 in five years' time, what would you reply? Well, 'Today!', without doubt. You'd have two reasons for your choice. The first is you're afraid that I may change my mind, and you'd prefer to get your hands on the cash while I'm still feeling generous. The second is that in five years' time the money won't be as valuable: it won't have the same spending power.

The further you go into the future, the less valuable money becomes. If you've read historical novels or watched films such as *Pride and Prejudice*, you'll know that people in England were once impressed because someone had an income of £1,000 a year. So if your project is forecast to get a benefit of £10,000 in Year 5, it won't actually be worth that much by the time you get to Year 5. What you need to do in order to have a more realistic view is to discount the value of future money; the further you go into the future, the more you need to discount it.

### Using discount factors – net present value

Depending on the current state of the economy and things like the rate of inflation, the discount factor varies. Ask your finance people what the current factor is or check on the Internet. Figure 3-2 uses a discount rate of 5 per cent so at Year 0, £1 is worth £1. By Year 3, though, £1 is only worth 86.4 pence. You express future money in today's values.

You can set up your discounted cash flow on a spreadsheet, and if you do you'll find a function that deals with discounts – *NPV*, which stands for net present value.

Using the same example as before, Figure 3-2 now shows that the project doesn't actually break even in Year 2 at all; by the end of that year, it's still £3,000 down. In fact, break-even occurs in Year 3, and you see that the overall benefits are lower.

Although it gives a more accurate view, discounted cash flow is still limited so don't get too carried away:

- ✔ It assumes that the economy will remain stable for the period covered by the cash flow, and so uses a uniform discount value over the period.

- ✔ It assumes that the projected benefits will be forthcoming. You can make adjustments to allow for known future events such as increased maintenance costs for existing equipment, but seeing into the future of a business isn't easy. If you can see into the future of the business world accurately and consistently, you're not only going to be very good at cost–benefit analysis, but you are also wasted in project management.

- ✔ It doesn't account for non-quantifiable benefits, of which some or all may be extremely important.

| £ '000s | Year 0 | Year 1 | Year 2 | Year 3 |
|---|---|---|---|---|
| **Costs** | | | | |
| Equipment | 105 | | | |
| Project teams | 135 | | | |
| Maintenance | 0 | 5 | 5 | 5 |
| **Total costs** | 240 | 5 | 5 | 5 |
| **Benefits** | | | | |
| Saved maintenance | | 15 | 15 | 20 |
| Higher productivity | | 35 | 35 | 35 |
| Increased order value | | 80 | 80 | 80 |
| **Total costs** | 0 | 130 | 130 | 135 |
| **Balance** | −240 | 125 | 125 | 130 |
| **Cash flow** | −240 | −115 | 10 | 140 |
| *5% discount factor* | | | | |
| **Discount factor** | 1.000 | 0.952 | 0.907 | 0.864 |
| **Discounted balance** | −240 | 119 | 118 | 117 |
| **Discounted cash flow** | −240 | −121 | −3 | 114 |

**Figure 3-2:**
Discounted
cash flow.

# Chapter 4

# Knowing Your Project's Stakeholders

. . . . . . . . . . . . . . . . . . . . . . . . . . . . . . . . . . . . . . . . . . . . . . . .

## In This Chapter

▶ Understanding that it's people who can often make or break your project

▶ Identifying your project's stakeholders and making a list

▶ Analysing stakeholders; seeing who can affect the project and how

▶ Deciding how to manage stakeholders

. . . . . . . . . . . . . . . . . . . . . . . . . . . . . . . . . . . . . . . . . . . . . . . .

*O*ften a project is like an iceberg: nine-tenths of it lurks below the surface. You receive an assignment and you think you know what it entails and who needs to be involved. Then, as the project unfolds, new people emerge who may affect your goals and your approach to the project.

Dick Parris, an experienced Project Manager and trainer, has a favourite expression: 'Projects are about people.' Dick's right. You can have a great project idea, be implementing the latest whiz-bang technology, and use a great project methodology, but if you don't get the people side right, you run a very real risk of failure.

On the inside of the project are the people involved in project management and then the teams that are actually doing the work. You need these people to be enthusiastic and empowered (check out Chapters 12 and 13 for more). Then, on the outside, you have a wide array of people with an interest in the project, and who can sometimes make or break it.

Unless your project is one of a small minority that only really affects you and your immediate staff, you need to carefully consider the various stakeholders. This chapter helps you establish who the stakeholders are, what their view of the project is, whether to involve them in some way and, if you do need to involve them, how. It also has a few hints and tips on handling any stakeholders who are opposed to your project and who may not be afraid of saying so.

# *Managing Stakeholders*

The area of project work you're involved in with stakeholders is called, not surprisingly, *stakeholder management*. Although that term has become a buzzword, don't dismiss it, because this part of project management can ultimately hold the key to success or failure in your project.

A *stakeholder* can be any person or group that supports, is affected by or is interested in your project. Project stakeholders may be located inside your organisation or outside, or both. In addition to making sure that your project has maximum support, knowing who the stakeholders are helps you to:

- ✔ Consider whether, when and how to involve them

- ✔ Understand your project communication needs

- ✔ Determine whether the reach and impact of the project is bigger or smaller than you originally anticipated

You risk compromising your project in two ways when you don't involve key people or groups in your project, and in a timely manner:

- ✔ You may miss important information that can affect the project's performance and ultimate success.

- ✔ Usually more painful, you may upset someone. And you can be sure that when people feel slighted or insulted – or just plain overlooked – they're more likely to oppose your project than become wildly enthusiastic supporters.

In UK business (which includes the public sector), opposition isn't always a direct frontal assault, with someone saying that your project is a heap of garbage and the worst idea ever to contaminate the planet. Often, opposition comes in the form of an apparently restrained but negative comment, or just a lift of an eyebrow, or simply a stony silence when a very senior manager mentions the project. It's worse when the opposer knows a senior manager well and can play on the manager's fears. In the *Yes, Minister* TV series, the civil servant Sir Humphrey Appleby can always stop the minister, Jim Hacker, in his tracks on any course of action by smiling and uttering the words, 'That's a very brave decision, minister.' The very last thing the minister wants is to be brave and risk his position, and those awful words guarantee frantic back-pedalling.

Do stakeholder problems mean you should give up immediately? No, of course not. But such people issues do mean that in order to be successful you need to manage the 'soft' people side of the project as well as the 'hard' skills side that includes things like planning.

In his poem 'The Elephant's Child', Rudyard Kipling wrote some well known and often quoted lines:

*I keep six honest serving-men*
*(They taught me all I knew);*
*Their names are What and Why and When*
*And How and Where and Who.*

The six serving-men questions are useful throughout a project, and in this chapter they provide a great framework for stakeholder management.

# Identifying stakeholders – the 'who'

Identifying stakeholders can simply mean that you sit down and think through the project and its environs, but it's often useful to talk to other people in the project who may think of important people or groups that don't immediately spring to your mind.

### Developing a Stakeholder List

As you identify the different stakeholders in your project, you may find it helpful to record them in the form of a *Stakeholder List*. It's important that you don't lose sight of any of the stakeholders, and unless you only have a very few stakeholders in your project, a list is a simple and obvious way of keeping track. As you develop your Communications Management Plan (covered in detail in Chapter 15), for example, you can quickly scan the Stakeholder List to make sure you haven't left anyone out.

In some more formal project environments you may hear people refer to the Stakeholder List as the Stakeholder Register.

A Stakeholder List is a living document. You can start developing your list as soon as you begin thinking about your project and people come to mind, rather than risk forgetting them when you come to consider the full communications later on. When you discuss your project with other people, ask them who they think may be affected by or interested in your project.

### Using specific categories

To help ensure that you include all appropriate people, you may find it sensible to structure and develop your list with categories. You're less likely to overlook people when you consider stakeholders department by department or group by group instead of trying to identify everyone from inside and outside the organisation at random.

You can work out your own list of categories, but here's one example:

✔ **Internal:** People and groups inside your organisation:

- **End users:** People who'll use the things that the project will produce

- **Groups needed just for this project:** Teams and individuals with special, often technical, knowledge related to this project

- **Project Manager:** The person with overall responsibility for successfully completing the project

- **Requesters:** The person who came up with the idea for your project, and all the people through whom the request passed before you received it

- **Senior management:** Executive-level management responsible for the general oversight of all organisational operations

- **Specialist interests:** Groups typically involved in most projects in the organisation, such as the human resources, finance, contracts and legal departments

- **Team members:** People assigned to the project, whose work the Project Manager directs

✔ **External:** People and groups outside your organisation:

- **Business partners:** Groups or organisations with which you may pursue joint ventures including, perhaps, this project

- **Clients or customers:** People or groups that buy or use your organisation's products or services

- **Professional societies:** Groups of professionals that may influence or be interested in your project

- **Regulators:** Government and agencies that establish regulations and guidelines that govern some aspect of your project work

- **Staff associations and unions:** Partly because they can often make valuable contributions to the project, but also because they may get direct enquiries from staff about it and need information to respond

- **The public:** The local, national and international community of people who may be affected by or interested in your project

- **Vendors, suppliers and contractors:** Organisations that provide staff, raw materials, equipment or other resources required to perform your project's work

### Spotlighting senior management

All of the interest groups in the preceding bullet list are important, but a particularly important one is senior management. Surveys of project failure show that a very common cause of problems is lack of senior management buy-in. If your project is anything other than small or is going outside the boundaries of your own work area, you must do your very best to secure this buy-in. Otherwise, senior management is likely to undermine your efforts on the project, such as by seeing the project as unimportant and transferring staff or funds to other areas part way through. Such undermining often happens because the senior managers were never seriously committed to the project in the first place.

Many project methodologies, including PRINCE2 and PRIME (see Chapter 2 for more on these), have senior management representation on the project management team (senior, that is, relative to the project), and usually in the powerful position of having ultimate responsibility for the project. The Project Manager is then accountable to that senior manager. That representation and structure is no coincidence and helps lock in senior management commitment to the project.

### Considering areas that are often overlooked

As you develop your Stakeholder List, be particularly careful to think through the following areas, because they're easy to overlook:

- ✔ **End users of your project's products:** People or groups who'll use the goods and services your project produces. Involving end users at the beginning and throughout your project helps ensure that the products and services delivered by the project are as easy as possible to implement and use and are most responsive to users' true needs. It also confirms that you appreciate the fact that the people who'll use a product may have important insights into what it should look like and do, which increases the chances that they'll work to implement the products successfully.

  In some cases, you may omit end users from the list because you don't know who they are, such as potential buyers of a new retail product. Instead, you may have people who understand and represent the interests of those end users, such as sales and marketing staff.

- ✔ **People who'll maintain or support the final product:** People who'll service your project's final products affect their continuing success. Involving these people throughout your project gives them a chance to make your project's products easier to maintain and support. It also allows them to become familiar with the products and prepare for the future maintenance.

- ✔ **Support staff:** These people don't tell you what you should do; instead, they help you accomplish the project's goals. If support staff know about your project early, they can fit you into their work schedules more readily. They can also tell you information about their capabilities and processes that may influence what your project can accomplish and by when. Such support staff work in areas include:

  - Facilities
  - Finance
  - Human resources
  - Information services
  - Legal services
  - Procurement or contracting
  - Project management office

- Quality
- Security

Specialists, such as legal specialists, prefer to be involved early on so that they can check that things are right and give you a steer if needed. Involving specialists early on is much better than not consulting them but then calling for them later in a flat panic because you've encountered serious legal problems and need the specialists to put in huge effort to dig you out of the mess. If you think that your project may have a legal dimension, put your organisation's legal advisers on your Stakeholder List.

### Keeping the Stakeholder List up to date

As the project develops, you may well discover more people who have a genuine interest in it. Keep the Stakeholder List up to date and then review it periodically to see how you need to keep those additional people informed or how you need to involve them. You may be able to cover any new information needs with a slight adjustment to your Communications Management Plan, such as by inviting the additional people to a monthly lunchtime project briefing; if the additional people need to be involved, however, it could lead to changes to the project and stage plans.

## Talking to the real end users

In the UK, headquarters staff in a prestigious hotel chain decided to run a project to upgrade the furniture in the conference rooms in all the chain's hotels throughout the country. They consulted designers and style specialists and chose smart new tables, chairs and other conference room fittings. They checked data for each hotel to find the number and capacity of its conference rooms and then ordered the appropriate number of items for each one. Towards the end of the project, hotel managers were informed that they were to have new furniture and that the existing furniture would be taken away when the new furniture was delivered.

Unfortunately, the new-style tables and chairs were larger than the older, but perfectly acceptable, existing furniture. In the smaller conference rooms with little or no spare space, the new furniture immediately reduced the capacity and therefore the profitability of the conference space. The project team had failed to talk to hotel managers, who were important stakeholders and, in fact, end users.

In one hotel, the manager was particularly upset because all his conference rooms were small. He was being held accountable for the profitability of his hotel – including the conference business – but the new furniture had been imposed on him with no consultation at all.

If you need to develop a Stakeholder List for most of your projects, consider setting up a template. The template is simply a pre-designed list that contains typical categories and stakeholders. You may even have specialised variants for particular types of project. You can develop and maintain your own templates, or your organisation's project management office may develop and maintain them for the entire organisation. Regardless of who maintains the template, it reflects people's cumulative experiences. As the organisation continues to perform projects of this type, it can add stakeholders that were overlooked in earlier projects and remove those that proved unnecessary. Using a template can save you time and improve your accuracy.

Suppose you prepare the budget for your department each year. After doing a number of these budgets, you know most of the people who give you the necessary information, who draft and print the document, and who have to approve the final budget. Each time you finish another budget, you revise your Stakeholder List template to include new information from that project. The next time you prepare the annual budget, you begin your list with your template. You then add and subtract names as appropriate for that particular budget preparation.

## Analysing the stakeholders – the 'where'

Stakeholders are those who have an interest in the project because it will affect them in some way, and who may have an influence on it. *Stakeholder analysis* is considering each stakeholder to ask where she is with the project – frequently in the two dimensions of degree of influence and then their positive or negative view of the project. You may set out to actively change the position or outlook of certain stakeholders, but to do that you clearly need to establish first where they are now. Having two dimensions may lead you to wonder whether you could even plot the position of each stakeholder on a matrix. If you do wonder that, you'll really like the next section.

### Developing a Stakeholder Matrix

The Stakeholder Matrix is an extremely simple idea, but a powerful one because it helps you see where stakeholders are in terms of their support of the project and the degree of influence over it. It helps you consider where you need to try to change that position. You simply plot each stakeholder's position on the matrix by evaluating what degree of influence the stakeholder has and whether she's generally for or against the project.

Figure 4-1 marks in four people as examples, suggesting four different approaches to stakeholder management.

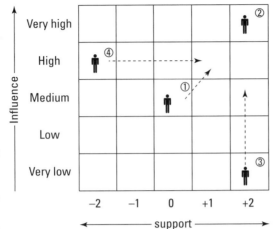

**Figure 4-1:**
The
Stakeholder
Matrix.

1. This person is neither for nor against the project and has medium influence over it. Your priority is to make this person much more positive about the project and then, if you succeed, you can move on to try and make the person more influential.

2. This person is a project champion, very much in favour of the project, and is also in a position of significant influence. Be careful how you think about people in this area of the matrix. An initial reaction may be that you don't need to do anything, but actually you must work to make sure that they stay on-side and enthusiastic.

3. The third person is really for your project but doesn't have much influence. The question for this person is whether you do something to increase her influence and so make her support more effective.

4. Here is the opposition, and quite serious opposition too. Not only is the person firmly against your project but she also has a high degree of influence. You need to work to convince her that the project is worthwhile and so get her support. If you're a more political player, you might also be looking to see whether you can reduce this person's influence.

Although the matrix is extremely useful in getting a picture of where individual stakeholders are, it's also useful for seeing the overall distribution. For example, you may see that the majority of the stakeholders are in favour of your project but that relatively few of them are in a position of influence.

If you want to, you can also make the matrix more sophisticated by showing the position of stakeholders before any management action, and your assessment of their position after management action is in place.

# Understanding positions – the 'why'

Before you can try to maintain or change a stakeholder's position, you need to understand why a person or group has taken a particular stance.

### Understanding a negative stance

When someone has objections to the project, it's important to hear those objections. And *hearing* means listening very carefully, working hard to understand, and trying to see things from the stakeholder's position. In some cases, those making the objections reduce their opposition when they feel that they've at least been heard rather than just plain ignored. In other cases, the concerns may be entirely valid and you need to do something about them. When people see that you've taken their objections seriously and addressed them, they may come on-side and support the project, or at least move to a neutral stance from a negative one.

## Look for the underlying causes

When starting an IT project in a UK government agency, Nick Graham was informed that the senior user representative on the project was to be a certain manager. Nick was told by the Project Manager of a project just finishing that this manager had been a real problem throughout that project and had constantly blocked progress. It wasn't so much opposition in his case, but rather inertia. When an important specification was to be signed after it was circulated, the manager would attend the approval meeting and sit quietly. At the point he was asked to sign off the specification he refused, saying that he couldn't sign it because he hadn't read it yet. When asked when he would be able to read the specification, he replied that he was very busy and didn't have time to read it.

Thinking about the problem, Nick decided that time pressure wasn't the issue because the manager was involved with less important things and dealt with them without any apparent difficulty. So Nick's conclusion was that the manager was scared. He didn't understand what he was being asked to put his name to,

but knew that he'd be held accountable if the documentation was later found to be wrong and he'd signed it off.

Before any significant document was circulated on the new project, Nick took to calling in to this manager's office for a chat. The manager was always happy to talk for a while – so not that busy then. The first time Nick did this, he noticed a pile of aircraft magazines on a shelf and so talked to him about an air show he'd recently been to . . . and he waited. The manager wasn't rude, so it was just a matter of time until he asked, even out of mere politeness, how the project was going. Nick's reply was that it was going really well and the work to map the current business functions was nearly complete and in fact, he 'happened' to have a copy of the main diagram with him. Nick put the diagram on the desk and talked the manager through it in a low-key way. The manager was very interested and asked a few questions. When Nick held a meeting a few days later to sign off the description of the current functions, the manager was the first one up with a pen.

Another reason for a negative stance is lack of understanding about the project, or even misunderstanding. People tend to react against something, or show inertia and a lack of positive support, when they don't fully understand it. Sometimes they're scared to commit, because they aren't sure exactly what they're committing to. Where you spot this, the action you need is communication to explain things clearly and in terms that the people involved can understand, but always taking care not to sound patronising.

If you do have significant opposition to the project, you can find a bit more help in the section 'Handling Opposition' towards the end of the chapter. Also check out the nearby sidebar 'Look for the underlying causes'.

### Understanding a positive stance

If a stakeholder has a positive stance then, perhaps strangely, you also need to understand why. You can't protect a position until you know the underlying reasons for it. The stakeholder may be a massive fan of your project because it will deal with a problem that's plagued her staff for years. If the project comes under pressure of time and budget, and the plan shows that you need to reduce the scope, you'd do well to think twice before cutting the part that deals with that stakeholder's problem.

Even if you do have to make a reduction that will remove an important benefit for a key stakeholder, you should be very aware of the impact when thinking through the changes. Then you can at least go and explain beforehand why you need to make the reduction, and so work to soften the blow. That way the stakeholder's reaction may be one of understanding and disappointment rather than cold fury and opposition.

### Understanding the power base

Your analysis of stakeholder positions must now look at their power base in relation to the project. You can think of this in categories:

- ✔ **Affected:** A person may be affected by the project, but she doesn't have the authority to give input or affect the results. However, you want the person to be positive and accepting of the project. An example is with operational staff who'll use the new business procedure, or another organisation or department that needs to fit in with new procedures in this one.

- ✔ **Approvers:** Those who aren't always directly involved in the project but whose approval is needed, often to confirm compliance with regulations. This includes legal and financial specialists.

- ✔ **Decision makers:** Those who can affect what the project does and what it will deliver, and who may even hold the purse strings and so can affect financial and staff resource.

- ✔ **Interest:** Such as customers wanting to know about new developments, but they don't have any influence over the project.

✔ **Those with a veto:** Some organisations contain people who can't make things happen but they have the power to stop things happening. Keep your eyes and ears wide open when working on this category, because sometimes the veto isn't through direct authority but disproportionate influence, and sometimes by surprisingly junior staff – 'Well, if Mary down in customer services doesn't think it's a good idea . . .'

Be careful how you document information about stakeholders. Your director of finance may have a mean, narrow-minded, 'bean counter' view of project benefits, and could cut project funding on a whim or in a fit of temper. However much that's a problem to the project, it may be counterproductive to document the stakeholder using those exact words: it's probably not the best way of getting the finance director on-side!

## Deciding action – the 'what'

Your stakeholder management now moves clearly from the analysis part into the action part as you consider *what* you need to do. On the one hand, you may want to consolidate a stakeholder's current position to make sure, for example, that the person stays enthusiastic and on-side. On the other hand, you may want to try and change the stakeholder's position, particularly if it's currently against the project. Now this is getting onto slightly dangerous ground because, as a Project Manager, you don't want to be seen as a political game player. However, you'll be pleased to know that you can be successful in changing the outlook of problematic stakeholders without becoming a cut-throat and devious greasy-pole climber. Skip down to the section 'Handling Opposition' to find out how.

### Looking at the possibilities

Your responsibility as a Project Manager is to deliver the project. What you can't afford is to manage your stakeholders superbly but fail in that project delivery. So you have to balance out stakeholder management. Exactly what effort is needed and how much work can be justified? In turn, part of that is looking at your chances of success. It's simply not worth a lot of effort trying to change someone's view of the project if she's dead set against it, and any attempt to change her view will simply be a non-starter or, worse, add fuel to the fire – 'Now they're trying to manipulate me as well!'

### Involving others

Don't think that working with stakeholders is all down to you as a Project Manager. If you have more senior managers involved in the project, perhaps on a project steering committee or as sponsors, talk to them about stakeholder issues. They may be better placed than you to take the agreed actions and so be much more effective.

# Working with stakeholders – the 'how'

Having decided that you need to involve some of the stakeholders, or at least communicate information to them, you need to decide *how* best to do that. This is where your analysis of both the stakeholders' positions and the stakeholders themselves pays dividends. Think about:

- ✔ **Approval:** Before completing the project, or even some key deliverables within it, you may need to get approval from stakeholders who have authority to make decisions. An example is the approval of a design before the building works start to modify the offices.

- ✔ **Communication:** How you'll communicate information such as on the impact the project will have, its progress and benefits projections – particularly on benefits to the stakeholders.

- ✔ **Consultation:** Do you need to get agreement from stakeholders at particular points in the project? How will you do that or, if you're constrained by procedures, how must you do that?

- ✔ **Participation:** When making organisational change, you get people on-side more easily if you involve them in the change process, so how will you do that? For example, you may get operational staff involved to help design new procedures. That helps ensure that the procedures work but also that the operational staff 'own' them from the outset.

You need to think through the detail of how best to involve stakeholders; in turn, that can affect the plans. Taking the example in the bullet list above of getting operational staff to help design new procedures, you can do that by having them submit suggestions and then check over the final design, or you can add some operational staff to the team that's working on the design.

The Stakeholder List comes into its own here, and you can use it to help think through whether you've considered the needs of all stakeholders on the project.

## Linking with communications

A lot of the stakeholder management actions relate to communications. It follows that as you think about the stakeholders, you adjust the Communications Management Plan. When passing on information, don't just add names to email lists. ('Well, we told you about xyz; you were on the distribution list.') In medium to large projects particularly, consider:

- ✔ **Briefings:** Such as a lunchtime 20-minute illustrated talk once a month

- ✔ **News sheet:** An illustrated project bulletin circulated to everyone with an interest in the project – and it can be electronic, not printed

✔ **Roadshow:** Going around to the regional offices before the product launch

✔ **Website:** A dedicated website for the project, with news and progress information, excluding anything sensitive

Use these strategies with care because they take effort, but one or more may be a really effective way of communicating information to important stakeholders.

# Planning the work – the 'when'

Some work to manage stakeholders is effectively continuous, such as keeping everyone up to speed with progress and new developments on the project. Other work focuses on particular points. Here are some examples that are at fixed points, but you need to think through your own project, come up with your own requirements, and then build the actions into the plan at the appropriate points:

✔ **Customers:** When the project is confirmed, to tell them changes are coming, and then towards the end of the project to explain, for example, how the new ordering procedures will work and when they'll become operational

✔ **Donors:** With communications at the front end to catch the imagination and drive up donations for the work, but then at regular intervals to maintain interest, show the impact of money given so far, and explain the current financial needs to encourage further gifts

✔ **Interfacing departments and organisations:** When you know the design, so that others can work out the impact of it, and then in testing to be sure that the interfaces function properly

✔ **User staff:** Towards the front of the project to provide input into the design, then a few users towards the end of the project to help with testing

# Handling Opposition

If one or more people are dead set against your project, then you won't need this book to tell you that you've got problems. However, although serious, such problems aren't insurmountable; this section gives a bit more help.

Before reading on, check out the 'Understanding positions – the why' section, earlier in the chapter. People rarely take action or hold a position without a reason, no matter how valid or invalid you think that reason is. Try hard to find out why a person is opposing your project.

## Solving the problems

If opposition exists because your project will cause genuine problems, do your best to make adjustments so that the project won't cause problems. Remember that sometimes objections are valid. Taking this approach can result in a win–win; not only do you avoid the problems, but the people who raised the objections are now really impressed that you've listened and then worked with them to solve the difficulties.

## Focusing on the common areas

Try to identify common areas and major on what you have in common, not on points that divide, especially if those points are minor. Sometimes people lose all sense of proportion when making negative arguments. Minor issues that are molehills assume the proportions of mountains and then obscure nearly everything else.

In the UK, there was widespread amazement at the formation of a coalition government between the Conservative Party and the Liberal Democrats after the 2010 general election. Many asked how people at all levels in both parties could be so friendly and co-operative when the week before they'd deeply criticised the other side and seemed to be at each other's throats. When this question was put by a TV interviewer, one person in a local Lib Dem party office answered it both simply and wisely. She said that in the elections, both sides had been focused on their differences but now, when forming a government, they were focused on the much greater amount that they had in common.

## Understanding that you're a threat

When looking for underlying reasons for a negative stance, consider the idea that people are probably seeing you, your project, or both, as a threat. Projects, by definition, are usually changing something, and generally people don't like change. You may not notice people's dislike of change at first because:

- ✔ You probably like change or else you wouldn't be involved with projects. It's natural enough to think that other people see the project the way you do, so you may be puzzled as to why they don't share your enthusiasm.

- ✔ 'Operation cover-up' is underway. If a managing director promotes a project at the company meeting by saying it will 'change the face of our whole operation', everyone may clap and smile and say 'wonderful idea' to each other, while saying secretly to themselves 'over my dead body!' It doesn't do to be seen to be opposed to something backed by senior managers, but what about what's unseen?

You need, then, to reduce the threat. Try the following:

- ✔ **Be scrupulously honest.** One thing guaranteed to heighten threat and fear is distortion. People need to know that when you say something, it's true. That way they learn to trust you instead of the rumour mill.

- ✔ **Be open.** Make as much known about the project as possible. If people think you're hiding things, they imagine all sorts of nasty threatening reasons why. That's completely unnecessary if the information wasn't secret in the first place.

- ✔ **Act open.** It's surprising how little things can increase or decrease the feeling of threat. If you're talking to someone and want to take notes, ask her permission, even if she's very junior. The person is highly unlikely to say no, but the act of asking gives her the feeling of being in control, which runs counter to feeling threatened. Also, hold your notes in a way that the person can see what you're writing, and ask if you can send her a copy afterwards to check that you've got the details right. Again, all of this signals openness, which does a lot to play down threat.

- ✔ **Involve people as much as you can.** Okay, maybe you could do it faster and a bit cheaper with less involvement, but that small saving comes at a high cost if you end up with huge opposition that could kill your project. Involvement is a key component in change management, and your project is about change. Nobody likes things being imposed on them, and a hugely different dynamic exists where people are involved.

- ✔ **Understand the extent and strength of opposition.** You can use techniques such as Force Field Analysis to model the forces at play so that you can understand them and also the overall dynamic of the project better. You can find information on this technique on the Internet or in publications like Inspirandum's *The Project Techniques Toolbox,* by Nick Graham.

## *Spotting facts and emotions*

It can be both puzzling and sometimes infuriating when you've countered a fear or an argument with rock-solid fact and unassailable logic, and *still* the stakeholder you're talking to doesn't come around. If that happens, think about emotion.

People make some decisions emotionally, and equally hold some views emotionally. Sir Richard Branson runs Virgin Atlantic Airways, but why? Did he think it was the best option for a business? That's debatable, because when asked how you become a millionaire, he's reported to have said, 'Start off as a billionaire and buy an airline!' No, although he no doubt checked out the business position, he started Virgin Atlantic because he'd always wanted to run an airline; at its root it was an emotional decision.

So why, when it's so obvious that the move to new offices would help opera-tions and be so much cheaper, is one of the founding partners so opposed to the project? Well, the old building that you're closing down and selling off is where the whole business started off 30 years ago with her and a team of five friends and five new employees who quickly became friends too. The place is part of her history and holds many memories of both good times and struggles through tough times, and it's so very hard to let go.

So what could you do about an emotional attachment to the old building? You need to think creatively and even if the solution adds to the project costs a bit, that's likely to be less than the cost of delay caused by reluctance or opposition. In the case of the founding partner, just going to talk to her for an hour so she can reminisce may be a start. Then, how about changing the plan for the décor of the reception area in the new building? Instead of that modern art of dubious taste, have some great graphics panels with photos of the earlier life of the company. They could include pictures of the original staff and building and progress to more recent times, and all be nicely lit with downlighters. Such a display, with some of the photographs having been pro-vided by the founding partner herself, may help satisfy her understandable need to stay in touch with the company roots. And it will probably be rather impressive to customers visiting the building to see how the company has grown and developed. Perhaps it will be cheaper than that modern art too.

## Overriding the opposition

Well, that's it for the kind stuff; now on to the tough stuff. If you have serious opposition but the project must get done, you need to stamp on the opposi-tion. Such stamping presupposes that you've done everything possible to win over the opposing stakeholders.

As a Project Manager, you probably won't have the personal authority to do much stamping! Even if you're a fairly high grade, the chances are that your project is cross-functional and the opposition is coming from another depart-ment where you don't have any authority. The answer in this case is to go higher. To take a simple case, you work with your project sponsor to get the managing director to issue a notice from the management board to say that this project is going ahead and that she requires staff in all departments to cooperate to ensure that the project is successful. Now if anyone opposes you or the project, they put themselves in opposition to the management board.

Having gone over the heads of the opposing stakeholders, you win out. But be vigilant because although opposers may now appear to cooperate, their involvement is unwilling and so is likely to be half-hearted at best. At worst, they may secretly work to undermine the project so that if they succeed they'll be able to say, 'I told you it was a bad idea and would never work.'

It is better to convince than compel, so don't stamp unless you really, really need to and all else has failed. After you've got heavy, you'll almost certainly have eliminated any further possibility of winning people over. Also, the bad feeling it creates will last long after the end of the project.

Have you heard the story of the sun and the wind arguing about who was more powerful? They decided to have a trial of strength and, looking down, they saw a man wearing a coat. They decided that whoever could get the coat off the man would have proved to be the stronger. The wind went first and blew and blew. But the more fiercely it blew, the more the man held his coat tightly around him. Eventually, the wind invited the sun to have a try. The sun simply shone on the man, who got hotter and hotter and took the coat off himself.

# Handling Multiple-Stakeholder Projects

This section refers to stakeholders who have power to authorise things in the project and who may also have a power of veto. If you're working in the public sector, you may face this where you have multiple government agencies involved or multiple organisations.

Two examples are:

- ✔ A project to reduce street crime that could affect several government departments, police, courts and probation interests
- ✔ A group of local authorities working together to share the development of a new system for keeping track of large maintenance works in schools

## Getting multiple approvals

In a multiple-agency project, instead of just getting approval for something in the project from your own organisation, you may need to get the approval of all the stakeholders. Getting that approval can prove difficult when the different agencies have different agendas, different priorities and different perspectives. What's important to one stakeholder may not be important to the others. But even worse, what if the requirements conflict? If you don't manage a conflict well, stakeholders with opposing views can bring the project to a standstill, each refusing to give approval unless you meet her requirements.

Where multiple organisations are equal financial stakeholders in a project, such as with local authorities or hospital trusts working together, life can get more difficult still. In effect, each organisation has the power of veto because if it pulls out, the others are faced with a higher financial overhead; if the remaining stakeholders don't have the budget for the project, then they're forced to cancel it, thereby losing both the project and all they have invested to date.

## *Developing management strategies*

The area of approvals can be an extremely difficult area to manage, but following are a few strategies that can help, at least as a starting point:

- ✔ **Checking out compatibility of interest:** Make sufficient effort in the project, or ahead of the project, to establish that the organisations are genuinely compatible in the project they're looking to run. It's all too easy to rush into joint agreements using the same sort of words and assuming that everyone means the same thing. You must do sufficient work to give confidence that the needs, outlooks and even cultures of the participant organisations are compatible.

  In planning, you might include a product that's a signed joint agreement. That product then makes a good bottleneck in the Work Flow Diagram – Chapter 5 has the detail.

- ✔ **Deciding up front how to handle conflicts:** Decide how you'll resolve conflicts of interest long before the first one happens. If you try to work out a mechanism for dealing with conflict during a conflict, then it's harder because people are already entrenched in positions and are possibly emotional about them, despite the apparently professional exterior. People can think dispassionately and more logically when nothing is at stake – yet – but when the conflict is already underway, then they're inevitably distracted by trying to come up with a mechanism that will work in their favour for the current problem.

  Again, the 2010 general election in the UK is of interest because for the first time in some 70 years a coalition government was formed. A committee was established at the outset for resolving any policy conflicts that would emerge in the future. The mechanism was put in place at the start.

- ✔ **Agreeing the casting vote:** Negotiate up front who has the casting vote. In government, this might be a lead department. In the event of disagreement, everyone works at trying to find a solution that satisfies all the participants. But if no such solution exists, then the lead department makes the call, and the other agencies have all agreed up front that they'll accept that decision.

- ✔ **Deciding priorities:** You can reduce arguments if you grade requirements at the outset so that it's clear for each agency what's essential, what's preferred and what's nice to have. Although this won't prevent clashes on major items, it serves to lessen conflict on minor ones because they've already been labelled as minor.

# Part II
# Building the Plans

# In this part . . .

**Y**ou have the greatest chance of achieving project success when you have a good plan that shows it's possible to accomplish everthing on time, to budget and to the right level of quality.

This part explains the very powerful 'product led' approach to planning, how to do activity planning and then resource planning, including the finances. And last, but definitely not least, it shows how you can identify and deal with potential project risks.

# Chapter 5

# Planning with Deliverables First

*I*f you've been around projects for a while and come across other books or used project management software (actually it's usually only scheduling software), you've seen the planning approach in which you first list all the activities or tasks for a project and then draw up a Gantt Chart with its familiar horizontal bars (see Chapter 6 for more on this chart). To help you get to your task list, you may also have used a hierarchical diagram in which you can break down the major activities into more detail to determine a working list of tasks.

This chapter, however, starts the planning up front of the activities: it starts with thinking about, understanding and defining what you need to deliver. Then, when you're as clear as you can be on what you're going to deliver, you can start thinking through what activities you need to build those deliverables.

This chapter makes the case for the *product-led* or *product-based* approach to planning and also gives you some extremely powerful techniques. The product-led approach is extremely logical, and it's hard to overstate just how very good it is. Not only is it an enormous help in planning, but it also opens the door to particularly effective quality management and progress control.

The product-led approach to planning isn't intuitive, so you may need some time to get your head around it. If you're reading this book because you're completely new to project management, then you'll be delighted to know that you'll probably find the technique fairly straightforward and easy to use. If you're a more experienced Project Manager, you may take to the product-led approach easily too, but don't be worried if you have a bit of a struggle, and don't give up, because the benefits of product-led planning hugely repay your efforts in getting to grips with the approach. Keep at it and suddenly you find everything clicks into place; after that, planning with products will seem easy and it will simply become the way you think and work.

# Seeing the Logic of Product Planning

You can't really argue with the logic of the product-led approach. How can you possibly determine activities and time durations with any accuracy if you're unclear about what it is you're going to build?

Many approaches to project management refer to deliverables as *products*. What you produce are the products. For more on products, see the later section 'Knowing What a Product Is – and Isn't'.

## Thinking 'product' before thinking 'task'

To show the logic of looking at deliverables, or products, first, you're best following the process of activity-led planning to show where it can create some problems.

Okay, we're working on a project and our computer software tells us to list the activities first. We write on our list 'Build the wall', because that's going to be an important element in this project, which involves some alterations to our headquarters building. After we've entered this and the other tasks, the next step is to draw bars on a Gantt Chart to indicate the time duration. Please say then, how long it takes to build a wall.

You probably want to start asking questions about the wall, such as how high it will be and how long, and the sort of finish required. But you missed the question and aren't helping. The software says that step two is to enter the time duration, not start a debate, so please give your estimate. How long does it take to build a wall?

The example shows a significant problem that exists when you start planning with the activities. Activities are a comfortable place to start, but not a logical place. The comfort comes because people normally think *activity* when faced with a project. 'Oh, I need to do this, and I must remember to do that, and I mustn't forget to ask Fred to do the other.' It's do, do, do. But how can you accurately determine the activities needed to build a brick wall and how long they're likely to take unless you've first defined what it is you mean by *brick wall*. So, you were right to want to ask questions.

The sorts of questions that you may think about are:

- ✔ How long is the wall and how high? The height is significant because we'll need scaffolding if the wall is higher than about 2 metres.
- ✔ When you say *wall*, does that include the foundations?

✔ Where's the wall going to be? If it's at the front of the building and in full public view, it needs to be neatly finished, but if it's a supporting wall that'll be covered by an earth bank, we can leave it rough.

✔ Will the wall be one brick deep or two?

✔ If the wall is in public view, is it to be plain brick, Flemish bond or some intricate design with the company logo in 3D?

Whatever the product, you need to define and understand it so that you can determine what tasks you need to do to create the product and how long those tasks will take.

If you're already deeply into activity-driven approaches, your response may well be that you do this sort of thinking already. If you do respond like that, great, because you're already halfway there. The product-led approach just emphasises that line of thinking and gives you some particularly powerful techniques to help.

# Who's using product-led planning?

The product-led approach is in increasing use, but not always to its full extent. In its PMBOK (*Project Management Body of Knowledge*), the American Project Management Institute (PMI) refers to products as a key focus. NASA, the American space agency, developed a product-based approach to avoid problems it had experienced with activity-based planning; in a guidance paper on Work Breakdown Structures, available on the NASA website, you see that, for the most part, the structure shows products. Some academic bodies working in the field of project management have developed the product approach, and although they've re-invented the wheel in some cases, they've helped establish the technique. Product-led planning is also built into some project methodologies such as PRIME, where it's a key focus, and PRINCE2, which expects you to use the product-led approach (for more on PRIME and PRINCE2, see Chapter 2).

It's worth commenting briefly on PRINCE2 because it's in such widespread use. The method is a little strange because although the product-planning approach was well developed at the time of PRINCE2's creation, it's never been explained very effectively in the method's manual. That weakness has led to a lot of PRINCE2 users ignoring product planning completely, and a great many more failing to use it well. In the latest manual edition (2009), the implementation has been rolled back, taking out some of the useful refinements developed for an earlier edition. The new manual also describes the very powerful progress-monitoring element of product planning as 'optional' and confuses how you should carry out progress monitoring. Why those responsible for the method should want to abandon useful refinements is something of a mystery. If you're using PRINCE2 and want to know more about how to incorporate product planning without losing its power, you might like to buy a copy of *PRINCE2 For Dummies* by Nick Graham (Wiley).

## Understanding the problems of an activity focus

Please note carefully that taking a product-led approach doesn't do away with activity planning. Activity planning is powerful and isn't only advantageous but also absolutely essential. But product planning provides a very logical and powerful front end.

Starting instead with activities brings two problems:

- Until you have a clear idea of what you need to build, you aren't going to have a clear idea of the activities needed and are highly likely to miss some out. In turn, that means that you're likely to underestimate the effort and time needed for the project, which, indeed, is a very common cause of project problems.

- Even where you correctly identify activities, time estimates are likely to be wrong. Returning to the example of the task to build a wall that we use in the previous section, clearly a great deal of difference exists between the time needed to build a small garden wall and the time needed to build something on the scale of the Great Wall of China.

Many projects, encouraged by books and software, plunge into activity planning without proper thought about what is to be produced. It's no wonder then that estimates of time and cost are inaccurate and the project is then plagued with problems where essential work is identified during the project that isn't on the plan. Many time sheets built into project scheduling software have a section for 'Unscheduled activity' where project staff can report work they're having to do that wasn't foreseen. Such problems lead to projects being late in delivery and overspent on budget.

# Knowing What a Product Is – and Isn't

There are a few refinements on what products are, but the starting point is extremely simple. A *product* is something that one of your project teams (and that may be just one person) builds. When a team leader comes up to you and says, 'We've finished it, here it is,' what is *it*? A product is something that you can hold in your hand or, if it's too big for that, walk up and kick.

Products in your projects might include:

- Brick wall – you can kick it

- Computer program – you can print it out and hold it

- Decorated room – you can stamp around it and kick the walls, though try not to dirty the new paint

> ✔ Installed network – you can kick the computers, hold the cables and see from the screens that the computers are talking across the network
>
> ✔ Instruction manual – you can hold it

Things that aren't products, but are commonly mistaken for them, are:

> ✔ Designers – that's a staff resource. The designers are the people who create your product 'Office design document'. Unless your project is quite long and rather exciting, you won't be making people!
>
> ✔ Money – that's a resource. Unless you work for the Royal Mint or your own country's equivalent, actually producing money is illegal and you can spend years in prison for it, causing substantial project delay.
>
> ✔ Jobsworth Office Furnishings Ltd – that's a source of supply. The products are likely to be desks and chairs, and Jobsworth Office Furnishings Ltd is where you bought them.
>
> ✔ Walls built – that's a point in time when the walls have all been built. You don't kick 'walls built'; instead the products that you kick are 'built walls' – or more simply 'walls', because if they aren't built, then they aren't walls.
>
> ✔ Writing programs – that's a task or activity; notice the verb *write*.

# Finding Good Product Names

As you think about your project's products, you may come up with better and more appropriate names for some of them. In the bullet point in the previous section, if you're particularly fast-thinking, you may have said to yourself that 'Jobsworth Office Furnishings Ltd' might well be a product if the project includes setting up the company. That's true, but then the product name isn't a particularly good one. The product that you hold in your hand isn't going to be the company, but rather something like 'company registration document'. As you work through the products, you're likely to think of better, more descriptive names for some – so change them.

Product names should be short and descriptive. Later on you'll be drawing up some diagrams, and you need short names to go into the boxes on the diagrams. If you have long, unwieldy names, you'll be tempted to use numbers instead, and that can cause problems.

Where you're working on a project that involves other people, which is usual, then stick to the terminology in use in their part of the organisation. If the engineering staff refer to something as the 'upgrade plan' and in your diagrams you call the product 'modification schedule', the engineers won't recognise the product and won't be able to say whether the diagrams are correct. Stay with their names and note down separately the definition of them if it's not obvious to you from the product titles.

## Good and bad product names

Here's a snapshot of some great and rubbish product names:

✔ **28** – bad because you don't know what product 28 is without looking it up

✔ **Fully detailed specification of the engineering operations procedure** – bad; it's too long

✔ **New user manual** – good; it's short and descriptive

✔ **15. Approved design** – good; it's short, descriptive and has a reference to its Product Definition – number 15.

# Using a Business Project Example

This part of the chapter uses an example to show how the product-planning sequence works. The example is a small business project to review and improve a business process in an accounts department, including a small update to some computer software.

## Identifying the products

In the project example to review and adjust an accounts procedure, the initial products – just in the order they come to mind – are:

✔ **Problems and requirements list:** A list of things that the staff say are causing difficulties with the present way of doing things, and their wish list for how they would like a new one to work

✔ **Updated computer system:** Adjusted to deal with any changes decided on in the revised procedure

✔ **Draft of new accounts procedure:** An outline of the intended new approach

✔ **Final new procedure design:** The agreed new procedure and the one that will be implemented

✔ **Training plan:** A list of staff who need to be trained in the revised procedure and what they need to know

✔ **Training course:** The short course of two to three hours to explain the new procedures to staff

✔ **New accounts procedure:** The implemented new procedure, complete with the upgrade to the computer

For your projects, you can make up a product list from your own knowledge if you already know the business area, but even then you'll probably want to involve some other people to check that the list is correct. If you don't know the project at all, don't worry. You can do this work in a workshop format and facilitate the product planning by briefly explaining the product-planning approach and then guiding the session.

Some techniques can help bring some structure into your thinking about products – see the later section 'Using a Structured Product List'. For now, it's enough to work with a simple list.

# Developing a sequence

The next step is powerful; seriously powerful. You develop a very simple sequence diagram. This is called a Work Flow Diagram or sometimes a Product Flow Diagram.

The Work Flow Diagram simply shows the products in the order that they will be created in the project. Figure 5-1 is a first attempt at the sequence.

### Checking the Work Flow – bottom up

What comes next is the most important part of the activity in drawing a Work Flow Diagram. It's called the bottom-up check. Guess where you start on the diagram? Ah, well done, you're getting the hang of this rapidly.

You do two tests in the bottom-up check:

✔ For each dependency arrow, are you absolutely sure that you can't begin the later product until the earlier one is finished?

✔ To build a product, you've established that you need the products feeding into it. The next question is, do you need any products other than those already connected by an arrow? You may find that a dependency arrow is missing from another product already on the diagram or, very commonly, you discover one or more new products that aren't on the diagram at all at the moment.

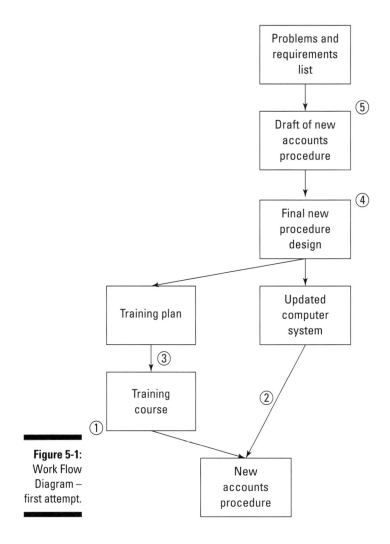

**Figure 5-1:**
Work Flow
Diagram –
first attempt.

Five locations are labelled on the first attempt at a Work Flow Diagram in Figure 5-1. These mark some problems that you discover in the bottom-up check:

1. You realise that 'Training course' isn't very good name. You can't hold a training course in your hand or kick it. A better product name is 'Trained accounts staff'. In the bottom-up check, you decide that it's correct that you need a training plan to produce the trained staff, so the dependency arrow is correct.

2. You realise that you also need the updated computer system for the training course. Unless that's available, the staff won't be properly trained because they won't have seen the changes and won't know how to work the changed system. The dependency from 'Updated computer system' to 'New accounts procedure' looked right at first, but now you see that you need to change the arrow to feed into the new 'Trained accounts staff' product. The trained staff also need sight of a new procedures manual for the training, which in turn can't be produced until the computer updates have been done so that screen shots can be included in the manual; so you discover a second missing product, 'Revised procedure manual'.

3. When you check the 'Trained accounts staff' (previously called 'Training course') product further, some thinking reveals that you don't just need a training plan, but also training materials. That's yet another new product that you need to put up front of the 'Trained accounts staff' product and after 'Training plan'.

4. It was clear that people would need to look at the draft design before it was finalised, but you now see that you need a formal response from some staff, such as your finance specialists, to confirm that the new procedure complies with the latest finance regulations. Because other staff comments really should be written down so that you can keep track of them and make sure they've all been considered, you identify a new product of 'Staff comments'. These comments are a product; they can be printed off and held in your hand.

5. Finally, on looking at the 'Draft of new accounts procedure', you see that the team will need a copy of the existing procedure manual to be sure they're clear on how things work at the moment in order to be able to correctly specify what the changes are.

The bottom-up check has discovered the missing products of Training materials, Current procedure manual, Revised procedure manual and Staff comments, and has also revealed that you need to change some dependencies.

Time for a re-draw of the Work Flow Diagram then – see Figure 5-2.

### *Seeing what's inside the project and what's outside*

In Figure 5-2 you may have noticed that most products are in a rectangle but two are in ovals. The shapes discriminates between internal and external products. An *internal product* is product that will be developed by one of the project teams. An *external product* is one that won't be developed by a project team, although it may be a very important product. Two sources of external products exist:

✔ **Products that already exist** (like the Current procedure manual in Figure 5-2). If the product already exists at the start of the project, clearly a project team isn't going to build the product during the project.

✔ **Something supplied from people outside the project** (like the Staff comments in Figure 5-2). The product may be very important, but it won't be built by one of the project teams. In a computer project, it is unlikely that your organisation will build the computer, but it's a very important product and the project can't go ahead without it.

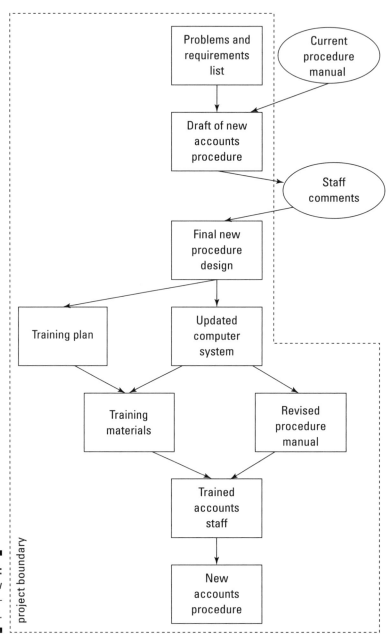

**Figure 5-2:**
Work Flow
Diagram –
adjusted.

The ovals and rectangles make the project boundary clear. In Figure 5-2 the ovals are to the outside of the diagram – although it isn't always possible to do that – so the boundary is particularly clear and can be shown with a dashed line.

### Sticking to a limit of 30 products

The number of boxes in the diagram should be between about 15 and about 30. If you go much beyond 30, the diagram gets too complicated and you find that you can't see anything; it all starts to look like a ball of string. In a small project, you have space to go into quite a lot of detail. If, however, your project is to review the business processes throughout John Wiley & Sons publishing worldwide (and no, we're not hinting, although project consultancy services are available from both authors at a very reasonable rate), then the project is so enormous that the 30 products will be quite chunky, to use a technical expression.

It's normal for a project to be coming up to the 30 limit quite nicely when the bottom-up check reveals big areas of the project that you hadn't realised were there, and you suddenly find that you have 50 products. The answer in that case is to combine some of the products and so show less detail in the diagram. Don't worry about combining products to stay within the limit. When you develop a more detailed stage plan later on for that part of the project, you can then show that greater level of detail. Chapter 9 has more on the levels of planning, including stage planning.

Where you have combined products, note down now what sub-products are contained in the new higher level one, so that you don't lose the more detailed thinking you've already done. You can note it on the Product Definition (see the section 'Defining the products'), and the information will be safe until you need to use it.

### Using names, not numbers

It's extremely important to use names on the diagram and not numbers. If you replace text with numbers (perhaps because you've chosen very long product names), the diagram loses meaning. If you have to look up the product numbers, you'll only ever understand a part of the diagram at a time.

You're likely to miss dependencies because you can't remember what all 30 product boxes are. Sooner or later you'll make a bad mistake, and sure as eggs is eggs, it'll be sooner.

The problem with numbers reinforces the point that you should find short, descriptive product names so that they fit easily into the boxes and so you won't be tempted to replace the names with numbers (see the earlier section 'Finding Good Product Names'). If you want to use numbers as well as names, that's fine, and actually an advantage because you can quickly look up the relevant Product Definition, as covered in the next section.

# Defining the products

For each product on the diagram, you now write a Product Definition, sometimes known as a Product Description. Product Definition is really a better term because it includes a description but rather more besides.

Have you ever heard a conversation that included the words, 'Oh, I thought you meant . . .'? It's that sort of conversation, with the accompanying problems of wasted money and of project delay, that the Product Definition does so much to avoid.

The *Project Definition* simply defines what the product is and also includes information on the quality criteria it must satisfy and how it will be tested to make sure that it does meet them. As with the rest of product-led planning, the case for the Product Definition is logical. If you're going to ask a team or an individual to build something for you, you're going to have to define what it is.

You may find this simple list of headings useful as a default, but you can always alter the headings to suit your own particular organisation or even a specific project.

- ✔ **Reference:** A product number.

- ✔ **Author and date:** The person responsible for this particular Product Definition.

- ✔ **Description:** A textual description of the product.

- ✔ **Sub-products:** If this product is made up of any lower-level components.

- ✔ **Quality criteria:** What quality criteria must the product must satisfy to be acceptable?

- ✔ **Tests:** To ensure that the product meets its quality criteria.

- ✔ **Required resource:** What team hours, skills and costs you anticipate you need to build the product and to test it.

- ✔ **Responsibilities:** As you get into more detailed planning, you can enter the names of the people (or team) who'll be building the product and those who'll be testing it.

If you're using the PRINCE2 methodology, you'll find that it refers to this document as a Product Description; the content is slightly different, although the concept is the same. If you're working to PMI standards, you'll find that the product details are stored in what the PMI calls the Work Breakdown Structure (WBS) Dictionary. Although the PMI mixes information on tasks and products, the same underlying thought exists that you need to set down information on deliverables somewhere.

## Taking the time to get the Project Definition right

In the UK, a large company asked Inspirandum to provide consultancy support to facilitate a product-planning workshop for a big, business-critical project to replace machines in an industrial environment. Six staff were flown in from overseas to take part in the workshop, and three more were from within the UK, then there was the Inspirandum consultant making ten in all. Part of that workshop was to produce Product Definitions for all the products. One Product Definition took four hours to produce with all ten people involved – that's 40 staff hours. What was the reaction of the participants at the end of the four hours do you think? That product

planning is long winded? No, actually they were delighted. The project was extremely important and this particular product was absolutely vital, yet at the outset nobody really understood it. At the end of the four hours everyone understood the product and was agreed on exactly what it was. In a difficult, business-critical project that was going to last some 18 months, everyone thought that pinning this product down so precisely was 40 staff hours very well spent. In the same workshop, two staff produced a Product Definition for a less contentious product in just over ten minutes.

# Using a Structured Product List

In the planning example used in the earlier section 'Using a Business Project Example', the initial list of products was compiled at random as products came to mind. In many projects, it can be a real help to use a bit of structure and think through the project in an orderly way, looking at different categories of product in turn.

For example, if the project is a house build, you might first list all the brickwork products, then all the electrical products, then woodwork products and finally decorating products. For the electrical products, you might find it easier still if you break that into two sub-categories and think first about the lighting circuit products and then the power circuit products.

Using categories provides some helpful structure and forms a hierarchy. You might write that down in the form of indented paragraphs. Taking just the first two of the four categories for the house build, the list might look like this:

Brickwork products

    Foundations

    Outer walls

    Garden wall

Electrical products

    Lighting circuit products

        Lights

        Switches

        5-amp lighting cabling

    Power circuit products

        Fuse board (consumer unit)

        13-amp power cabling

        Power sockets

If you like Mind Maps, you might prefer to list products using that format, which is essentially a hierarchy bent around in a circle. Again, you might prefer a hierarchy diagram such as that shown in Figure 5-3.

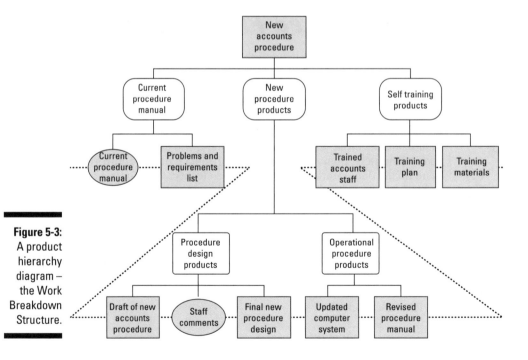

**Figure 5-3:** A product hierarchy diagram — the Work Breakdown Structure.

The hierarchy diagram is just like the indented list or Mind Map, only this time you show the categories and products in boxes. The advantage of this format is that you can use the same symbols as on the Work Flow Diagram (see the earlier section 'Developing a sequence') and show whether products are internal or external. Figure 5-3 uses the example of the new office procedure from the earlier section 'Using a Business Project Example'.

The bottom level of the Work Breakdown Structure hierarchy forms the list of products that you'll carry forward to the Work Flow Diagram. In Figure 5-3 a dashed line identifies the bottom level, with the products shown in grey, even though some products are physically higher up in the diagram. The key point is that there is nothing underneath each of the boxes along that dashed line, so those boxes are all bottom level no matter where they are physically. The top box on the diagram is the whole project, and that maps to the last box on the Work Flow Diagram.

The grouping or category boxes, shown with a rounded rectangle symbol in Figure 5-3, are effectively headings and not products and so don't form part of the product list. The category boxes simply show why that set of products have been grouped together.

No rules exist about the groupings or categories; they're just what help you to think through the project systematically. In larger projects involving contracts, a common grouping is by contract. If the subject of the whole project is unfamiliar to you and you don't know what the high-level categories are, just go straight for the Work Flow Diagram and don't do the Work Breakdown Structure. The Work Flow Diagram is helpful in that case because it is a network diagram and you don't have to start at the top; you can start anywhere with the information you have.

# Working at different levels of detail

This chapter focuses on project planning where you're setting out the whole of the project in the list and diagrams. However, you can use the same techniques for more detailed planning, if you need it, at stage level and at a lower level still for very detailed team or work pack plans. Chapter 9 has more on working with these different levels of plan when you need them in larger projects, and also discusses when you produce the different plans.

The levels of plan bring in huge power. In a ten-stage project with up to 30 products in each phase, you'll have capacity for 300 products even before you go down to work assignment level; that's an awful lot of products, considerably more than you're likely to want on your projects.

Some conflict exists over the use of the term *Work Breakdown Structure*. In activity-led planning approaches, Work Breakdown Structure is a diagram showing the decomposition of activities, where high-level activities are broken down into lower level activities. However, project guidance from the American space agency NASA shows the Work Breakdown Structure as products, with the very last level being the activities needed to build the products. NASA's approach is excellent, and we refer to it later when we discuss activity planning in Chapters 6 and 7.

# Unleashing the Power of the Work Flow Diagram

The Work Flow Diagram (which we explain in the section 'Developing a sequence', earlier in this chapter) is extraordinarily useful and powerful. A big advantage of using the Work Flow Diagram is finding missing products. The diagram is great for this and reveals missing parts of the project that other techniques such as the Gantt Chart and activity network just don't show, or don't show very well. Now that's significant because if you establish the real scope of the project at the beginning, you can then think what activities are needed to build the products and so have a more complete Project Plan. Some projects fly off the plan almost as soon as they start, and the problem isn't with the project, it's with the incomplete plan that significantly understates the project.

In a large project in a multinational company, the Project Manager decided not to use the product-planning approach and went straight in with activities and the Gantt Chart. At a progress meeting one month into the project, the project team had already discovered a lot of additional but essential work and they estimated that that after one month the project was already one month behind!

## Using the Work Flow Diagram for risk

Your organisation is probably unique in that you have absolutely no problems with external supply. Suppliers – other organisations and other projects – always provide you with exactly what you need, exactly when you need it; they never, ever let you down. No? Oh, so you live in the real world as well then!

The Work Flow Diagram is superb for revealing dependencies on things that are coming in from outside the project. Simply look for the ovals and you see products crossing the project boundary. For each one, you can ask yourself whether the supply is likely to be a problem. In some cases, if that supply fails, you can quickly and easily get an identical or similar product from somewhere else. In other cases, though, you find that you can't easily replace the supply, and so that external dependency needs to be risk managed.

A second use of the diagram in risk management is to use it as part of the risk analysis. You can work systematically through the diagram and ask, for each product, 'What can go wrong with developing this one?' It flushes out risks that other risk analysis techniques may not find.

## Using the Work Flow Diagram for control

Another powerful use of the Work Flow Diagram is to bring a highly effective control point into the project by deliberately creating a bottleneck. In the UK, Inspirandum used this when providing project consultancy to a power company. The company had a project to bring a new and novel approach in to control part of the operational side of power supply, but the project team members weren't sure that what they were trying to do was even theoretically possible. What they needed was a *proof of concept product* fairly early in the project. Only if they could demonstrate that the idea was at least theoretically possible would the Project Manager allow more substantial work on the project to go ahead. The team manager made this product into a bottleneck in the Work Flow Diagram.

You can get the idea of the bottleneck from the diagram in Figure 5-4. The product dependency lines originally flowed around the proof of concept product, but they were deliberately changed to create this powerful control bottleneck. Only when the proof of concept product was accepted and demonstrated that the idea was workable would authority be given to start on generating further products. And yes, if you're already thinking about delivery stage boundaries (Chapter 2 has more on stages), this product makes an ideal one because it's a major decision and commitment point in the project.

## Using the Work Flow Diagram to show stages

The Work Flow Diagram is sequential, and because of that you can map phase or stage boundaries on it. You can mark them on with dotted lines and so see them clearly.

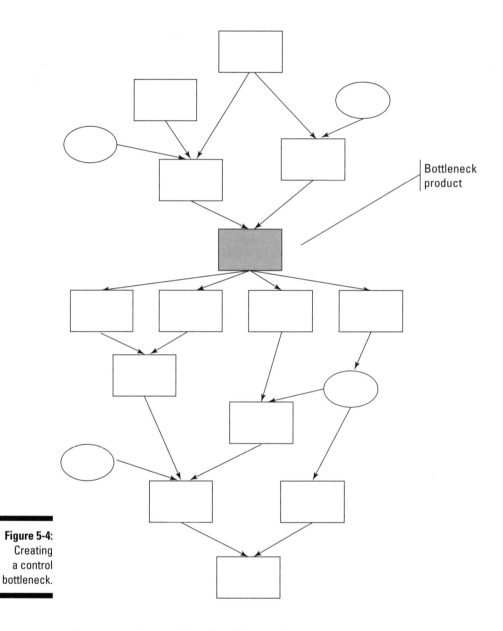

Bottleneck product

**Figure 5-4:**
Creating
a control
bottleneck.

# Using the Work Flow for progress reporting

Many, or actually most, project planning tools and books suggest that you monitor progress using 'percentage complete' on activities. So, this particular activity is '60 per cent complete'. Computer planning software often shows the percentage complete on Gantt Charts by filling up the activity bar like a thermometer. Very pretty, but known to be generally unreliable. Who says the activity is 60 per cent complete; can you prove it? No, normally it's somebody's guess – sorry, somebody's estimate.

In his book *A Guide to the Successful Management of Computer Projects* (Associated Business Press), Hamish Donaldson came up with a highly amusing but very real rule that he calls the *90 per cent rule*. Hamish's rule is simply that the first 90 per cent of the activity takes 90 per cent of the time, and the last 10 per cent of the activity also takes 90 per cent of the time! It's that last little bit that goes out, and out, and out. The work is 'nearly finished', and a month later it's still 'nearly finished'.

When they're saying that their task is nearly finished, perhaps the team really think it is. Then they find a huge problem and they have to do a lot of the work all over again. Or perhaps, though not in your organisation, of course, the team say 'nearly finished' to keep the Project Manager happy and off their backs for another week or two!

The thing about products is that they're either delivered or not delivered. *Delivered*, by the way, means checked and signed off. If the product hasn't been checked and signed off, then it isn't delivered. Progress monitoring, then, becomes a matter of factual reporting: which products are complete and which aren't.

 You can make a useful Delivery Checklist listing all the products in a stage as milestones and, after you complete the activity planning, recording the target completion date for each product. Then, when the product is signed off, you can record the actual completion date.

Taking the progress monitoring a bit further, you can also colour code the project or stage Work Flow Diagram as suggested by Philipp Straehl, a senior Project Manager and co-developer of the PRIME method, who has used this approach to great effect on large projects. To show just how effective this visual Progress Checklist is, imagine that you're a senior manager looking at the diagram for a project. Look at Figure 5-5 and ask yourself where the project is at this point in time.

No brainer, isn't it? Using colour or shading turns the Work Flow Diagram into a superb visual progress chart based not on an opinion or estimate of progress, but on factual reporting of what has been delivered and what hasn't.

You can make the diagram even more meaningful by having three states of product indicated with three colours such as:

✔ **Red:** Those products that haven't been started yet

✔ **Amber:** Those products that are currently being worked on

✔ **Green:** Those products that have been quality checked, signed off and delivered

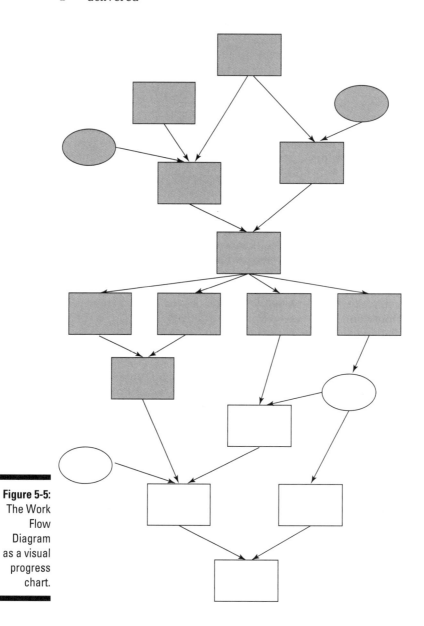

**Figure 5-5:**
The Work
Flow
Diagram
as a visual
progress
chart.

Using the Work Flow Diagram for progress reporting makes the point that all products on a plan should be used as milestones; in other words, 15–30 milestones (see the guidance in the earlier section 'Sticking to a limit of 30 products'). You can find more on the value of products as milestones for progress control in Chapter 14.

## *Getting a picture of the project*

If you've been involved in project management for a while, think about the Gantt Chart from the project before the one you're currently working on. Can you remember it? Can you remember the one from the project before that? Can you even remember the Gantt Chart from your current project? Your answer to all three questions is likely to be 'no'. Gantt Charts are excellent, but they all look pretty much the same.

A further advantage of the Work Flow Diagram is that it provides a picture of your project that's memorable and that you can hold in your head. As you work on the project, you can bring up your Work Flow Diagram in your mind's eye as you discuss developments with a team leader or perhaps another Project Manager; when you talk about the inter-project dependencies, you can think of the two ovals that represent products coming in from his project.

# Chapter 6

# You Want This Project Done When?

*P*roject assignments often have deadlines, but even if you don't have a deadline imposed on you, you'll want to know when the job will be finished. For one thing, you have other work to move on to, but then other people may need to know when your project will deliver in order to fit in with what you're delivering or changing.

When you find out the required end date, your immediate reaction is often one of panic: 'But I don't have enough time!' Don't worry, one major reason to do the planning is to make sure that you can meet any required end date with time to spare.

In Chapter 5 the planning started with *products*: what it is you're going to build and deliver. But products don't have durations – a wooden table doesn't have a time span; rather, it's the activities to build the table that have the time span. To calculate the length of the project and to know what work is to be done, activity planning isn't only extremely helpful, it's essential.

The first part of activity planning is to build an Activity Network. Some people think this first step is very difficult, so much so that computer project management software tools usually have an option to avoid the network and instead model the activity dependencies with arrows on the Gantt Chart. You don't need to miss out on the power of the Activity Network technique, though. Switch off the Gantt arrows option if you're using a computer tool, and prepare for something that's powerful and basically very easy. In this chapter you find out how to move from products to activities, and how to draw up an Activity Network that you can use to work out how long the project will take and that you can work with to help meet any fixed end date. Then, finally, you see how to move all the information onto a Gantt Chart.

# Moving From Products to Activities

Having established what the deliverables or products of the project are (Chapter 5 guides you through this work), moving to activity planning is very easy. You simply ask, 'What do we need to do to build this product?' Bear in mind that you personally may not know. Don't worry, just go and ask people who do know. You can ask team members, specialists, suppliers – in fact, anyone who knows the answer. You probably already have a good idea about who to ask because you consulted them when listing and defining the products in the first place.

## Having multiple tasks to build a product

There may be a single activity or task to build a particular product, but for many products you can expect to have more than one task. A simple example is with the two tasks of 'Build it' and 'Test it'. These are two tasks for a single product, probably using different staff resources.

## Listing the activities or tasks

You can produce a list in one of three ways: as a simple list, by noting the tasks on the Work Flow Diagram (see Chapter 5) or by noting the tasks on the Work Breakdown Structure (also see Chapter 5).

Here's an activity list for three products in a project to revise a company's accounts procedure. The product name forms the heading, and the indents list the activities.

> Problems and requirements list
>> Analyse existing procedure
>> Interview staff
>> Prioritise problems and requirements list
> Draft of new procedure
>> Draft the new procedure
>> Circulate the draft

Staff comments

[Await comments]

The third product, Staff comments, is an external product coming from people outside the project. By definition, then, there is no project work to be done. However, staff aren't going to send in comments in one-thousandth of a second, so a time allowance is needed in the activity plan. There are two ways of showing the delay on the Gantt Chart, and you'll find more on that later in the chapter in the section 'Understanding dependency types', under the heading of 'The lag'. For now, the waiting time is in the task list as a reminder that it will have a duration that may affect other activities. However, it's not an active task, in the sense that it doesn't require project work.

Instead of writing a list, you can just add the tasks onto either of the product diagrams. If you use the Work Flow Diagram, write the tasks alongside the boxes (see Figure 6-1).

Alternatively, you can show the activities beneath the bottom-level boxes – the products – on the Work Breakdown Structure. This is a good way of listing activities, because you will usually have more space than on the Work Flow Diagram. You can group all the activities neatly in their own area of the Work Breakdown diagram towards the bottom, as shown in Figure 6-2.

Then again, if you used a Mind Map (see Chapter 5) to add structure when thinking through the list, you can now extend this with further branches, perhaps in a different colour, to show the activities to build each of the products, around the outer edge of the Mind Map.

It really doesn't really matter which approach you use as long as you end up with a list of tasks needed to build the products. It's these tasks that you'll then use to create the Activity Network (see the following section) and, after that, the familiar Gantt Chart (see the later section 'Going for Gantt').

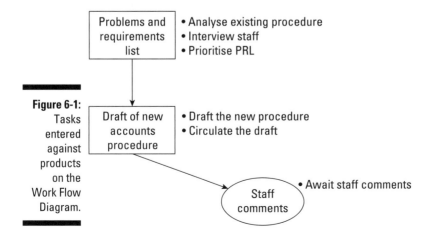

**Figure 6-1:** Tasks entered against products on the Work Flow Diagram.

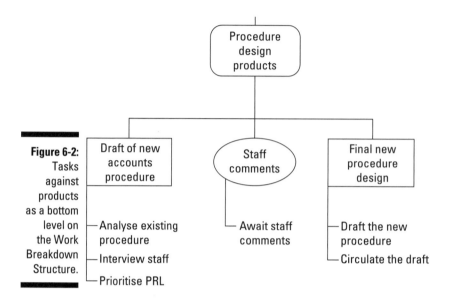

**Figure 6-2:**
Tasks
against
products
as a bottom
level on
the Work
Breakdown
Structure.

# Drawing Up a First Activity Network

To determine the amount of time you need for any project, you have to decide the following two aspects:

✔ **Sequence:** The order in which you perform the activities

✔ **Duration:** How long each individual activity takes

For example, suppose you have a project consisting of ten activities, each of which takes one week to complete. How long will it take you to complete your project? The truth is, you can't tell. You may finish the project in one week if you can perform all ten activities at the same time and have the resources to do so. You may take ten weeks if you have to do the activities one at a time in sequential order. Or you may take between one and ten weeks if you can do some, but not all, activities in parallel.

To develop a schedule for a very small project, you can probably hold the durations and sequence in your head. But projects with 15–20 activities or more – many of which you can perform at the same time – require an organised method to guide your analysis.

The technique that's really helpful here is the *Activity Network*. Although finally the diagram will deal with project timing, you start by focusing on the sequence – the dependencies between the activities.

Computer tools are a particular help with Activity Networks, and in Chapter 18 you can find out more about the software that's available. Even if you're intending to use a tool, though, it's important to understand the technique so that you properly understand what the computer tool is doing for you.

## Seeing how you build up an Activity Network

The Activity Network Diagram isn't at all difficult to understand, so, as your starter for ten points, what do you think the diagram in Figure 6-3 means? The project has just two activities so far, A and B.

**Figure 6-3:**
**Basic**
**activity**
**dependency.**

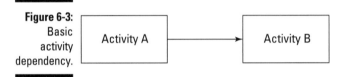

If you think A must be done before B, you score the ten points; well done. An equally acceptable answer is that B comes after A, so ten points for that too. Difficult, isn't it? Okay, because you're so good, here's another. Figure 6-4 shows a third activity, C, added to the project. So what can you say about when this activity is done?

Hopefully, you see that C will be done after A, or again that A must be completed before C can be started. On, then, to the really tough stuff with the addition of a final activity, D, to the project in Figure 6-5.

Figure 6-5 shows that you need to complete both B and C before you can start work on D.

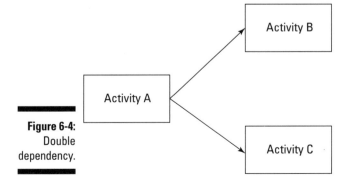

**Figure 6-4:**
**Double**
**dependency.**

So that's it, the diagram that people find so difficult. Really, as you've seen, it's very easy and is just a network diagram showing the tasks and the dependencies between them. You can, and will, go on to put some timings onto the activities and work out things like the project duration, but you have the main part of the technique clear already.

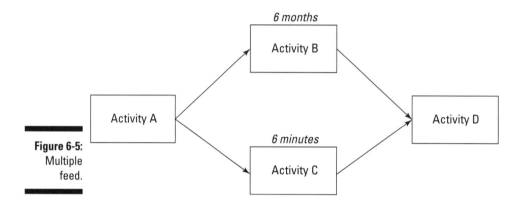

**Figure 6-5:**
Multiple
feed.

Before getting into the full detail of timings, try one more question on the examples with the letters. In Figure 6-5 you'll see a time duration above the boxes for Activity B and Activity C. For ten more points, what do you think the time span is between the end of Activity A and the beginning of Activity D? Look back at the diagram before you read on.

# Seeing circles – the PERT Chart

In Figures 6-3 to 6-5 the diagram notation shows the tasks in rectangles and then arrows showing the dependencies between those tasks. Nearly everyone uses this type of *activity on the node* network and its correct name is *Precedence Network*.

You may occasionally come across an older variant of the diagram, which uses circles and arrows instead of rectangles and arrows. It actually works the other way around to the Precedence Network, with the arrows representing the tasks and the circles being the junction points between the tasks. The Activity Network with circles is *activity on the line* and is usually called a *PERT Chart* (Programme Evaluation Review Technique).

PERT has problems compared with the Precedence Network and requires dummy activities to show some dependencies correctly, and is also cumbersome when showing overlaps between activities. That's why just about everyone now uses activity on the node – the Precedence Network.

Getting the right answer to the question requires you to bear in mind that both B and C must be completed before D can start, so the time duration is six months between the end of A and the beginning of D. There seems to be quite a lot of slack time for Activity C, so it's a good one for you to do personally and have an easy time of unless, of course, C is dangerous.

If the task is dangerous – and please take careful note because self-preservation is a vital project management principle – you must delegate it to some junior member of the project team who's expendable. Clearly, it's very important that you stay alive and safe so you're available to run future projects – in the very best interests of the organisation, of course, and also to maximise your investment in *Project Management For Dummies*.

## Using the Work Flow Diagram

The Work Flow Diagram (see Chapter 5) is a great help when moving on to the Activity Network. If you take the Work Flow Diagram and lie it on its side, you have the basic framework of the Activity Network already.

For a particular product, you may now have two or three activities, so you may have two or three boxes where you used to have one. You need to think through and then draw in any dependencies between those tasks.

You lie the Work Flow Diagram on its side because, by convention, Work Flow Diagrams go from top to bottom whereas Activity Networks go from left to right. Although the orientation of the diagram may be mere convention and seems unimportant, if you're ever going to have to work with other people who use to these diagrams, it's best to get used to the standard approach. Reading a diagram that's flowing in a different direction from the one you're used to is surprisingly hard.

Where the dependency lines used to flow between the 'outer' product boxes, you're now attaching them to the 'inner' activity boxes. The link from a previous product may not always be to the first activity within a succeeding product box, so think carefully. Figure 6-6 provides an example in which a flow from 'Test and adjust system' feeds into 'Produce training materials' and not into the activity 'Design training materials'. That dependency is because in this project the design doesn't need screen shots from the adjusted system, but the finished materials do.

Figure 6-6 uses the procedure change project example from Chapter 5, but only part of it to keep the diagrams to a manageable size for the book. You can see that tasks have been identified for each product and the activity dependencies worked out. Although the dependencies are more detailed than those on the Work Flow Diagram (there are more boxes to deal with), the underlying dashed boxes of the products show that the main framework of these dependencies was already in place.

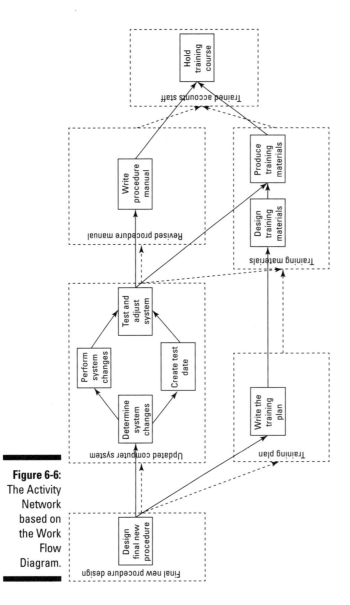

**Figure 6-6:**
The Activity
Network
based on
the Work
Flow
Diagram.

Activity planning is much faster to do if you've done product planning first. If you're clear about what you're producing – the products – then either you or team specialists can more easily determine what activities are needed and estimate how long they are likely to take, rather than just guessing.

# *Putting in the time durations*

So far, you may think 'interesting, but the Activity Network hasn't taken me very far forward'. However, now comes the bit where this technique starts to reveal some real power. Having established the dependencies between activities (see the previous section), the next step is to put some times onto the activities and, among other things, work out how long the project is going to take. For each activity, you need an estimate of how long it will take to do it – its *duration*.

### *Understanding staff hours and elapsed time*

The Activity Network works with calendar time, sometimes referred to as *elapsed time*. That's not the same as staff hours. To give a couple of simple examples, if you have a task to do that requires ten days' effort, but you can only spare half of each day to work on it, it's going to take you 20 elapsed days to do it. Equally, if you can work on it full time and a colleague can work with you and can also devote full days, then that ten days of staff effort will only take five days of elapsed time to complete – provided you don't get distracted and start arguing about the football or pop idols.

At first, you can put in a provisional duration based on the amount of staff resource you expect to be available. If it turns out that the project will take too long, and some extra staff time can be freed up to work on the project, then you can adjust the network and reduce the elapsed time for activities for which there is now more resource. That's all in the fine tuning that comes later though, and the first thing is to get the initial timings in.

### *Estimating – the tricky bit*

There's no way out of it – estimating is difficult to get right. If you find a way of getting accurate estimates every time, then patent the idea quickly and prepare yourself to be very rich.

Different industries have different approaches to estimating, but the bottom line is that the most useful information you can have to hand is how long it took last time you did an activity like this. It's worth keeping historic information from past projects because they can be an invaluable source of estimating data for future projects. Where you don't have that information, you do the best you can, but remember you can always ask other people too, such as technical specialists in the organisation (see the later section 'Getting the best information'). This is where product planning (see Chapter 5) comes in useful, because you can say exactly what it is you're building, and in turn that helps the specialists estimate more accurately based on their experience.

You'll find more detail on estimating in the section 'Estimating Activity Durations', towards the end of the chapter, but if you're new to Activity Networks, then stay focused on the technique itself for the moment.

### *Thinking a bit more about duration*

The following can all affect an activity's duration:

- ✔ The amount of work effort required to complete the activity
- ✔ People's availability
- ✔ Whether people can work on the activity at the same time
- ✔ Capacity of non-staff resources (for example, a computer's processing speed), and availability of those resources
- ✔ Delay (for example, if your boss spends one hour reading your memo after it sat in her inbox for four days and seven hours, the activity's duration is five days, even though your boss spends only one hour on it)

In many cases, you can see up front that the duration of an activity is dependent on something other than work effort. This situation is quite common in business projects where a manager who's both very senior and very busy must do something. That manager may tell you that she'll do the three days' project work you need from her, but she can't tell you exactly when she'll do it within a given two-week period because her availability depends on the other demands on her time. In that case, you can enter the activity into the plan as 'fixed duration' of two weeks, and note separately for project costing that in fact it involves only three days of that manager's time.

Understanding the basis of a duration estimate also helps you work out ways to reduce it. For example, suppose you estimate that testing a software package requires that it run for 24 hours on a specialised computer. If you can use the computer for only six hours in any one day, the duration for your software test is four days. Doubling the number of people working on the test won't reduce the duration to two days, but getting approval to use the computer for 12 hours a day will.

## Calculating the length of the project

The next bit is very easy, provided that you've mastered basic addition and subtraction, like 2 + 3 = 5. So, assuming that you're aged 6 or over, this step in building the Activity Network shouldn't present too much of a problem. (If you're under 6, then you're getting a real jump start in your project management career – and it isn't just police officers who are looking younger these days.)

In Figure 6-7 you now see some smaller boxes inside the activity box – in fact, seven of them. You may think that these smaller boxes will make the diagram look busy, but in fact they make all the calculations very easy and very mechanical. The duration goes in the top-middle box and you choose your scale. The scale is normally elapsed days or you can use weeks; the examples that follow use weeks.

| 0 | 3 | 3 |
|---|---|---|
| | Activity A | |
| | | |

**Figure 6-7:** Calculating the earliest finish date.

In Figure 6-7 you can see that the top-left box has been set to zero, which is the beginning of the project and which is the earliest start date for that first activity. The top-right box is the earliest finish date. So, the activity starts at zero and is three weeks long. So when is the earliest the activity can finish? Here's the formula you need:

Earliest start date + duration = earliest finish date

Well, 0 + 3 = 3, so the answer is the end of Week 3. Tricky, huh?

You can use calendar dates rather than day or week numbers. You'll find more about working with calendar dates in the nearby sidebar named, with normal *For Dummies* precision, 'Working with calendar dates'.

Now, you know from the dependency arrow that the next activity can start the moment that the first activity finishes: in the example, the end of Week 3. You may think that sounds a little weird and it should be the beginning of Week 4, but stay with 'end of week' for the moment because it makes the calculation very easy and very mechanical. So, just copy the figure from the top-right box of the first activity into the top-left box of any other activity coming after it and directly connected with an arrow.

Stick to the arrow pathways at all times. Take care not to jump across the network to an activity that isn't directly connected by an arrow, or your network will go horribly wrong.

You can see the whole Activity Network calculated forwards in Figure 6-8.

The earliest start date of an activity is the same as the earliest finish date from the activity directly in front of it. Figure 6-8 reveals a bit of a problem with the last activity in the project, because three activities feed into it, not just one. In the case of more than one activity feeding in, take the highest figure or, if you're working with calendar dates, the latest date. Flick back to Figure 6-5 where the time gap across the middle of that simple network was six months, not six minutes. The point is that all the preceding activities must be finished before the current one can start, so it's the highest number from all the feeder activities that determines the start point of this one.

## Working with calendar dates

An option with the Activity Network is to work with calendar dates rather than day or week numbers. That's fine, and all the computer tools do that. In one way it makes the network easier to understand, but in another way it's more difficult, so don't expect to find a perfect approach. If you're using a computer tool to plan the project, which is sensible if the project is anything more than very small, just one of the problems you encounter is with the start date.

Imagine you want to plan the project out but you haven't got approval for it yet, so you don't know exactly when it will start. You go to your computer tool, and as soon as you've got the project name in, it starts demanding to know the day on which you'll start the project. You don't know, but you find to your annoyance that the tool won't move off that screen until you've entered a start date. In frustration, you enter '1 November', which is in two weeks' time. As you then put in durations, the tool tells you that you can't schedule work for certain days because they're end-of-year public holidays and aren't working days. 'But,' you explain patiently to the screen, 'those activities may not clash with holidays because I may not get approval for this project until January anyway.' Then you look more closely at your computer and realise it doesn't have ears.

Nick saw a great cartoon of a bear sitting in front of a PC having just smashed a huge paw through the screen. The caption was, 'Please enter your response'. Automated tools for project scheduling are great but they can be really frustrating sometimes and make you want to emulate the bear.

The Activity Network now starts to earn its keep because you can see that this project is going to take ten weeks. The total of the activity durations is 16 weeks, but the project will complete in less time because some activities can be done in parallel.

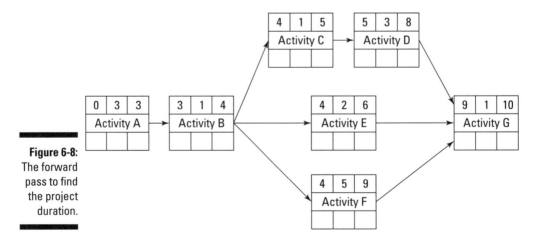

**Figure 6-8:** The forward pass to find the project duration.

# *Understanding Float and Its Impact*

It's useful to know which activities have some slack time, and that's the next thing to find out. This is a great help when managing the project, because if someone reports that her activity is more difficult than she thought and will take a week longer than planned, you know immediately whether you can absorb that week or whether it may cause a problem. Going back to the example of doing a six-minute activity in parallel with a six-month one (see the earlier section 'Seeing how you build up an Activity Network'), you aren't going to lose a lot of sleep if the six-minute activity ends up taking ten minutes, because you still have a vast amount of time to spare.

The term *slack* is a very descriptive one for the amount of spare time for an activity. However, the international word for this time is *float*. Computer scheduling tools mostly refer to slack as float.

The first step in working out the float is to copy down the earliest finish date of the last activity – as shown in the top-right box – into the box at the bottom right, which is the latest finish date. In the example in Figure 6-8, the time shown for Activity G is ten weeks. Then you work back on the bottom line, going from right to left. What you want to calculate and put in the bottom-left box is the latest start date for that activity.

So, if the activity must finish at the end of Week 10 and is one week long, when is the latest you could start it without going beyond the ten weeks?

Given that the activity will take one week to complete, if you start any later than the end of Week 9, you won't be finished by the end of Week 10. Remember, you're working with 'end of week' figures here. To calculate the latest start, you simply subtract the activity duration from the latest finish date:

Latest finish date – duration = latest start date

So, the mind-boggling calculation is 10 – 1 = 9; the latest start date is the end of Week 9.

Now copy that latest start date into the bottom-right box of any activity directly connected to this one by an arrow, to provide its latest finish date; follow the arrows backwards. As before, take care to follow only the arrow pathways, and whatever you do, don't jump across the network where no direct arrow connection exists. Figure 6-9 shows the result.

Activity B is tricky because three activities feed back into it, so which of the three different figures is the right one? The answer on the backwards pass return trip is to take the lowest figure or, if you're using calendar dates, the earliest date. In Figure 6-9 the three options for Activity B were 5, 7 and 4, so the correct figure is 4.

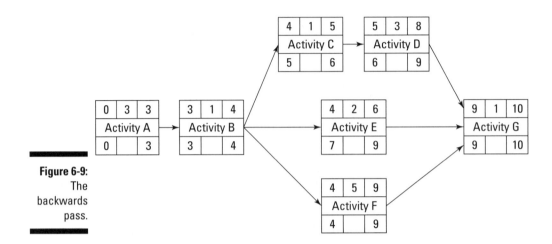

**Figure 6-9:**
The
backwards
pass.

If you've done all the mathematics correctly and stuck carefully to the arrow pathways, you should end up back on the far left-hand side of the diagram with zero as the latest start date of the first activity. In Figure 6-9 it is; whew!

Now, this is where the diagram gets more interesting and even more powerful. It shows, for example, that people can start working on Activity F at the end of Week 4. But the network also shows that the start of Activity F can be postponed right up to the end of Week 7 without causing a problem, because the end of Week 7 is the latest start date. That's three weeks of spare time. You can work out the float on each of the activities, and that's what the box in the middle of the bottom line is for.

You can calculate float in different ways, but the safest one is to compare the figures in the two right-hand boxes for each activity: the earliest finish date and the latest finish date. Here's the formula:

Latest finish date – earliest finish date = float

The next figure, Figure 6-10, shows the result.

Knowing the float is actually a bit better than just knowing whether you can delay the start of an activity, as you may have already realised. The float tells you how much spare time you have for that activity, whether it's in postponing the start date or the activity taking a bit longer than estimated.

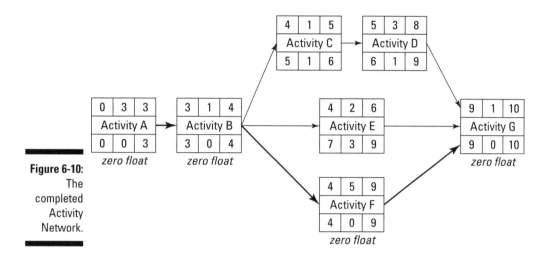

# *Identifying the Critical Path*

You may have heard of Critical Path Analysis (CPA) — or Critical Path Method (CPM) – and think it sounds daunting. However, the good news is that Critical Path Analysis is very easy; in fact, if you've made an Activity Network (see the previous sections), then you've done most of the work already.

The *critical path* is simply the longest chain of dependent activities going through the Activity Network. You can see it clearly, because critical path activities all have a float of zero (the previous section explains float). So, looking at the float boxes, just trace the zeros through the diagram and you've got it. Figure 6-10 shows this path with the heavy arrows. The critical path is significant because, as the longest path, it determines the duration of the project. If you add up the durations of the activities along the heavy lines in Figure 6-10, you find that the total is ten weeks, the length of the project.

The critical path is important in managing the project, because if you get a delay on a critical path activity, the longest path gets longer. If the longest path gets longer, that means that the project end date goes out. So slippage on a critical path activity doesn't just affect that activity but the entire project.

As you manage the project, monitor all the activities carefully, but especially look out for the critical path. You also have to consider the resource dependencies – but see Chapters 7 and 8 for more on that aspect.

# *Watching the critical path*

Planning isn't just something you do at the start of a project, but rather something you do continuously right the way through. Things change, and unless yours is the first, no project ever goes *exactly* to plan. Strangely, that's what makes the plan even more important: it's something you adjust in order to keep the project on track.

Staying with the example of the network used in Figures 6-8 to 6-10, imagine there's a problem part way through the project as Activity C is being done. The team leader reports two delays: one because a supplier was late delivering something needed for C, and one because half the team have suddenly become ill and have gone home. The team leader tells you that Activity C is now going to take three weeks instead of the planned one week and she can do absolutely nothing to pull the time back. So what's the impact on the project of this two-week delay?

Your first reaction may be that there is no overall impact, because there is a week of float on C and also on the following activity, D, so these will offset the two-week delay. However, if you look at the calculations on the top of the boxes in Figure 6-11, you'll find they tell a rather different story, and the project has been extended by one week.

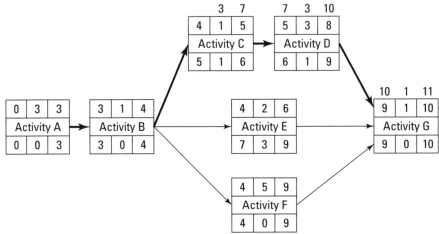

**Figure 6-11:**
A changing
critical path.

The reason for the project delay is that Activities C and D are in an uninterrupted chain (no dependency arrows between C and D going out to other activities or coming in) and the one-week float on each of these two activities is actually the same week. So, of the two-week delay, one week has been absorbed by the float and the other week has pushed the project out by a week. Because of this change in C and D, that chain has now become the longest one in that part of the project, so the critical path moves as shown by the heavy arrows in Figure 6-11. If you recalculate the diagram on the backwards pass (see the section 'Understanding float and Its impact'), you find that Activity F, which used to be on the critical path, now has one week of float.

Be careful if, on your project's Activity Network Diagram, you have, for example, an uninterrupted chain of three activities each showing five days' float (the float figure will always be the same on each activity in an uninterrupted chain). Along that chain you have five days' float, not 15. This is known as *dependent float*. If you use all or part of the float in one activity, you've lost that much on the remaining activities in that chain.

## Finding a split critical path

For good measure, here's one final twist. Suppose the team leader doing the work on Activity C comes to see you again, but this time with some good news. There's still a problem with the supplier, but the sick team members are now all back at work having had a 24-hour stomach upset after a dodgy takeaway (carryout, if you're a Scot) lunch. The team leader tells you that there is still a delay on C, but it will now only be a one-week delay, not a two-week delay. The activity will now take two weeks instead of the original planned one week.

The one-week delay is now completely taken up by the float, and the project reverts to ten weeks, but now both the top and bottom branches of the network are the same length, so the critical path splits into two for this part of the project. It's unusual for the critical path to split, and you normally have a single path. But if the critical path does split into two or even more for a while, don't worry – it can happen, and in the example it just did.

### Two types of float

The Project Management Institute (PMI) identifies two types of float:

✔ **Total float:** The total amount of time by which a scheduled activity may be delayed without delaying the project end date or a schedule constraint. So in Figure 6-11, Activity C has a week of total float because it can be delayed for that long without

affecting the overall project. That is the float that you enter in the bottom-middle box.

✔ **Free float:** The amount of time by which a scheduled activity may be delayed without delaying the early start of any immediately following scheduled activities. In the case of Activity C, that would be zero. Any delay at all on C would affect the start of the following Activity D.

# *Being More Precise with Dependencies*

The Activity Network Diagram you create with the help of the previous sections provides some great information, but sometimes you need to be more precise. You can enhance the diagram notation to give you that greater precision with the dependencies.

## *Understanding dependency types*

The examples in all the Activity Network Diagrams so far in this chapter have needed a dependency where an activity cannot start until work on the previous one(s) has been completed. This isn't the only type of dependency, but it's the most common.

### *Finish to start*

So, the most common sort. When you have finished one activity, you can start the succeeding one(s). It's good to know that project management isn't bound up in a lot of jargon, and this type of dependency is known as a *finish to start*.

### *The overlap, or lead*

This is in which you don't have to wait for the first activity to be completely finished before you start the next one. Figure 6-12 shows the notation.

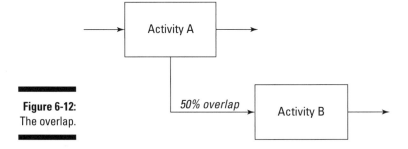

**Figure 6-12:**
The overlap.

Think of a project to write and test computer programs. You don't usually have to wait until all the programs are written before you can start testing. As soon as a set of programs are finished, you can start testing them while programmers are still writing other programs. It's important that you spot overlaps, so you don't build unnecessary delay into your plan.

### *The start to start*

A *start to start* dependency is like the ultimate overlap. You can't start Activity B before Activity A, but as soon as you've got going with A, you can begin B.

That means that the earliest start date of Activity B will be the same as the earliest start date of A. Have a look at Figure 6-13.

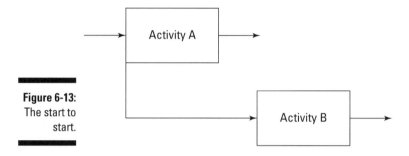

In a 250-kilometre gas pipeline project, a trench was dug for the pipe, but optical fibre was also put in the trench to carry control signals such as those needed to operate the valves. The optical fibre couldn't be put in first, because laying the gas pipe would have damaged it, but there was no need to lay all the pipe and then go back to the start to lay the optical fibre. As soon as the first length of pipe was in, the optical fibre could be put in on top.

### The lag

Sometimes there is a delay after an activity before a second one can start. You can show this in two ways.

First, you can put in a dummy activity of 'waiting time', which can be good because it makes the waiting time visible rather than having a weird gap in the project when you come to look at the Gantt Chart. In the example in the section 'Listing the activities or tasks', earlier in this chapter, the dummy activity is in square brackets so it can be seen at a glance that it doesn't involve project work.

The second way to show a delay after an activity before a second one can start is to put a lag time on the dependency line. You need to adjust the earliest start date of the following activity if there is a lag. If Activity A can finish at the end of Week 6, then Activity B doesn't begin at the end of Week 6 but rather at the end of Week 10 if you have a four-week lag, as with the example in Figure 6-14.

**Figure 6-14:**
The overlap.

An example is with sending out contracts to newly recruited staff and holding the induction training. Unless you're recruiting people who are currently unemployed, you're likely to have to wait at least four weeks before they arrive, because they need to work a period of notice with their current employers.

### The finish to finish

The final dependency type to look at is the finish to finish. You may be able to start Activity B early on, but you can't finish it until Activity A is finished. Figure 6-15 shows this finish-to-finish notation.

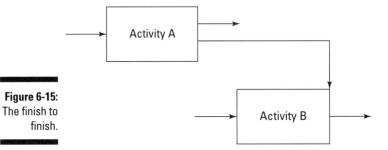

**Figure 6-15:**
The finish to finish.

Consider a project to produce a four-page company brochure. Activity A is to write the text and Activity B is to design the brochure. Now, because the text is important stuff, the managing director wants to write it herself. You can get a long way with the design of the brochure, but you can't finish it with that last tweak to the layout until you know exactly what the final text is.

# Using computers

Having hit out a bit at computers in the sidebar 'Working with calendar dates', earlier in the chapter, it's time to redress the balance and praise them up a bit. When you have anything more than a small Activity Network, and when you start to use the more sophisticated dependencies, the computer tools come to the fore despite their limitations. They perform in a blink of an eye calculations that would have you scratching your head for quite some time – just make sure that you've entered the dependencies and timings absolutely correctly.

Using computer tools for activity planning is a bit like using a spreadsheet. Provided you have double-checked your data and your formulas, you can trust the spreadsheet to come up with the right answers, because computers are pretty good at that stuff. Chapter 18 has much more on using computer software in projects, and to whet your appetite you can get some of it for free.

The finish to finish affects your calculations because the end of Activity B will be determined by the end of Activity A, not the addition of the earliest start date of B to its duration.

## Staying in touch with reality

There is a danger that you can get very focused on your network and become so absorbed in the times and dependency arrows that you lose touch with reality. You might look at a diagram for a project and think it isn't right because one activity finishes at the end of February and the next one that's dependent on it starts in the first week of April. That's got to be a mistake . . . or has it? The problem is that the organisation works to the standard fiscal year, and the money needed for the second activity won't be available until the new financial year, which starts on 6 April. So the network is actually correct: the activity's start is dependent on funding, not just on the previous activity.

If you're using a computer tool, you can deal with this situation quite easily by specifying a fixed start date for an activity – in this case 6 April. Make a note in the plan to remind yourself both that you've anchored the start date (in case circumstances change) and the reason, which in this case is the availability of finance. Other reasons include interaction with other projects where staff won't be available to work on your project until they've finished work on another that's higher priority. Flick to Chapters 7 and 8 for more on resourcing.

## Thinking a bit more about sequences

In thinking through the dependencies for your network, you will find that some things are fixed but others are a matter of choice:

- **Mandatory dependencies:** These relationships must be observed if project work is to be a success. They include:

  - **Hard logic:** Certain processes must logically occur before others. For example, when building a house, you must pour the concrete for the foundation before you erect the frame.

  - **Legal requirements:** Some laws or regulations require that certain activities be done before others. As an example, a pharmaceutical company develops a new drug in the laboratory and demonstrates its safety and effectiveness in clinical trials. The manufacturer wants to start producing and selling the drug immediately but can't. The law requires that the company obtains government approval for the drug before selling it.

- **Procedural requirements:** Company policies and procedures require that certain activities be done before others. Suppose you're developing a new piece of software for your organisation. You've finished your design and want to start programming the software. However, your organisation follows a systems development methodology that requires the formal management and audit approval of your design before you can develop it.

✔ **Discretionary dependencies:** You may choose to establish these relationships between activities, but they aren't required. They include:

- **Choices:** Sometimes you make arbitrary decisions to work on certain activities before others. Imagine that you have to perform Activities C, D and E. Your work will be too fragmented if you work on all three at the same time, and there's no legal or logical reason why you should work on one or the other first. You may choose to work on Activity D first, then E and then C out of personal preference, perhaps getting the most difficult one out of the way first.

- **Logical dependencies:** Performing certain activities before others sometimes seems to make the most sense. Suppose you're writing a report. Because much of Chapter 3 depends on what you write in Chapter 2, you decide to write Chapter 2 first. You could write Chapter 3 first or work on both at the same time, but that plan increases the chance that you'll have to rewrite some of Chapter 3 after you finish Chapter 2.

✔ **External dependencies:** Starting a project activity may require that an activity outside the project be completed. For example, imagine that your project includes an activity to test a device you're developing. You want to start testing right away, but because you don't want to hire in equipment and increase project costs, you can't start this activity until your organisation's own test laboratory receives and installs a new piece of test equipment that's currently on order.

Discriminate very clearly between activity dependencies that are mandatory and those that you've chosen, and note the details in your plan. Where you've chosen to do things in a particular sequence, you can alter it later if you change your mind. You can't change your mind about the legal constraints affecting activity sequence, though; they're fixed and you must live with them. Notes in the plan also help other people to understand why you've set up the dependencies in a particular way.

To give a more meaningful example than A's, B's and C's, Figure 6-16 is the activity network for part of the business change project example from the earlier chapters.

The example in Figure 6-16 is still a 'first cut' and now needs to be examined to see, for example, whether some of the relationships are something other than finish to start.

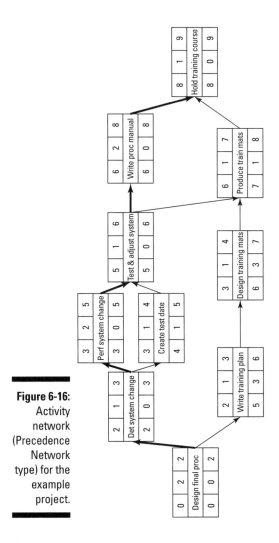

**Figure 6-16:**
Activity
network
(Precedence
Network
type) for the
example
project.

# Working with the Activity Network

With the network you build up through the guidance of the previous sections, it's still early days with the activity planning but the network already reveals useful information. Even before you finish the network, you can see whether you can meet any required end date. You can also get useful preliminary information from the critical path.

In the project example in Figure 6-15 in the section 'Being More Precise with Dependencies', it's clear that computer work is going to determine the length of the project. You may already be making a mental note, then, to make doubly sure that the computer people have the time put aside for this job so that it won't get delayed. Such thinking is actually a start into risk management (see Chapter 10). A lot of risks come to light during planning; note them down and start thinking about them now.

Something else you may notice from the network, if you already know who'll be doing what, is a resource constraint. If you happen to know that the person who's making the adjustments to the computer system is the same person who'll be producing the test data, then although these two activities aren't dependent on each other logically, a resource dependency exists because one person can't do two full-time jobs simultaneously. That resource conflict foreshadows the resource planning of Chapters 7 and 8.

You may be starting to think that this planning stuff is really interesting, but it's also getting rather detailed. The answer to both issues is, 'Yes, it is, isn't it?' The detail is important, however, because it recognises the reality of the project. Taking the example of the resource conflict for the person adjusting the computer system, it's just not possible to do two full-time jobs on the project simultaneously. The resource issue is a genuine project-planning problem that needs to be resolved; it's not merely a matter of fine detail that's over the top and not really necessary.

## *Working back to meet end dates*

If your network shows you can't meet a required date, don't panic. With the product and activity plans, you have powerful tools you can work with to adjust the project so that it will fit – and with time to spare for contingency.

Inspirandum project management courses are fun as well as hard work. Nick often teases groups when their case study plans (often for one of the organisation's live projects) fail to meet the required end date. He talks in low 'gloom and doom' tones and asks whether the plan has failed. The group members invariably say that it has, to which he responds that, on the contrary, the plan is already a huge success. Even before finishing the Activity Network, the group hasn't only discovered that at present the project won't work, but it can say exactly what the shortfall is. Now that the problem is visible and sized, the group can work on the plans to get the project in balance.

You can't finalise the plan when you've done the Activity Network because there is still the whole area of resource planning to consider. You do get early warning of a timing problem, though, if your Activity Network shows that you will miss the end date. There will be things that you can do, and not least to identify activities that could be shortened or *crashed* by adding extra resource (usually, but not always, extra staff). If you do find activities that can be crashed, you can try to get some extra resource for your project and take that into account when starting the resource planning.

You may well be looking to reduce the duration of a number of activities, but clearly your primary focus will be the critical path (see 'Identifying the Critical Path', earlier in this chapter). Being the longest path and the one that determines the length of the project, that's the set of activities that you must ultimately reduce in duration. That may even mean leaving some out and so reducing the scope of the project to fit the time available.

When looking to see whether you can crash an activity to reduce its duration, think carefully. On some activities, you simply make things worse if you add extra people. If you need the inside of a small walk-in cupboard painted and it will take one person half an hour, then it's sad but true that putting 30 people on the job won't get it done in one minute. That's a light-hearted example, although it does illustrate the impact of a physical constraint. One you're more likely to come across is a complex task where you need just one or two people to focus on the job and where the work just doesn't lend itself to being done by a bigger team.

Ultimately, your aim is to have a plan that shows everything can be done by the end date, and with a bit to spare for contingency because you can be confident that something's going to go wrong somewhere.

## Avoiding backing into your schedule

When working with the schedule, it can be tempting to try and make the activities fit the time available instead of calculating the time needed to do those activities. Don't do it! If you reduce the estimates to fit, you simply end up with an unrealistic plan and a late or even failed project.

In the States, Stan Portny was reviewing a colleague's Project Plan a while back and noticed that she had allowed one week for her final report's review and approval. When he asked her whether she thought this estimate was realistic, she replied that it certainly wasn't realistic, but that she had to use that estimate for the Project Plan to work out. In other words, she was using time estimates that totalled to the number she *wanted* to reach rather than ones she thought she *could* meet.

# Going for Gantt

At last, something that's likely to be more familiar territory: the Gantt Chart with its horizontal bars showing activities against a time scale. You may have wondered what *Gantt* stands for. Graphical Analysis Network Timing Tool, perhaps? No, it actually stands for *Henry*. The chart was devised by the American management consultant Henry Gantt getting on for 100 years ago. He came up with a number of innovations but is most remembered for the chart named after him that's at the hub of most project management computer tools today.

The Gantt Chart is powerful but, perhaps predictably, it doesn't do everything. Used in combination with an Activity Network, it's extremely useful.

If you're using a computer tool, getting to the Gantt is automatic. As you draw the network, you find that you can switch view and see the same data in the form of a Gantt Chart. In line with the overall approach of this chapter, though, it helps if you see how to do it 'by hand' so that even if you do end up using a computer tool, you fully understand what it's doing for you.

Here's how to produce a Gantt Chart:

1. **List the activities.**

   This is simple because you just copy in your activity list with the products as milestones or headings, and the activities to build each product listed under its heading.

2. **Draw the bars.**

   Simply take three figures from each activity box on the Activity Network: top left, top right and bottom right, which are the earliest start date, earliest finish date and latest finish date. These three figures mark the three points on the Gantt bar showing the activity being done as early as possible, but with float at the back end showing how far it can extend before it starts to knock on into other activities. Critical path activities, of course, don't have float, so the earliest and latest finish are the same.

Figure 6-17 shows how the figures on the Activity Network map onto the Gantt bar. Because the figure is using week numbers, the position on the Gantt bar relates to 'end of week'. If you're using calendar dates, then the bottom scale will be actual dates not just week numbers.

To give a more complete example, Figure 6-18 goes on to show the activities for the sample project plotted onto the Gantt Chart.

Gantt Charts are both powerful and popular because you can easily see the project mapped out, and they provide a view of where you are (more on that in Chapter 14, which covers progress control). You can use the chart at more than one level of detail, and computer tools allow you to 'roll up' part or all of the chart to show less detail, such as only displaying project-plan-level activities. You can also open out the task list to work on the more detailed activities when you get into planning at a lower level for each stage, as you approach that particular part of the project.

Although senior managers such as those on steering committees must normally approve stage-level plans, they often like to focus primarily on the project level to keep sight of the big picture. So it's the project level of detail that senior managers often ask for in progress reports.

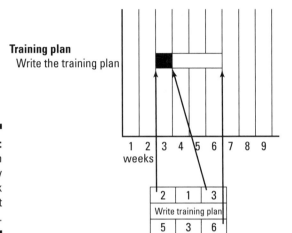

**Figure 6-17:**
Moving from
the Activity
Network
to a Gantt
Chart.

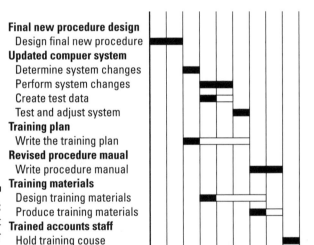

**Figure 6-18:**
The Gantt
Chart for
the example
project.

Gantt Charts are excellent, but as Figure 6-18 demonstrates, they don't show everything. For example, the critical path is hard to see, but also if it moved because of a change in the duration of an activity, where would it go? You can see the critical path easily enough on an Activity Network, but you can't see it on the Gantt. Use the two tools together, though, and you have a very powerful combination. It's a huge shame when people miss out on the power of an Activity Network because they think networks are difficult. As you've seen in this chapter, networks are really quite straightforward. All the major computer scheduling tools support both techniques.

# Estimating Activity Durations

An *estimate* is your evaluation of how long you need to actually perform an activity. The estimate isn't how long you want the activity to take or how long someone tells you it must take; the estimate is how long you think it really will take. Because estimating is quite difficult to get right, and because if the estimates are significantly out it undermines the plan, this last section of the chapter focuses on some issues to bear in mind and outlines some techniques that may help.

Unrealistically short duration estimates can lead to an interesting array of serious project problems:

- ✔ The work simply can't be done in the time set down on the plan, so after the project is underway it goes wildly off track and becomes very hard to control. This isn't because of a problem with the project but because the plan is hopelessly unrealistic and virtually useless as a management tool.

- ✔ Because unrealistic estimates appear to meet your schedule's targets, you don't seek realistic alternative strategies that increase the chances of accomplishing activities in required durations.

- ✔ Because the work actually takes longer than the plan allows, delivery will be late – delivery of the end product but perhaps also intermediate products that are being taken into operational use during the project. That causes disruption to other parts of the business, including dependent projects, that expected things to be in place at a certain time.

- ✔ If people believe duration estimates are totally unrealistic, they stop trying to achieve them. When delays occur during an activity, people accept them as inevitable instead of seeking ways to overcome them.

- ✔ Quality goes out of the window as team members struggle to throw things together to get somewhere near to the deadlines – all those planned tests and checks just become a joke. However, those on the receiving end of the project deliverables don't share the humour when things don't work properly and cause operational problems.

- ✔ When your project fails to meet the end date or quality has suffered badly, both the project and you are perceived as failures.

## Getting the best information

If you're running a small project in an area that you're thoroughly familiar with, you can probably come up with the estimates yourself. However, after the project moves beyond small and starts to involve more skill sets and people, you almost certainly need to consult others. Where you don't know the project area at all (and that doesn't mean that you shouldn't manage the project), you'll need a lot of input from other people.

Don't be scared to ask others for estimates, but then don't be surprised if you get significantly different ones for exactly the same activity. And remember that it's very difficult to get estimates right.

When estimating an activity's duration, consider past experience, including any records of previous projects you can get your hands on, expert opinion and other available sources of information. The more important your project and the more significant the deadline, the more you need to do to clarify the different components of the activity:

- **Physical processes:** Physical or chemical reactions, such as concrete curing, paint drying and chemical reactions in a laboratory.

- **Time delays:** Time during which nothing is happening; for example, you may need to reserve a conference room two weeks before a meeting. (Time delays are typically due to the unavailability of resources.)

- **Work needing physical resources:** Activities that computers and other machines perform, such as testing software on a computer or running a trial batch on the production line.

- **Work performed by people:** Physical and mental activities that people perform, such as writing a report, assembling a piece of equipment and thinking of ideas for an ad campaign.

When you look for information and advice to help with estimating, consider the following sources:

- Experts familiar with the type of activity, even if they haven't performed the exact activity before

- Historical records of how long similar activities have taken in the past

- People who'll be working on the activities

- People who've performed similar activities in the past

## Using estimating techniques

The problem with projects is that they happen in different industries, and these industries tend to have their own specialised techniques for estimating. But you can use a couple of techniques in any project, including business projects where often the closest anyone gets to a specialised estimating approach is using a blindfold and pin.

### Delphi and Modified Delphi

Had you been an ancient Greek, you might have sought guidance from the oracle at Delphi. How the oracle actually worked is lost in the mists of time, but one theory is that it was a group of wise people who consulted between themselves and then gave a single answer. Similarly, you can ask people for estimates using the Delphi technique. As to whether they're wise or not . . .

The *Delphi technique* works well in a workshop. You explain an activity and then get everyone to write down how long they think it will take to carry out the activity. You then gather up the individual estimates, calculate the average and use that as the estimate in the plan.

*Modified Delphi* is where you take the estimating a step further. Having got everyone's opinion, you identify the person who gave the most optimistic estimate and the person with the most pessimistic estimate and ask them to explain their thinking. The pessimistic person may say that she's done this sort of work before and it tends to be more complicated than everyone thinks because of particular factors. Everyone listens carefully. Then the person with the most optimistic estimate explains her thinking. She may say that a team that she worked with before came up with an easier way of doing part of the work. Again everyone listens and, with the explanations in mind, they estimate again. You take the average and put it in your plan.

### Three-point estimating

Three-point estimating establishes the best case, worst case and most likely case. It sometimes helps to think about the best and worst case to help you come up with the most likely. Although you will almost certainly use the most likely value for the plan, it may help to note the best and worst cases so other people can see the range and not get too worried if the work goes a bit beyond the estimate, in either direction, during the project.

### The PERT formula

A technique that comes with the PERT approach (see the sidebar 'Seeing circles – the PERT Chart', earlier in the chapter) is a formula that's based on three-point estimating. It returns a single value for a range of estimates. The formula loads the most likely time by a factor of four against the extremes of optimism and pessimism, which have a factor of one. So with the most optimistic estimate being 'o', the most pessimistic 'p' and the most likely (or mode) being 'm', the formula is:

Estimate = (1o + 4m + 1p)/6

In a workshop involving 20 staff, one person says that an activity will take 8 days, one says that it will take 20 days and the most common response is that it will take 11 days. The PERT formula will give a final estimate of 12 days:

$[(1 \times 8) + (4 \times 11) + (1 \times 20)]/6$

The weighting gives a bias to the most likely estimate but allows it to be pulled a bit either way by an extreme of optimism or pessimism. The interesting thing about this formula is that it tends to work. If you find during a project that the formula produced an estimate that was wrong but consistently so, then for a future project you can adjust the weighting: you might take twice the most optimistic and only three times the most likely plus the most pessimistic, and divide by six.

## Putting a health warning on estimates

You can't always get accurate estimates, and that's both a worry and a comfort.

It's a comfort because you don't need to beat yourself up if, having done your best, you aren't too sure of the accuracy of your estimates. If your project is going into entirely unfamiliar territory, then you're not going to be totally confident about how long things will take. You can sometimes ask other organisations, but knowing how long it took them to do something doesn't tell you exactly how long it's going to take you to do something slightly different with the people in your organisation. You need, then, to accept that if the work is uncertain, then the estimates are likely to be uncertain too.

Not having accurate estimates is also a worry because your project may quickly go off track. While you won't find an easy answer to the problem of estimates being uncertain, you can do three things about that uncertainty:

- ✔ **Allow additional contingency.** The more uncertain you are about the estimates, the more time you need to allow for things taking longer than anticipated. Of course, they may take less time than anticipated too, but that is inherently containable and usually much less of a problem.

- ✔ **Warn people.** Simply put a note in the plan to warn those reading it that the estimates may be incorrect. You can state a degree of confidence in the estimates, such as that in one part of the project you're 90 per cent confident that the estimates are broadly correct, but for another you're only 20 per cent confident. Your plan shows the most likely duration of each activity, but you can also include a table to show the best case and worst case estimates as well as the most likely. Then those reading the plan have some warning about the likely range and it won't come as a shock if things don't quite work out as set down on the plan.

- ✔ **Update the estimates and the plan.** When better information comes to hand as the project continues, feed that new information into the plan. For example, if by stage 3 your estimates for earlier work were fairly close, you can probably increase the confidence rating for remaining stages and be more sure of the overall project delivery date.

You can find out more about the human factors side of estimating in Chapter 7.

# Chapter 7

# Looking At Staff Resources

. . . . . . . . . . . . . . . . . . . . . . . . . . . . . . . . . . . . . . . . . . . . . . . . .

## In This Chapter

▶ Understanding the dynamics of staff scheduling

▶ Focusing first on people's abilities

▶ Accurately planning your project's staff needs

▶ Striking a balance among all your resource commitments

. . . . . . . . . . . . . . . . . . . . . . . . . . . . . . . . . . . . . . . . . . . . . . . . .

*S*tan Portny remembers reading the following from a stressed-out Project Manager: 'We've done so much with so little for so long, they now expect us to do everything with nothing!'

The truth is, of course, you can't accomplish anything with nothing, and in the context of project resource planning, you need people as well as money. Getting the people planning right is essential both in terms of getting the right staff onto your project in the first place and then using the project staff in the best possible way. Although staff resourcing can be tricky – and many Project Managers tend to underestimate this resourcing – don't be daunted by it, but instead allow time to think it through and plan thoroughly. By the way, using project staff well isn't selfish either. Good project management includes giving team members opportunities to succeed and develop alongside you getting a successful project, and that needs careful thought and planning too.

This chapter covers the first part of the resource planning: the staff. It helps you understand the dynamics of scheduling and includes areas such as availability to show that full-time staff aren't really full time. The chapter also covers topics such as individual performance, multi-tasking and the working environment, all of which can have a big impact on your Project Plan. Chapter 8 then goes on to deal with the next part of resource planning, which focuses on the physical resources such as equipment and financial resource.

You live in a world of limited resources and not enough time, which means you always have more work to do than time and resources allow. After you decide which tasks to pursue, you need to do everything possible to perform them successfully.

# Seeing Why You Need to Plan Staff Use

Before you roll your sleeves up and get stuck in to the detail of how to plan your use of staff on the project, it's helpful to be clear about *why* you need to do this planning.

## Dealing with resource conflicts

The first reason that you need to plan staff resource is that your use of staff can conflict in several ways with something else. Resource conflicts make your plan completely unworkable if you don't deal with them.

The activity plans such as the Activity Network and the Gantt Chart covered in Chapter 6 deal at first with the logical dependency of tasks, and they don't take account of resource availability until you add that in – the subject of this chapter.

Here are three areas of potential resource conflict, using an employee, Sue, as an example:

- ✔ **Multiple tasks:** We make a plan that has a number of activities including three which will take a month each. My Activity Network shows that the three can be done in parallel and each one involves Sue working full time. However, unless Sue is Superwoman and can work three shifts a day of eight hours each – 24-hour working – for a whole month, we seem to have a problem.

- ✔ **Calendar events:** A task is three days' duration and Sue is required to work eight hours a day. On the plan, the task is to be done from 1 to 3 January. But now we have a problem with the calendar. Because 1 January is a public holiday, there are only two working days in that period, not three, so the task can't be achieved. If we don't sort this out, our plan isn't going to work because the offices are shut on 1 January and Sue just won't be there. Oh yes, and four months ago she booked annual leave for 2 and 3 January because it's her husband's 30th birthday and she's booked a surprise trip to Paris, and although Sue appreciates that the project is quite important . . .

- ✔ **Other projects:** For another task, we need Sue for five days for the week commencing 8 February. Oh joy, she isn't working on any other project activity during that week and neither are there any public holidays or birthday surprises. But just when we thought it was safe to go back in the water, we find that another project also needs her for five days in the week commencing 8 February. Unfortunately, that other project has a much higher priority than ours.

The last of these conflicts reveals the messy but realistic situation that you sometimes find yourself in: sorting out resourcing between projects, not just within your own. That can take time – so allow some. You must allow sufficient time for planning at the front end of your project, because if you don't sort these problems out on the plan they'll hit you later on during the project when they'll be even harder to deal with. Picking up the last example again, Sue isn't going to be at work on 8 February even if it's on the plan in red letters, bold type and underlined. If we leave it on the plan that she'll be at work, the plan is unrealistic and the project will hit a major problem on 8 February.

Having, hopefully, convinced you that resource conflicts can cause problems and that it's important to resolve them, you may now be wondering how you actually do that. The later section 'Smoothing the resource' will help, after a closer examination of the dynamics and nature of staff resourcing.

## Making sure that people are available

Another reason you need to plan staff resource is so you can tell people when you'll need them and arrange, if necessary, for their managers to release them to work on the project. A number of people both inside the project and outside it may need to see the resource plan and agreed it up front to be sure that it's acceptable and realistic. The finance manager may be more than happy to give 40 hours of finance staff time to a project. However, he may be rather less happy if a Project Manager then marches up to him at the start of the last week of the financial year when things are really busy and says, 'Okay, I need those 40 staff hours you promised, starting at 8:30 tomorrow morning.'

The staff resource plan makes everything visible, and people who are taking part in the project or who are authorising the staff hours can make sure they can meet the commitment in terms of the number of staff, the particular skills and people involved, and the dates that you actually need them. That word *commitment* is significant because you don't want empty promises that cause you problems later when the resource doesn't materialise.

## Monitoring use of staff on the project

Some organisations have procedures and even systems that detail and track every resource on every project. Other organisations don't formally plan or track project resources at all (see the nearby sidebar 'The "we pay our staff anyway" argument'). However, even if your organisation doesn't require you to plan your resource needs and track your resource use, doing so is vital to your project's success. Even in terms of progress and control, how can you tell whether the project is on track if you don't know whether the actual use of staff hours on work so far is as you expected?

## The 'we pay our staff anyway' argument

Organisations that don't track project staff resource are, to be kind and understate the point, odd. Even if they aren't interested in the cost of staff, which they surely should be, having staff hours information is useful to help assess the likely staff effort needed for future projects. But anyway, time is money, as the saying goes. The normal excuse that 'we're going to pay the staff anyway so we don't need to track their hours' just doesn't stand up to scrutiny. If the staff weren't working on this project, they could be doing something else, so it's not as if their project work comes for free. Then there is an impact on the Business Case (see Chapter 3), because if you don't record staff hours, then you leave out a major – and, in a lot of projects, the biggest – project cost.

Nick Graham was advising a major organisation that had a policy not to record staff hours. On one project, the Project Manager was looking at the Business Case and said that the project was great and would pay for itself because it would save a lot of administrative staff hours. Nick asked how she knew that, if nobody knew the number of staff hours expended on the project. The number of project hours spent could exceed the number of administrative hours saved and it could be years before the balance tipped, if it ever did. The Project Manager couldn't answer Nick's question, but the project effort was considerable and involved some very senior and expensive people, so the question was surely valid.

# Matching People to Tasks

Your project's success rests on your ability to get the right people to perform your project's work. That may be in terms of suitably qualified staff or simply just getting enough people – which isn't always so easy. You begin your project planning by looking at what you need to deliver (see Chapter 5 for details on how to do this). Next, you decide what activities you'll need performed to create the deliverables (see Chapter 6). Your third step is to decide what skills and knowledge people must have to perform the activities.

## Working out the skill sets and knowledge that you need on the teams

To determine the skills and knowledge that people must have for your project, you can work from the Product Definitions produced as part of your planning (refer to Chapter 5). You now develop that thinking as you consider the staff resource needs in more detail.

You determine the skill and knowledge requirements by reviewing what is to be built, but as with planning, don't panic if you aren't sure or simply don't know. Remember that being a Project Manager doesn't usually mean that you're a technical expert, so go and talk to other people including:

✔ Any Project Managers who've run similar projects in the past

✔ Possible external supplier companies

✔ Staff who've worked on similar projects in the past.

✔ Subject matter experts

✔ Your project office, which may have plans and other documents showing staff resource on similar past projects

For most situations, you need to know two pieces of information about a task to determine the qualifications that a person must have to perform it:

✔ The required levels of proficiency in the needed skills and knowledge

✔ Whether the assignment entails:

- Working under someone else's guidance when applying the skills or knowledge

- Working alone to apply the skills or knowledge

- Managing others who are applying the skills or knowledge

If you'd like to think in a more structured way about the staffing needs for each task, you can use scales such as the following two-dimensional measure:

✔ What level of proficiency is needed for the task?

  1 = Requires a basic level of proficiency

  2 = Requires an intermediate level of proficiency

  3 = Requires an advanced level of proficiency

✔ What's the management requirement?

  a = Will be supervised, so doesn't need independent working ability

  b = Needs to be able to work independently but doesn't entail managing others using the skill or knowledge

  c = Entails managing others using the skill or knowledge

## Growing your people

As you think through the tasks and who you will assign them to, you'll normally need to consider staff development. You want to progress in your career, and so too do your project staff. You need to bear in mind individual needs for development and organisational needs for increasingly skilled staff, as well as the need to get the project delivered.

### Developing skills

As you look through the project tasks, you can look to see what flexibility exists for people to work on things where they can learn new skills and develop more competence in existing ones. Your efforts pay off in two ways:

✔ You help the organisation develop its skills base.

✔ You interest and motivate staff, who are enjoying what they're doing and are challenged by it.

For example, you might allocate someone to something that's new for him but where the task has got a bit of spare time, or put him alongside someone else who's already experienced.

### Using the critical path

Chapter 6 covered the critical path technique, and that comes in useful here. If a task is on the critical path, by definition there's no spare time on it; you'll therefore usually want to assign very competent and experienced people to do the work. Equally, if a task has a lot of float (slack) time, it may be more suitable for less experienced staff. If the less experienced staff take a bit longer to do it than planned, then there won't be any time impact because of the float time on the activity.

### Explaining yourself to experienced staff

In your project, you'll want to protect the critical path and also grow your less experienced staff. However, don't now neglect your more experienced people. More experienced staff like a challenge, and if you only allocate them to the mundane tasks that all happen to be on the critical path, they're going to get bored and demotivated. Try to make sure that experienced staff get some of the more juicy project work, and where you do need them to work on something boring because it's critical or helping to develop a more junior team member, you can at least explain why and hold out the promise of something more substantial later on.

If you're now thinking that there's a lot to bear in mind when dealing with staff resource on a project, yes, there is. But that's why we dedicate a whole chapter in this book to staff resource to help you.

## Developing a Skills Matrix

Whether you're able to influence the people assigned to your project team, people are assigned to your team without your input, or you assume the role of Project Manager of an existing team, you need to confirm the skills, knowledge and interest of your team members.

If you're working on a project of any size, then it's usually helpful to document each person's skills and knowledge and verify their interests. That skills and interests information may prove really useful later when something unexpected comes up and you need to switch people between tasks or add a new task, or if you have to replace a team member unexpectedly.

A *Skills Matrix* is a table that displays people's proficiency in specified skills and knowledge, as well as their interest in working on assignments using these skills and knowledge. Figure 7-1 is an example of a portion of a Skills Matrix. The left-hand column identifies skill and knowledge areas based on two dimensions (as we suggest in the earlier section 'Working out the skill sets and knowledge that you need on the teams'), and the top row lists people's names. At the intersection of the rows and columns, you identify the level of each person's particular skills, knowledge and interests.

| | Bill | | Mary | | Sue | | Ed | |
|---|---|---|---|---|---|---|---|---|
| | Proficiency | Interest | Proficiency | Interest | Proficiency | Interest | Proficiency | Interest |
| Technical writing | (0,0) | 0 | (0,0) | 0 | (3,2) | 1 | (0,0) | 1 |
| Legal research | (0,0) | 1 | (0,0) | 1 | (0,0) | 0 | (3,3) | 0 |
| Graphic design | (3,3) | 1 | (0,0) | 0 | (0,0) | 1 | (3,3) | 1 |
| Questionnaire design | (1,0) | 0 | (0,0) | 0 | (0,0) | 0 | (0,0) | 1 |

Proficiency rating is expressed as (X,Y), where

X = Person's level of skill or knowledge
Y = Level of responsibility applying the skill or knowledge

**Figure 7-1:**
Listing people's skills, knowledge and interests in a Skills Matrix.

Skill or Knowledge Level (X)

0 = No capability

1 = Basic level of capability

2 = Intermediate level of capability

3 = Advanced level of capability

Application of
Skills/Knowledge (Y)

1 = Must work under supervision

2 = Can work independently with little or no direct supervision

3 = Can manage others applying the skill or knowledge

Interest

0 = Has no interest in applying this skill or knowledge

1 = Is interested in applying this skill or knowledge

Figure 7-1 shows that Sue has an advanced level of proficiency in technical writing and can work independently with little or no supervision. In addition, she's interested in working on technical writing assignments. Ed has an advanced level of proficiency in the area of legal research and is capable of managing others engaged in legal research. However, he'd prefer not to work on legal research tasks. Instead, he'd like to work on questionnaire design activities, but he currently has no skills or knowledge in this area. This is one of the interests you may try to satisfy when you're considering staff growth.

Or if you're trying to find more people who can develop questionnaires anyway, Ed's a prime candidate. Because he wants to work on these types of assignments, he's likely to be willing to put in the extra effort to acquire the skills needed to do so.

The following steps help you prepare a Skills Matrix for your project:

1. **Discuss with each team member his skills, knowledge and interests related to the activities in your project.**

   Explain that you want this information so you can take it into account when assigning team members to project tasks. However, be careful not to build up expectations that you'll be allocating each person only to the most prestigious, interesting and career-enhancing activities. Someone has to do the boring, routine stuff.

2. **Determine each person's level of interest in working on the tasks that you propose.**

   At a minimum, ask people whether they're interested in the tasks for which you've scheduled them. If a person isn't interested in a task, try to find out why and whether you can do anything to modify the assignment to make it more interesting to him.

   If a person isn't interested in a task, you can either not ask and not know the reason, or ask and (if you get an honest response) know the reason. Knowing that a person isn't interested is better than not knowing, because you can consider the possibility of rearranging assignments or at least you can show you understand, explain the importance of the activity and point out the more interesting stuff coming later.

3. **Consult with team members' functional managers and/or the people who assigned them to your project to determine their opinions of the levels of each team member's skills, knowledge and interests.**

   You want to understand the reasons why these managers assigned the people they did to your project.

4. **Check to see whether any areas of your organisation have already prepared Skills Matrices.**

   Find out whether existing Skills Matrices give any information about the extent to which team members have the skills and knowledge that you feel are required for your project's activities.

5. **Incorporate all the information you gather in a Skills Matrix and review with each team member the portion of the matrix that contains his information.**

   This review gives you the opportunity to verify that you correctly recorded the information you found, and gives the team member a chance to comment on or add to any of the information.

# Honing Your Task Duration Estimates

When drawing up the Activity Network and Gantt Chart (see Chapter 6), you already made some estimates of how long each activity will take. The estimates may be based on good information such as where you already know exactly who'll do that task and his level of experience. However, it may have been little more than a guess just to get the basic framework of the plan in place. Now's the time to work on the detail of the estimates and fine-tune the plan.

Changing something in your plan may have knock-on effects on other aspects, so make sure you allow plenty of time for planning.

## Documenting your estimates

Here are three basic ways to document the resource requirements and estimates:

- ✔ Make a list on paper. Given the ready availability of computer tools, this isn't a great option unless your project is very small.

- ✔ Use a project-scheduling software tool with facilities for entering people's names and work estimates against each task. Good though these tools are, they do have limitations.

- ✔ Work out the information on a spreadsheet and just put basic information into the project-scheduling software. Many Project Managers prefer this approach. (You'll find more information on using computer software in Chapter 18.)

Either way, you need to show who you're assigning to each task and how long that task will take. Then you need to resolve any resource conflicts to make sure that the plan is workable.

If you're using a computer-based project management tool, it will almost certainly include a calendar facility, so you can avoid some of the areas of resource conflict. For example, it should already know about public holidays and so won't let you schedule work on those days unless you've overridden the default and declared particular holidays to be working days. You can even have a calendar for each person working on the project, so you can enter booked holidays and other assignments, and again the tool then prevents you allocating project work involving particular staff members on days when they aren't available. Good news for Sue's husband then (see the earlier section 'Dealing with resource conflicts').

# *Factors in activity timing and estimates*

Resource scheduling is inherently complicated, so don't get worried if things start to look difficult. Just work through in a methodical way and everything will come right in the end. It's tempting to focus simply on the figures when scheduling staff resource, but other factors can have an impact. Here are a few things to bear in mind as you work through the activity estimates:

- ✔ **Irregular availability:** Some staff may suddenly be less available than anticipated, so be aware of what their other duties are. If, for example, some of your technical staff are also involved with support, and a major breakdown of a vital piece of production line equipment occurs, they'll suddenly disappear from your project no matter what their percentage availability is on your plan. If the whole factory has come to a standstill, you can't insist that the staff come back to give their 50 per cent of the week to your project and finish fixing the production line next week.

- ✔ **Multiple staff:** If two or more people are working on a task and must work together on it, then the duration will depend on the one with the least availability. If part of the work can be done without everyone involved, then that impact is reduced. A simple example is where there are two people on a task, of whom one is available for part of his time and one is available for all his time. If only part of the task requires both people working together, then clearly the one who's full time can get on with some stuff when his fellow team member is unavailable.

- ✔ **Project dependencies:** Sometimes, work can't start until staff are released from other work such as work on other projects. So, although three of the four people on a team are ready to roll, a fourth person, who's essential, is several days late arriving because of a delay in another project. The impact of that one person's delay is that the whole team gets held up.

- ✔ **Speed of working:** Some staff members perform faster than others, and some organisations perform faster than others.

- ✔ **The team size:** If a task involves a lot of people, they tend to work more slowly than if it just involves two or three people. That's not least because of the communication and organisation needs within the team.

- ✔ **Working environment:** People in some working environments are hassled with noise and interruptions (such as phones ringing). Be realistic in assessing the duration of activities, and don't expect the same productivity from staff in a disruptive environment that you would from the same staff in a peaceful environment where they can focus and work with few distractions or interruptions. We offer more on this point later in the section 'Factoring in productivity'.

## Working from home

Where people can work independently for at least some of the time, it is often better if they can work at home. Not only is there a saving in travelling time and hassle, people often work better at home where there are fewer interruptions than in the office. The reduction in interruptions not only means that the working time itself is more productive, but also the increased concentration generally means that they make fewer mistakes, which in turn saves even more time on the project.

Some years ago, Nick Graham was doing some work that was very modular. On one day he needed to be in the office in Central London as cover for someone else, though in the event he wasn't needed and could get on with his own stuff. He had his red flag up on his desk to indicate that he wanted to concentrate and shouldn't be disturbed unless the office was on fire, and possibly not even then. He had a good day and was pleased with how much he had accomplished. The next day he worked at home. When he took a break at about 11 a.m. and was thinking about the work done so far that morning, he realised to his amazement that he had done as many modules that day up to 11 a.m. as he had all the previous day in the office. He struggled to believe it until he thought back and started to remember the noise in the office, the distractions with people coming and going around him, and the interruptions – 'Hi, Nick. Oh, sorry, I didn't notice your red flag. But as I've broken your concentration now anyway can I ask you about . . .'

## *Estimating required work effort*

As you develop your work-effort estimates, do the following:

- ✔ **Think through the detail of all work related to performing the activity.** Examples include:
  - Sending out an agenda in advance of the planned meeting and booking the room and refreshments
  - Preparing and rehearsing a presentation to be given at the meeting

- ✔ **Consider history.** Past history doesn't guarantee future performance, but it does provide a guideline for what's possible. Find out whether similar work has been done before. If it has, review any written records to determine the work effort spent on it. If written records weren't kept, ask people who've done the activity before to estimate the work effort they invested.

When using prior history to support your estimates, make sure that:

  - The people who performed the work had qualifications and experience similar to those of the people who'll work on your project.
  - The facilities, equipment and technology used were similar to those that'll be used for your project.

- The time frame was similar to the one you anticipate for your project.

✔ **Have the person who'll actually do the work participate in estimating the amount of work effort that will be required.** Having people contribute to their work-effort estimates provides the following benefits:

- Their understanding of the activity improves.

- The estimates are based on their particular skills, knowledge and experience, which makes them more accurate.

- Their commitment to do the work for that level of work effort increases.

If you know who'll be working on the activity, it really helps if you can involve those people in the initial planning, perhaps in a planning workshop. If people don't join the project team until the start of the project or during it, have them review and comment on the plans you've developed. Then update your plans as needed.

✔ **Consult with experts familiar with the type of work you need done on your project, even if they haven't performed work exactly like it before.** Incorporating experience and knowledge from different sources improves the accuracy of your estimate.

Accurate estimating can be difficult, to say the least. You can find more help on estimating, including a few techniques, towards the end of Chapter 6, which covers activity planning.

## Factoring in productivity

A good estimate is one that's close to how long a task eventually takes. If the estimates are good, then the project will stick pretty close to the plan and will be a whole lot easier to manage than if it keeps veering wildly off plan.

It's worth spending some effort getting the task durations as close in as you possibly can, because it saves a lot of corrective work, and probably time, later. A more accurate plan saves time because if project tasks don't take the time you anticipated, then you have to keep re-scheduling everything else. 'Sorry Cheng, I know I said I needed you on Week 12, but it's now going to be Week 14. Oh sorry, something else has just shifted so it's Week 11; oh wait a minute, more breaking news . . .'

### Defining 'full time'

Being assigned to a project full time doesn't mean a person can perform project work at peak productivity 40 hours per week, 52 weeks per year. Additional personal and organisational activities reduce the amount of work that people produce. During your project, your staff will probably:

✔ Take annual leave.

✔ Go sick occasionally.

✔ Read and respond to emails on non-project work.

✔ Talk about the football, or their holiday, or the weather. If you work in an office with other people, do you always sit straight down and start working at full capacity the moment you get in?

✔ Read professional journals or web feeds.

✔ Have organisational things to do, such as read staff notices or attend departmental meetings.

So don't ever think of staff as 100 per cent available to the project. The reality is that they won't be, and if you schedule them for five full days a week then your plan won't work. Someone working full time on a project is probably available, on average, four days a week, but watch out because it could be even less (see the nearby sidebar 'The truth is out: How workers really spend their time').

Don't use overtime when planning. Plan using normal working hours only, because that way if you come under pressure during the project you have overtime working as a fallback. If you've already planned in overtime, you've got nowhere left to run. Also be careful of how you think about overtime if you do come to use it later. Staff who are working long hours aren't usually as productive in the overtime hours as they are in the normal ones, because they get tired. But they may not be as productive in the normal hours either. If someone knows he has a really long day ahead, he'll tend to pace himself in the early part of the day.

## The truth is out: How workers really spend their time

A number of years ago, Stan Portny read a study that determined that the typical employee spends an average of four hours of an eight-hour working day on planned project activities and work assignments. In other words, the typical employee in this study averaged a work availability of 50 per cent! The interviewers in this study spoke with people with a wide range of job responsibilities from more than 100 organisations.

Since then, Stan has found several organisations that conducted similar studies of their own operations. These organisations all found

workers' project time to be about 75 per cent of total time. You may think the workers in these companies were more efficient than the ones in the previous study, but, in fact, these studies were biased. The people surveyed wanted their organisations to think that they were spending most of their time working on project assignments, and the organisations wanted to believe that their employees were doing so. Still, the organisation studies found that people spent about 25 per cent of each day doing something other than planned project-related activities!

### *Making specific adjustments*

In thinking about how long something will take, you need to factor in productivity. Be especially careful where you're basing estimates on how long something took on a previous project in another organisation, or even in another part of your own organisation. What matters isn't how long it took to do an earlier job *there*, but how long it will take to do the job *here*. So, you may need to make a few adjustments, and that's in three areas:

- ✔ Adjusting for the exact nature of the task
- ✔ Adjusting for your people
- ✔ Adjusting for the working environment

#### *Adjusting for the exact nature of the task*

When thinking about the task you need done in comparison with similar work done previously on another project somewhere else, consider:

- ✔ **Degree of similarity:** Is the task on your project exactly the same as the one done on a previous project, or is it more or less difficult?

- ✔ **Size:** Is the task the same size, bigger or smaller? If it took two staff two hours to pack ten boxes on a previous project, then packing 1,000 similar boxes on your project isn't going to take two staff 200 hours. For a start, your people will need a lunch break each day. On the other hand, if the box packing is quite complicated, the unit speed on your project may increase over time because your staff will get more familiar with the task, whereas on the previous project with just ten boxes they didn't have time to.

#### *Adjusting for your people*

Consider each of the following factors when you estimate the number of hours that your people will need to complete assignments:

- ✔ **Ability to switch among several tasks:** A person's level of comfort moving to a second task when he hits a roadblock in his first one, so that he doesn't sit around stewing about his frustrations and wasting time.

- ✔ **Knowledge and skills:** The raw talent and capability a person has to perform a particular task.

- ✔ **Motivation:** Are your staff highly motivated and so likely to perform better, or less motivated – perhaps some were assigned to your project when they very much wanted to work on a different and much more interesting one – so are likely to work more slowly?

- ✔ **Multi-tasking:** This is the inverse of the first bullet point. When someone is constantly switching between tasks, the elapsed time of all tasks will be increased. Have a look at the sidebar 'The impact of multi-tasking' to see why.

✔ **Prior experience:** A person's familiarity with the work and the typical problems of a particular task. Trainees normally take longer than experienced team members, and make more mistakes.

✔ **Sense of urgency:** A person's drive to generate the desired results within established time frames. (Urgency influences a person's focus and concentration on an activity.)

### *Adjusting for the working environment*

Working conditions affect performance, and if you don't take that into account then your estimates are likely to be wrong. The area of working conditions covers an array of factors, and this point doesn't just mean avoiding Dickensian workhouse conditions. Consider also:

✔ **Availability of equipment:** Is the right equipment readily available and in good condition, or are staff having to make do with inadequate equipment or wait for a long time before they can get to use the right kit, because it is in such short supply?

✔ **The nature of other work:** Are staff involved in other work alongside the project work, for example providing support for computer systems or the production line? If they are and there are constant interruptions, performance on project activities will be severely degraded. Not only is time taken up on dealing with a support incident, but it then takes that staff member time to pick up the threads on the project task. If he's just done that and the phone rings again . . .

✔ **The quality of the environment:** Is it quiet and peaceful so that people can concentrate, or is it noisy and distracting with phones ringing and a lot of people walking through all the time? A lot of organisations have moved to open-plan offices and *hot desking* (where staff don't have their own permanent desks but are allocated one – if there's one left - when they arrive each day) to save money. However, the focus tends to be solely on reducing accommodation costs, and few organisations consider the wider dimension of staff performance.

✔ **The setup of the physical environment:** The proximity and arrangement of a person's furniture, the amount of space and the adequacy of lighting.

For the physical working environment, think about how you might improve it, including ways of working, and so improve productivity. When running projects involving support staff, Nick Graham set up a hot seat system. One person on the team was designated to take all of the support calls for a week. That person would be interrupted frequently, and although he or she did get some project work done, productivity was low. However, the rest of the team were sheltered and could get on without distraction unless a support problem was particularly severe and more help was needed. In the next week, a different team member was in the hot seat, so the hassle was shared out and everyone could work undisturbed most of the time.

# The impact of multi-tasking

When someone is working on several tasks at once, the elapsed time of all of them will be increased. The following diagram uses the example of someone switching between three tasks that he's doing at once; you may think, 'Only three things at a time? I wish!'

If you can organise the work so that people deal with one thing at a time, then the elapsed time of each task will be reduced. If you plan well, you can tell people exactly when you will need them, confirming it as you approach that point so they can clear the decks of other work and so give you faster delivery. As the diagram shows, even just working on one thing at a time gives an improvement, with C being delivered at the same time as before, but A and B both delivered earlier. But even that doesn't account for the extra time needed to pick up the threads if a team member breaks off work on a task and then goes back to it some time later.

Each two-week task takes four elapsed weeks

Each two-week task takes two elapsed weeks. A and B are completed earlier and C is no later than before.

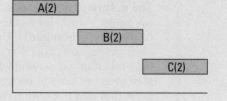

# *Taking care with historical data*

When completed properly, time sheets provide the most reliable source of past experience. However, it's with good reason that time sheets are often called 'lie sheets'. Before relying on past metrics, make sure that you fully understand the information, and that includes a careful assessment of the organisational culture, which in turn affects how time is recorded.

The following time-sheet practices can cause the data on them to be inaccurate:

- ✔ People aren't allowed to record overtime, so some hours actually spent on an activity may never be known.

- ✔ People are required to send in their time sheets several days before the reporting period is over, so they must guess what their hourly allocations for the next few days will be.

- ✔ People fill out their time sheets just before they go home at the end of the week. They're in a hurry to get away and can't remember with any clarity what they did in the early part of the week, so they take a wild guess and put that down.

✔ People are working on some non-project stuff during the week but are supposed to be allocated full time on the project. So they spread out the hours spent on the other work among your project time codes.

✔ People copy the work-effort estimates from the Project Plan onto their time sheets each period instead of recording the actual number of hours they spend.

If any of these situations exist in your organisation, don't use historical data from time sheets to support your work-effort estimates for your current project.

In a large civil engineering company, senior managers told middle managers that if their staff were having to working overtime it was a sign of poor management. A good manager should be able to achieve things within normal working hours by working smarter not harder. Fearful of damage to their promotion prospects, the middle managers promptly instructed their staff that the total weekly hours on the time sheets must never exceed 37.5 hours, the standard week. If they'd worked more than this, the staff were to allocate the effort proportionally among the relevant codes but keep the total at 37.5 hours. All the time-sheet information was fed into a computer system from which senior managers could get reports.

A very big contract came up that was similar to a project already done, and a senior manager decided to get a report on the previous contract from the time-sheet system. That data was used as the basis of the bid for the contract, which the company easily won because its bid was significantly less than that of any of its competitors. When the project got underway, the Project Manager was puzzled that everything was taking much more work effort than shown in the breakdown of work on the bid. He went to see the Project Manager of the previous contract to ask how they did things with far fewer staff hours. The reply was, 'Oh, we didn't do it with fewer hours. What you're looking at is just the time we put on the time sheets!'

## Accounting for availability in estimates

If you base work-effort estimates on the opinions of people who'll do the activities or who've done similar activities in the past instead of on historical records, you have to factor in a measure of availability.

First, ask the person from whom you're getting your information to estimate the required work effort, assuming he can work at 100 per cent availability. (In other words, ask him not to worry about normal interruptions during the day, having to work on multiple tasks at a time, and so on.) Then modify the estimate to reflect availability by doing the following:

✔ If the person will use a time sheet that has one or more categories for non-project-specific work, use his original work-effort estimate.

✔ If the person will use a time sheet that doesn't have categories to record non-project-specific work, add an additional amount to his original estimate to account for his availability.

As an example, suppose a person estimates that he needs 30 work hours to perform a task (if he can be 100 per cent available) and his time sheets have no categories for recording non-project-specific work. If you estimate that he'll work at about 75 per cent capacity, allow him to charge 40 person-hours to your project to complete the task (75 per cent of 40 person-hours is 30 person-hours – the amount you really need.) Bear in mind for your Business Case (see Chapter 3), though, that you're carrying organisational work overheads in your project, not just project work costs.

Failure to consider availability when estimating and reviewing project work effort can lead to incorrect conclusions about people's performance. Suppose your boss assigns you a project on Monday morning. He tells you the project will take about 40 work hours, but he really needs it by Friday close of business. Suppose further that you work really hard all week and finish the task by Friday close of business. In the process, you record 55 hours for the project on your time sheet.

If your boss doesn't realise that his initial estimate of 40 person-hours was based on your working at 100 per cent availability, he'll think you took 15 hours longer than you should have. On the other hand, if your boss recognises that 55 person-hours *on the job* translates into about 40 person-hours of work *on specific project tasks*, he will appreciate that you invested extra effort to meet his aggressive deadline.

The longer you're involved in an assignment, the more important efficiency and availability become. Suppose you decide you have to spend one hour on an assignment. You can reasonably figure your availability is 100 per cent, so you charge your project one hour for the assignment. If you need to spend six hours on an assignment, you can figure your availability is 100 per cent, but you must consider 75 per cent availability (or a similar planning figure). Therefore, charge one work day (eight work hours) to ensure that you can spend the six hours on your assignment.

However, if you plan to devote one month or more to your assignment, you'll most likely take some leave days during that time. Even though your project budget doesn't have to pay for your annual or sick leave, one staff month means you have about 97 hours for productive work on your assignment.

# *Smoothing the Resource*

The resource conflicts that we explain in the earlier section 'Dealing with resource conflicts' usually apply to staff. Sometimes, though, you encounter conflicts on things like accommodation or specialised equipment. Non-human resource is covered in detail in the next chapter, but the way you'll deal with such conflicts is the same as with staff resource conflicts.

# *Checking for resource conflict*

To check for resource conflict, you need to look at what each person is scheduled to do in each time period, usually each day. If a person has more to do than there is time available in the day, then there is a resource conflict. That may be because the person has 16 hours' work to do in an 8-hour day, or perhaps it's 8 hours' work to do in a day that has 0 work hours because it's a public holiday.

If you're using a computerised scheduling tool, it either prevents you scheduling in a way that creates a conflict, or it allows you to schedule how you like, but then highlights the conflicts so you can work through them and deal with them.

You can create a Resource Histogram for each staff member to show whether any conflicts exist. This shows the required hours if all the work is done as scheduled, and displays that against available hours.

Going to back Sue, the overworked team member from earlier in the chapter (see 'Dealing with resource conflicts'), Figure 7-2 shows a Resource Histogram for a few of the project tasks. Sue is clearly overcommitted and for two days is needed three days per day, which is asking a bit much. To resolve these resource conflicts, it's necessary to do some *resource smoothing*, sometimes known as resource levelling. Put simply, the level of required resource needs to be got down below the level of available resource.

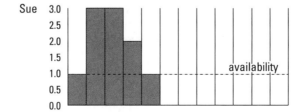

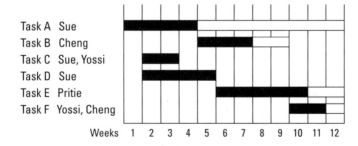

**Figure 7-2:**
A Resource
Histogram.

# Resolving resource conflicts – the steps

Here are some straightforward steps for resource smoothing:

1. **Check the activity dependencies and resource allocations to make sure they're correct.**

   Continuing the example from the last section, you don't want to solve the problem of Sue being overcommitted if you've put her onto the tasks by mistake and you meant to enter Sam.

2. **Adjust within float.**

   This is where the Activity Network (see Chapter 6) pays dividends. You may see from your network that the earliest start date of an activity is considerably earlier than the latest start date, so you can simply slide the activity along within its float to a time when Sue has plenty of availability.

   In Figure 7-2 it looks like the start of Activity A can be delayed as late as Week 9 without causing a problem. However, you'd need to be sure that it doesn't have a knock-on effect. In this case, if Activity B was dependent on A, you would now cause problems for both Sue and the project as a whole. Again, the Activity Network will be really useful, because it shows the dependencies clearly.

3. **Adjust resource.**

   This is where the Skills Matrix (see the earlier section 'Developing a Skills Matrix') may prove extremely useful. Is there someone else who has the same skill set as Sue? If so and he has more availability at this point, can you assign one or more tasks to him instead? Or alternatively, can you put that person on the task alongside Sue to help; in other words, can you raise the line of available resource?

4. **Move tasks downstream.**

   If you've made changes but still have a resource conflict, you need to move things downstream, and the project end date will go out. In theory, three tasks can be done in parallel, but because of a resource constraint that Sue must do all three, she'll have to do them one after the other, and the impact on the end date is accepted.

Computer tools, both project-scheduling software and spreadsheets, are great for playing around to try different things. But don't forget to save a copy before you start your 'what if's'. If everything goes horribly wrong, you'll want to be able to get back to your start point. It's so easy to save the work in the middle of the 'what if's' and forget that you're overwriting your main file.

## Plans make things visible

Nick Graham was running a project-planning workshop for a client in the UK, and the senior manager responsible for the project was insistent that the project be completed within nine months. The team was working with the Project Manager and Nick in the workshop and everything was fine with the product planning, but when it got to activity planning everyone got a bit suspicious. On doing the resource planning, it became absolutely clear that the project was going to take 15 months. The senior manager was due to visit the workshop on the third day,

the point when the team had just finished the resource planning. When the boss walked in, the Project Manager went up to him and told him about the 15-month duration on the plan. The boss said 'You're joking, it's got to be done in nine months.' The Project Manager took the senior manager over to the large whiteboard where the plan was drawn up. After studying it carefully for a few minutes, the senior manager said, 'You're right, it's going to take 15 months.' Plans make things visible.

Where you have staff who aren't full time on the project, you can sometimes squeeze out a bit more flexibility by talking to them about how they allocate their work. For example, if Sam is available to your project for 50 per cent of his time, that needn't mean he just works mornings. If you have a resource conflict in the early part of a week, you could ask if he could work the first half of the week full time on your project then spend the second half of the week on his other assignments. In other words, concentrate the 50 per cent into a shorter period of time rather than have it uniformly spread. Depending on the nature of the other assignments, you may find he can be even more flexible than that and, say, work a full week for you when you really need it, then the following week work full time on the other assignments; it's still 50 per cent. Involving team members in estimating and resource planning pays off when it comes to asking people to be flexible to meet the needs of both the project and any other assignments.

## *Co-ordinating assignments across multiple projects*

Working on overlapping tasks can place conflicting demands on a person, whether the tasks are on one project or several. Although successfully addressing these conflicts can be more difficult when more than one Project Manager is involved, the techniques for analysing them are the same whether you're the only Project Manager involved or you're just one of many.

In general, people on any of your project teams may also be assigned to other projects you're managing or to other Project Managers' projects. If Resource Histograms (see the earlier section 'Checking for resource conflict') or other loading information is available for each project your people are assigned to, you can manage each person's overall resource commitments by combining the information.

Figure 7-3 illustrates overall loading information that shows the commitments for each person on one or more of your project teams.

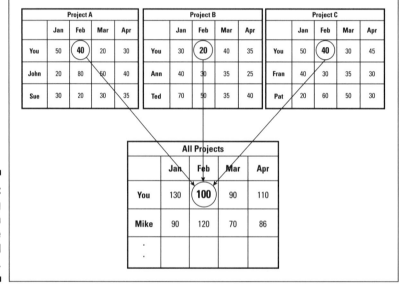

| Project A | | | | |
|---|---|---|---|---|
| | Jan | Feb | Mar | Apr |
| You | 50 | 40 | 20 | 30 |
| John | 20 | 80 | 60 | 40 |
| Sue | 30 | 20 | 30 | 35 |

| Project B | | | | |
|---|---|---|---|---|
| | Jan | Feb | Mar | Apr |
| You | 30 | 20 | 40 | 35 |
| Ann | 40 | 30 | 35 | 25 |
| Ted | 70 | 50 | 35 | 40 |

| Project C | | | | |
|---|---|---|---|---|
| | Jan | Feb | Mar | Apr |
| You | 50 | 40 | 30 | 45 |
| Fran | 40 | 30 | 35 | 30 |
| Pat | 20 | 60 | 50 | 30 |

| All Projects | | | | |
|---|---|---|---|---|
| | Jan | Feb | Mar | Apr |
| You | 130 | 100 | 90 | 110 |
| Mike | 90 | 120 | 70 | 86 |
| . . | | | | |

**Figure 7-3:** Staff loading information to plan time on several projects.

With all the resourcing issues, the key to success is good plans. If you have clear plans, you not only see the problems but you also have excellent tools to hand to resolve them.

# Chapter 8

# Planning for Other Resources and Developing the Budget

- - - - - - - - - - - - - - - - - - - - - - - - - - - - - - - - - - - - - - - - - - - - - - - - - - - - -

## In This Chapter

▶ Accounting for your project's physical resources

▶ Preparing a detailed budget for your project

- - - - - - - - - - - - - - - - - - - - - - - - - - - - - - - - - - - - - - - - - - - - - - - - - - - - -

*A* key part of effective project management is ensuring that staff resources are available throughout the project when and where they're needed, and we cover that in Chapter 7. But although staff resource is extremely important, it's not the end of the story, because you're going to need other types of resource for your project too. Unless your project is somewhat unusual, you'll need money, and often you'll need physical, non-staff, resources such as special equipment, accommodation and computers. That's where this chapter fits in.

Although you need to think about the physical resource and also budget, the thinking about physical resource mostly comes first. That's because the physical resource requirements have an impact on the budget, not just in total but in terms of the timing of when you'll need money. Just occasionally it can work the other way around and limitations on the budget and cash flow constrain your options for physical resource.

You need to build the physical resource needs into your plan just like staff resource needs. If people are available for a scheduled task but, for example, the necessary laboratory equipment isn't, your project can have costly delays and unanticipated expenditures. Also, your team members may experience frustration that leads to reduced commitment. So, to be successful, you're going to need to establish a clear list of physical resources, a schedule of when you need them, and a budget to cover both physical and staff resource.

This chapter helps you determine, understand and then specify the physical resource you need for your project, and then gives some guidance on how to develop your project budget.

# Determining Physical Resource Needs

In addition to staff, your project may require a variety of other important resources. You need to plan for these resources in the same way you plan to meet your staff requirements. (Check out Chapter 7 for more on meeting your staff needs.)

As always, when you're planning, you'll often find it helpful to talk to other people, to the point of involving them in a planning workshop. In the case of physical resource requirements, you may want to talk to:

- ✔ Potential team members who may do the project work
- ✔ Technical specialists within the organisation
- ✔ Potential or selected suppliers
- ✔ Project staff, including Project Managers from any similar projects

## Identifying resource needs

It's really important to think through *all* the resource requirements for your project and also identify any equipment your organisation already has.

Here are some physical resources to think about:

- ✔ Special equipment, tools and materials to:
  - Design products
  - Build products
  - Test products, such as specialised test rigs
- ✔ Team accommodation such as team rooms or a lab for:
  - Existing organisational staff who need to work together
  - Accommodation for contractors and supplier staff
- ✔ Accommodation for intermittent use for:
  - Workshops
  - Project meetings and briefings
  - Presentations
- ✔ Furniture and fittings:
  - Tables, desks, chairs, desk lamps
  - Whiteboards, flip charts, data projectors, screens

- Computers, scanners and printers, including any specialised ones
- Security containers, if you're working with confidential information

✔ Communications: landline phones, cell phones, computer data cards

✔ Transport:

- To move part-finished or completed products between sites
- To move team members around
- Project Manager's chauffeur-driven car – well perhaps, one day

It's usually safe to leave out standard equipment such as if your team already has a team room equipped with desks, computers and phones.

### Considering availability

It's dangerous to assume that a resource will always be there when you need it, and the more time critical your project is, the more careful you need to be. If you think that sounds a bit like risk management (see Chapter 10), you're right because it overlaps.

Things that can affect physical resource availability include:

✔ Bookings from other projects or for operational work

✔ Loans of equipment to another department or site

✔ Scheduled maintenance

✔ Breakdown and damage

✔ Likelihood of subsequent needs of a higher priority project

Don't kid yourself that the 'I booked it first' argument will unfailingly hold up in the face of a demand from a top-priority, business-critical project that has the backing of the whole board of directors, the chief constable, the secretary of state or, in the military, someone simply pulling rank.

### Using your plans to help

As you think through the physical resource needs, do include looking through the Product Definitions of what is to be built (see Chapter 5 for the full detail on product planning). The activity plans then give information on when that kit is likely to be wanted.

### Building a Physical Resource Matrix

It's helpful to produce a Physical Resource Matrix on a spreadsheet, with columns for the physical resources involved, the IDs of the products that the resources are needed for, how much of each resource is needed and when it's needed. You can make the list more refined by adding columns for equipment category, source of supply and cost, so that you can sort the list in different ways when it comes to letting other people know what you need or when placing orders.

## *Understanding physical resources*

Having thought through what you need, it's important to think next about the nature of each of those resources and the best source of supply, given those characteristics. That supply may be through your own organisation because the item is readily available, or by buying or hiring it.

Your thinking here should include:

- ✔ **Availability:** How easy is it to obtain the item? If it's easy to get hold of a piece of equipment, then you won't be too bothered if a source of supply fails, because you can get it somewhere else. However, if the item is in short supply and very hard to obtain, you may want to buy it rather than rely on hiring it, and if you're buying it, to buy it early to make quite sure you've got it.

- ✔ **Environmental:** Does the equipment need any special conditions or have special installation requirements such as needing a special power supply? Can it be affected by things around it? Far too many people have set up a computer installation in a room directly underneath the roof area where a main water tank is sited, and then the inevitable happens.

- ✔ **Lead times and delivery constraints:** If you need to book equipment, whether that's within your own organisation or from a hire company, how early should you do that? You may need to adjust your plan because although you need the kit in Stage 6, you need to book it in Stage 3. Similarly, on deliveries of equipment, how much notice do you need to give for the delivery of that large item, and do any limitations exist such as 'We only deliver to the South-West on Tuesdays'?

- ✔ **Operability:** Do the relevant team members already have the skills to use a piece of equipment, or do they need to be trained to use it?

- ✔ **Size and weight:** If something is big, do you also need to arrange some storage space while it's waiting to be installed? If it's big or heavy, are there any implications for getting it in place, like enlarging a gate or doorway or hiring a crane to get it in through a window? Do you need to have the floor reinforced?

- ✔ **Value:** Do you need secure storage and then booking-in and booking-out procedures? Is the item covered by your organisational insurance or do you need to take out specific insurance?

Check the spec. If someone in your organisation says 'We've got one of those – we can lend it to you,' then be grateful. But before you're grateful, make sure the specification is right. Don't assume it will be okay then find you've got a problem later when a team member reports that the equipment is an old model and won't do the job.

## Thinking a bit more about timing

Where you're using physical resources such as equipment, it's worth thinking a bit more deeply about when you'll need to get hold of them. The bullet list in the last section included lead times for booking when you may need to book equipment early in the project for use that will actually take place much later on.

The problem with booking things too far in the future, though, is that timings change – no project ever goes exactly to plan. A small delay in the project, quite normal and acceptable in terms of contingency allowances, could throw out booked slots for equipment. So you wanted the test rig in Week 23 and you booked it for Week 23. Unfortunately, a problem a bit earlier in the project resulted in a time slip, and now you need the rig in Week 24, but another project has it booked for that week. You can do three things about this problem:

- ✔ **Contingency:** Put some contingency time into your Project Plan just before you need the equipment. That way, if a delay occurs you can absorb the problem without missing the booked slot for the equipment. However, this option means that if the project doesn't hit a problem, your team may be hanging around waiting for the equipment if it's currently in use. That's like being hit by a reverse Murphy's Law – if it can go wrong, it won't!

- ✔ **Fallback:** Find alternative sources of supply in advance. That way, if you miss the booked slot and the equipment is unavailable when you now need it, you already have a list of other places where you may be able to get it.

- ✔ **Time buffer:** Book the equipment for longer than you think you'll actually need it. Depending on where you're getting it from, that could have an implication for project costs, but that may be preferable to a long delay while you wait for the kit to become available again.

Where equipment is vital and there could be delays in getting it, you may want to think about buying your own for the project, even if that's quite expensive. Suppose you need some equipment for three weeks and it will cost £8,000 to buy but only £500 a week to hire. Well, it may be worth buying it if the timing is particularly unpredictable and it's likely that your project will face a four-week delay waiting for the kit. If your project, when delivered, will save the organisation £250,000 a month, then the £6,500 extra spend is small compared with the loss of a month's benefits – and you may even be able to sell the equipment afterwards. The 'Part of Tens' at the end of this book includes ten tips for being a better Project Manager. One of those tips is to think about the big picture.

# Making Sense of Costs and Budgets

In a world of limited funds, organisations are constantly deciding how to get the best return for their investment in terms of both money and staff hours. Therefore, estimating a project's costs is important for several reasons:

✔ It's a vital element of the Business Case (see Chapter 3) to see whether the project is financially justified.

✔ It allows organisational managers to assess whether the project should be run by comparing the costs against the benefits for this project compared with other 'candidate' projects that could be run instead.

✔ It allows departmental or organisational finance staff to check that the necessary funds are available to support the project, and allocate those funds.

Managing project finance is an essential part of project management and one that's very high profile. If you work in an organisation of any size, you already appreciate just how important finance is. You also know how impressive it is when a Project Manager delivers a project on time, to the required level of quality and also bang on target with the finances. The following sections examine different types of project costs and offer helpful tips for developing your own project budget.

## Looking at different types of project costs

A *project budget* is a time-based estimate of all resource costs for your project. It normally gives a total projected spend for each stage then a total for the whole project. If some of the project's products are to be taken into use during the project, not all in one 'big bang' at the end, you may also start to see some financial savings during the life of the project. In that case, the budget usually needs to show inbound cash flow as well as outbound.

You typically develop a budget in three levels of detail as you move through the project:

1. **You develop a rough estimate – a ballpark figure.**

2. **When you're doing the more detailed project planning, you revise the budget to be more detailed and more precise using the information from the plans.**

3. **As you progress through the delivery stages and better information and more detailed plans are to hand, you update the budget to reflect that better information.** (Check out 'Developing a project budget at three levels', later in this chapter, for more on this.)

### Understanding direct and indirect costs

Your project's budget normally includes both direct and indirect costs.

*Direct costs* are costs for resources solely used for your project. Direct costs include the following:

- ✔ Salaries for team members on your project
- ✔ Specific materials, supplies and equipment for your project
- ✔ Subcontracts that provide support exclusively to your project
- ✔ Travel to perform work on your project

*Indirect costs* are costs for resources that support more than one project but aren't readily identifiable with or chargeable to any of the projects individually. Indirect costs fall into the following two categories:

- ✔ **General and administrative costs:** Expenditures on centralised things that keep your organisation operational. Examples include salaries of your contracts department, finance department and top management, as well as fees for general accounting and legal services.

- ✔ **Overhead costs:** Costs for products and services for your project that are difficult to subdivide and allocate directly. Examples include employee benefits, rent for office space, general supplies and the costs of furniture, fixtures and equipment.

  You need an office to work on your project activities, and office space costs money. However, your organisation has an annual lease for office space, the space has many individual offices and work areas, and people work on numerous projects throughout the year. Because you have no clear records that specify the proportion of the total rent that's just for the time you spend in your office working on just this project's activities, you treat your office space as an indirect project cost.

It's important to discriminate clearly between the different costs – not least because your finance director will! Indirect costs will already be in the organisational budget, but at least some of the direct costs will need to be specially funded.

### Understanding capital and revenue

Many organisations refer to costs as capital and revenue. *Revenue* is ongoing year-on-year costs such as building rental, equipment maintenance and staffing. *Capital costs* are one-off purchases such as equipment and contract staff.

Some organisations prefer to use contract staff for at least some of the project work, simply because it can be accounted for as a capital cost whereas recruiting more permanent staff would show up as an ongoing running cost. Higher revenue costs make an organisation appear less efficient because it's spending more on overheads, whereas the staff spend in capital expenditure is hidden. This may seem like political and budgetary manoeuvring, which it is, but be aware of it because it can affect the staffing and funding of your project.

### Understanding capex

Within direct capital costs you may also be involved in a particular type of capital expenditure, or *capex*. This is where you buy equipment or other things that have an extended working life. Identifying such items clearly is important because they become assets of the organisation and in turn that means that their value isn't offset against tax all at once. Instead, part of the cost is set against tax each year as the value of the item depreciates over its working life.

Be clear, then, on purchases of things that have an ongoing value (such as a new machine for the production line) and what things are fully expended in the current tax year (such as the use of contract staff), because your finance people will need to know.

### Seeing things from the financial manager's perspective

Although, as a Project Manager, you aren't supposed to be a career finance specialist, and perhaps even the thought of assets and capex makes your head spin, it does help if you develop a proper understanding of the nature of your organisation's finances. This not only helps with communication on budgets, but also helps you make the life of the finance people easier. Being totally selfish, if you understand how your finance managers see things, you're more likely to make your project pitch correctly and get approval for it.

Unless you're running a project that affects only a small area of the business and where the budgets are all dealt with by someone else, do go and talk to your finance people. That way you'll understand their needs, understand their view of the project and get them on side. Also, if you want to know more, you may consider investing in a copy of *Understanding Business Accounting For Dummies* by Colin Barrow and John A. Tracy.

# Developing a project budget at three levels

Organisational decision makers would love to have a detailed and accurate budget on hand whenever someone proposes a project, so they can assess its relative benefits to the organisation and decide whether they have sufficient funds to support it. Unfortunately, you can't prepare such an estimate until you develop a clear understanding of the work and resources the project will require.

Try to resist pressure to state a specific project budget up front before you've done any real thinking about a project. In some organisations, as soon as someone mentions the words *project* and *Business Case*, some finance managers start pushing for a specific project cost. You tell them that you don't really know, but they say, 'Well, tell us roughly how much you've got in mind – you must have some idea.' You say, 'Well, it's probably going to be about £100,000.' Unfortunately, the finance people then go away and put that figure in the accounts, and just you try changing it now; it's carved in stone. It's for that very reason that the PRIME project management method doesn't use the term 'Business Case' until the more detailed project planning is being done and more reliable costs are to hand (more on PRIME in Chapter 2).

In reality, decisions about whether to go forward with the early parts of a project and how to undertake them must be made before people can prepare highly accurate budgets. You can develop and refine your project budget at the following levels to provide the best information possible to support important project decisions:

- ✔ **Rough order-of-magnitude estimate:** This level is an initial estimate of costs based on a general sense of the project work in the Starting the Project stage. You make this estimate without detailed data. Depending on the nature of the project, the final budget may end up being much more (or less!) than this initial estimate.

    Prepare a rough order-of-magnitude estimate by considering the costs of similar projects (or similar activities that will be part of your project) that have already been done, and applicable cost and productivity information, if you have the luxury of such information being available.

    This estimate sometimes expresses what someone *wants* to spend rather than what the project will really *cost*. You typically don't detail this estimate by lowest-level project activity because you prepare it in a short amount of time before you've identified the project activities.

- ✔ **Detailed project budget estimate:** This level entails an itemisation of the estimated costs within each project stage. You prepare this estimate in the Organising and Preparing stage by developing the Project Plans. This budget is approved as part of the full project's approval (it usually forms part of the Project Charter; see Chapter 2) and now provides a baseline against which you can measure project finances. However, because circumstances can change, this budget may be modified during the project, which brings in the third level of budgeting and the next bullet point.

✔ **Stage budgets and revised project budget:** As the project progresses, the financial forecast is likely to change, and that's for two reasons:

- Often the fine detail of the work isn't known yet. For example, you don't know at the start of the project exactly what equipment you'll need to buy, because the capacity planning work hasn't been done yet.
- Projects are often going into the unknown, so the budget can't be exact at the outset.

As more information becomes available during the project stages and stage budgets are worked out in detail, you can calculate the implications and update the project budget. The next section covers this point in more detail.

## Refining your budget through the stages

As you work through the delivery stages, you prepare more-detailed costings as you build successive stage plans and, as explained in the last section, you also update the project-level budget with fresh projections. When looking for changes to see what adjustments and other actions you need, you may find the following steps useful:

1. **Review your approved budget as you plan successive delivery stages – when you identify the people who'll be working on your project and when you start to develop formal agreements for the use of equipment, facilities, vendors and other resources.**

   You need to review the budget as you develop the more detailed stage budgets, and to do this you may want to talk to the people who'll actually be doing the work to check that the initial estimates are okay. As you check to see what changes there have been, pay particular attention to the following items that often trigger changes in the budget approved for the project:

   - The work is different from that originally envisaged. Perhaps a problem emerged that required a change in the technical solution, or a very simple solution was found for a problem that everyone thought was going to need a lot of work.

- A stated planning assumption hasn't worked out. For example, you may have based the plan on the assumption that you would be able to use organisational specialists for some work. After that plan was approved, a high-priority project was set up by the chief executive officer, who instructed that the specialists were to work on that and their existing work was to be cancelled or covered by contractors. You're now going to have to hire some people in. That may change the total cost of your project and also the type of cost because the hire is capital, not revenue (see the earlier section 'Understanding capital and revenue').

- The work done so far in the project has consistently taken less effort or more effort than you expected. This may show that the estimates were unduly pessimistic or optimistic and so justify an adjustment for the rest of the project, based on this real-life experience. You can expect this adjustment if you're new to a particular type of project and you didn't have organisational experience on which to base the estimates in the first place.

- People assigned to the project team are more or less experienced than originally anticipated.

- Actual prices for goods and services you'll purchase have increased or, occasionally, decreased.

- Some physical resources required for the project are no longer available when you need them. For example, you were planning to borrow some equipment from another department, but it's now broken and beyond repairing. That department decides it doesn't need the equipment any more anyway, so isn't going to replace it, and you now have to buy or hire your own.

- Your clients want additional or different project results than those they originally discussed with you. This links in with the use of a change budget as well as revisions to the project budget. You can find out about change budgets in Chapter 14.

2. **Get approval for any required adjustments to the budget or other parts of the approved plan before you begin the actual project work.**

Submit requests for any changes to the original plan or budget. You may need to submit them to the same people who approved them or to one or more managers who have oversight of the project (such as a sponsor or steering committee) and whose authority includes budget change. Often that authority to approve changes will be within a specified limits, which is sensible because few projects run exactly to budget. The process of getting budget change approval will normally be part of the stage gate work at the end of each delivery stage. Chapter 2 has more on dividing the project into stages, with each stage ending in a stage gate.

3. **Monitor project activities and related occurrences throughout the carrying out the work and closing the project stages to determine when budget revisions are necessary.**

Sometimes problems and other issues that come up during the work have implications for the budget. For example, a team member may come up with an idea for doing something more simply and cheaply, or a problem may arise that will need money to resolve. This overlaps with the working of the change budget (see Chapter 14). If something is a change and money has been set aside for changes within the project budget, then making a change won't necessarily affect the total cost. However, if a problem goes beyond minor change, then it may have more substantial implications, including ones that definitely affect the overall budget. That impact may be to the point that it affects the Business Case and calls the whole viability of the project into question. Check out Chapter 14 for more on how to monitor project expenditures during the project and how to determine whether you need to make changes to the budget.

 You may not personally participate in all aspects of developing your project budget. If you join your project after the initial planning, be sure to review the work that's been done on the budget and resolve any questions you have and issues you identify.

## Creating a detailed budget estimate

After you prepare your rough order-of-magnitude estimate (see the earlier section 'Developing a project budget at three levels') and move into the Organising and Preparing stage of your project, you're ready to create your detailed budget estimate. You can use a combination of two approaches to develop this budget estimate:

- ✔ **Bottom up:** Develop detailed cost estimates for each lowest-level product (refer to Chapter 5 for more information on product planning), and add these estimates together to obtain the total project budget estimate.

- ✔ **Top down:** Make a target estimate for the entire project and apportion this budget, pro rata, among the main categories on the Work Breakdown Structure (explained in Chapter 5). For example, in a computer development project you may know from organisational records that the physical design usually takes around 15 per cent of overall project cost. For this size of development, you expect the overall cost to be £180,000; therefore, you anticipate that the physical design work will cost £27,000.

### Dealing with the unknown

As with project planning, you can make assumptions in budgets, but keep any assumptions to the minimum and state them clearly in the explanatory text. That way, if things don't work out according to the assumption, those managers who approved the plan knew that the final costs could be different.

Where you simply don't know a cost, put in an estimate based on the most likely. For example, suppose you need a graphic artist to design some visuals for your presentations to customers. The head of the graphics department estimates the person will spend 100 person-hours on your project. If you know that Harry, who has a salary of £20 per hour, will work on the activity, you can estimate your direct staff costs to be £2,000. However, if the director doesn't know who'll work on your project, use the average salary of a graphic artist in your organisation to estimate the direct staff costs.

### Listing the different costs

As explained in the 'Looking at different types of project costs' section, earlier in this chapter, your budget will be more accurate and more acceptable to those giving financial approval if you discriminate clearly between cost types. So, for each part of the project, you can list the forecast expenditures with columns against each one for the different types. Remember that for some work, more than one type of expenditure may be involved, such as staff costs and equipment purchase.

### Including indirect costs – or not

Whether you include indirect costs will be a matter of organisational policy. Some organisations simply ignore indirect costs for project budgets, but whether that's a good idea depends a bit on how big your project is and how many people are involved in it. If your project takes two staff three weeks to do, it's arguably not that significant to add in the appropriate share of the company's legal services. However, if you have 50 staff on the project for two years, then the indirect costs are significant and a strong argument exists for including them.

You'll need to get some guidance on whether to include indirect costs, but if you need to include them, then ask your finance people about the amount to put in. You won't be expected to do your own calculations on each team member's share of paying the CEO's salary – even supposing she was willing to divulge it.

Some larger organisations develop *weighted staff rates*, which combine hourly salary and associated indirect costs. As an example, suppose your salary is £20 per hour and your organisation's indirect-cost rate is 50 per cent. Your weighted staff rate is £30 per hour (£20, plus 50 per cent of £20).

### Showing the timing

Your budget needs to show timing in two senses:

> ✔ **By stage:** You'll probably want to give a stage breakdown to show the total cost of the project, and then the lower level detail of the expected cost of each stage making up that total.

> ✔ **Calendar timing:** If your project will have irregular spends (such as a few times when you're going out to buy a lot of equipment), you'll also need to show the spend against the calendar, so that finance staff can see when you'll need money to be available. A key divide is the financial year end, and your budget will need to show what's being spent in each financial year.

For calendar timing, you may need to think very clearly about when things are ordered, delivered, charged (invoiced) and paid for. You might order something in Week 5 that is delivered in Week 9, invoiced by the supplier in Week 10 and which must be paid for within 28 days so the money actually goes out around Week 14. Or, you might call into the computer shop on the way home to buy that special cable, pay for it on the spot and claim it on your expenses the following day.

Go and talk to your finance people about their information needs if you don't already know. Find out whether they want to know when money is committed as opposed to actually spent, and what cash flow detail they need. You can then build that into your financial control and reporting.

### Being clear on sub-budgets

Within the main budget, be clear what funds are for planned work and what amounts are set aside for a change budget and a risk budget. (We talk about the risk budget in Chapter 10 and the change budget in Chapter 14.) The distinction is important because the funds for planned work will be spent, but funds set aside for change and risk may be only partially used, depending on the amount of change and how many risks materialise.

## Avoiding drowning people in detail

When thinking through the format of your budget, consider who'll be looking at the different parts of it. Typically, the managers who'll approve the project budget won't want to know how many pencil sharpeners you plan to buy in Stage 23 for the user training.

An easy approach for bigger budgets is to set them down in three sections:

> ✔ **An overview:** The total project cost, costs of each project stage making up that total, any breakdown of the total such as revenue and capital costs and then perhaps a brief description of any major expenses. Given that the budget is likely to be seen by senior staff who like pictures, you might also show some graphics here, such as a pie chart to show how much project cost is equipment, how much is internal staff cost and how much is contractor cost.

✔ **A detailed budget:** An itemised breakdown under main headings such as 'staff', 'room hire' and 'travelling costs', week-by-week or month-by-month. This lends itself well to a spreadsheet.

✔ **The fine detail:** The rivet-counter's guide – or perhaps it should be the bean-counter's guide! This section can usually be set down in appendices showing all your calculations. It's unlikely that anyone will study this section from end to end, but some people may want to dip in to see how you arrived at a particular figure. This section is essential for you to keep track of project costs, but senior managers making a decision on the project won't want this detail, so you can present the budget to them without these detailed appendices. However, in a presentation you'd do well to have a copy with you, so if any detailed questions do come up, you can quickly refer to the calculations and be incredibly impressive by coming up with fast, accurate and confident answers.

# Chapter 9

# Planning at Different Times and Levels

. . . . . . . . . . . . . . . . . . . . . . . . . . . . . . . . . . . . . . . . . . . . . . . . . . . . .

. . . . . . . . . . . . . . . . . . . . . . . . . . . . . . . . . . . . . . . . . . . . . . . . . . . . .

*A* great temptation in project planning is to dive into the fine detail and start 'counting rivets' before you're even sure what the project is really about. That's certainly true of planning, and a danger for most people involved in projects is that they go too deep too quickly in planning. The approach in this book, though, is to work at different levels of planning detail at different times.

Here are a few reasons why it makes sense to get the 'helicopter view' before going into detail:

✔ You may be heading in the wrong direction and be doing all sorts of detailed planning on the wrong stuff. In Chapter 2 you may already have seen the quotation from Stephen Covey's *The 7 Habits of Highly Effective People* (Simon & Schuster), which is 'Begin with the end in mind'. It makes sense to check out the high-level stuff before you get into the detail.

✔ Things change, particularly in business projects. It doesn't make a whole lot of sense to do the detailed planning a long way ahead, because you can be sure that things will have changed by the time you get there and a lot of your work will be wasted.

✔ Until you've seen the bigger picture clearly, you're not going to get the detail right, because you don't properly understand what you're dealing with. For a start, you won't usually be absolutely clear on the scope of the project until the high-level Project Plan is agreed.

The chapters so far in this part cover the sorts of things you do in planning. This chapter brings the earlier chapters together to explain when you plan, at what level, and then how to integrate plans at those different levels of detail.

# Putting the Main Structure in Place

Just about all approaches to project planning and control break the project down into phases or stages. This allows you to concentrate on one part of the project at a time, while still seeing the big picture. Stages also create powerful control points, because between each stage everyone can take stock and check that the project is okay before going on to the next stage. People often refer to these control points as *stage gates*, although if you're working with the PRINCE2 project method you'll see that it still insists on using the unwieldy name of *End Stage Assessment*. You can find more on Stage Gates later in the chapter in 'Holding a Stage Gate'.

Stages are useful because of the control points, but also because they allow managers to drip-feed staff resource and money into the project. Although all the project funds and staff resource are earmarked at the outset, the sponsor or steering committee can specifically authorise the release of that resource one stage at a time, checking on each occasion that the project is still viable and on track.

## Deciding on the stages

Two basic sorts of stages exist in projects: management stages and technical stages. *Technical stages* relate to the nature of the project work, so you may have, for example, a design stage and a build stage. In terms of control, though, projects often use management stages. A *management stage* is simply a block of work that the sponsor or steering committee is happy to finance and authorise in one go; a management stage may include several technical stages.

If stages are being used for management control (so, management stages) then the decision on how many to have and where the stages should start and finish rests with the sponsor or steering committee. You can think of this in exactly the same way as ordinary business management. The sponsor is effectively the boss here, so how much does the boss want to authorise at a time, and how often will he check up on the work being done to make sure everything is okay? Of course, you can't answer the question because it's one that rests on personal judgement. It depends, among other things, on the management style adopted by the boss. A particular boss may exercise quite a lot of control and be happier doing that. However, if another person with a more laid-back management style had been appointed as boss, he might have supervised the same staff much less and checked up less frequently.

The Project Manager may recommend what he thinks are a suitable number of stages for the project and show where they should come, but with management stages it's for the sponsor to decide on the level of control he wants to take.

Having said that, there are a number of factors to take into account about how many stages there should be in a project and where one stage should finish and the next one start – the position of the stage gate. Here are a few factors to get you thinking:

- **Before a major investment:** If there is a point in the project where a considerable amount of money is to be spent, it makes sense to have a stage gate just before it. The project can be checked to make sure that it is still viable and on track, and then the next stage can be authorised and the spend can go ahead. That's better than spending a lot of money then having a stage gate that finds that the project is no longer viable and should be cancelled.

- **Experience of the Project Manager:** Just like in general management, if the Project Manager is inexperienced, the boss may want to check up on things more often and authorise less at a time. On the same project but with a highly experienced Project Manager, the sponsor may be happy with much longer stages and fewer stage gates.

- **Finance:** Stages are different lengths, but a sponsor may put a cash limit on them. So, the whole project will cost £12 million, but no one stage is ever to be more than £2 million. The sponsor will never specifically authorise more than £2 million worth of work at a time.

- **Risk:** If the project is high risk, a sponsor will tend to want shorter stages so that stage gate checks are more numerous and less is being authorised at a time. If the project is lower risk, the sponsor may be happy to authorise much more at a time and have much longer stages.

- **Sensible blocks of work:** Sometimes you can almost see the stage boundaries on a plan. The groupings of products and good control points are simply obvious, and it's hard to explain it better than that.

- **Time:** In the same way as for money, the sponsor may put a limit on the maximum length of a stage. In a two-year project, the maximum stage length could be, say, four months. If there is a block of work that will take six months, then it will need to be broken into two stages with a stage gate part-way through that work.

In exactly the same project, a different choice of people on a steering committee or a different choice of sponsor may result in very different decisions on the number of stages in the project.

No right or wrong answer exists when thinking about the number of stages; it's a management choice.

Some people, including well-paid consultants, get very confused about management and technical stages. If you're talking to a consultant who says 'Oh yes, in this type of project you should always have four management stages.' you know immediately that he doesn't understand management stages, despite his air of calm confidence and large bill at the end of each month. You can't ever say to a departmental manager, 'Well, if you have staff in your department doing accommodation work, you should always check up on them five times a year; never more and never less.'

To get this really clear, have a look at Figure 9-1. For the same project you can see that two different steering committees would choose different patterns of supervision, with the first wanting more stages and control points than the more laid-back committee in the second option. Perhaps the second committee is too laid-back, though, and it won't be exercising enough control.

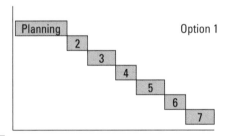

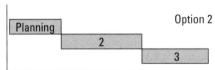

**Figure 9-1:**
Two options for stages of the same project.

## Holding a stage gate

Before going on to planning levels, it's worth saying just a bit more about the Stage Gate. The sponsor or steering committee holds the Stage Gate. The name is great because it gives the right concept of a barrier, but one that you can open to allow you through into the next section. The Stage Gate is a look back, a look at where you are now and then a look forward:

✔ **Looking back:** You look back to check how things went on the stage just finishing. Are there any warning signs that indicate future problems? How much change has there been compared with what was expected? Was the spending on track? What problems came up?

✔ **Looking at where the project is now:** You want to make sure that the project is still viable and on target to deliver the benefits expected of it. You also check that the risk is still acceptable.

For example, suppose that the projection of benefits has fallen, and where it was expected that the project would deliver £1 million of savings a year, it's now projected to save only £250,000 a year. Suppose also that the risk has gone through the roof with all the risk factors increasing and a number of new severe risks emerging. The steering committee or sponsor may now decide it isn't worth that level of risk exposure to deliver what is now only 25 per cent of the original benefits, and rather than authorise the next stage, they order that project be shut down.

✔ **Looking ahead:** You look at the stage ahead and, in particular, the stage level plan. Is that plan workable and achievable? Are the controls adequate? Is the staff resource confirmed to be in place?

If the look back, look at the present position and look ahead are all okay, the sponsor, committee or project board gives the green light and the Project Manager can go and get on with the next stage.

# Working with Planning Levels

It's a common myth that you do planning once only, and at the start of the project. With stages, plans are being prepared right the way through, one as you approach each Stage Gate. In any case, re-planning is needed throughout the project as things change. As we point out throughout this book, no project ever goes exactly to plan, unless yours is going to be the first in history – in which case, prepare to be very famous.

You can plan at three different levels:

✔ **Project Plan:** Covers all the delivery stages of the project. In other words, the period from the end of the planning stage until the end of the project.

✔ **Stage Plans:** One for each of the delivery stages. You usually prepare a Stage Plan at the end of the previous stage, just before the new stage commences. If you're in a small project with only one delivery stage, the Project Plan will also be the Stage Plan.

✔ **Delivery Plan or Team Plan:** The Delivery Plan or Team Plan covers a single work assignment or *Work Package* to build a single product or sometimes a small group of products where it makes sense to construct them together. The team leader usually produces the Delivery Plan on recognising that the Stage Plan won't offer sufficient detail to control that part of the development. Within a project, some Work Packages may need a Delivery Plan, while for other, simpler, Work Packages the level of detail in the Stage Plan is sufficient to exercise control over the build.

Figure 9-2 shows how the plans fit into the project at the three levels of detail.

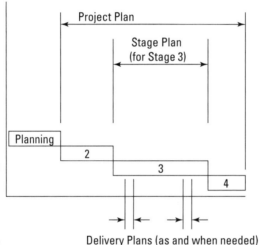

**Figure 9-2:** How plans fit the project.

## Drawing up new plans

Stage and Delivery Plans are both drawn up from the level above. Look ahead to Figure 9-3 to see the plans at the three levels. You develop a Stage Plan from the relevant section of the Project Plan, and a team leader develops a Delivery Plan (if needed) for a Work Package from the relevant section of the Stage Plan.

### Developing a Stage Plan

Developing a Stage Plan from a Project Plan is remarkably easy in overall concept, but quite a lot of hard work when it comes to the practicality. The Project Plan shows at a high level what products are being produced in each of the delivery stages. Overall, the Project Plan shows between about 15 and 30 products.

When you're approaching the Stage Gate for a stage, it's time to start thinking about the Stage Plan for the following stage and identify the high-level, project-level, products for that stage. There may be two or three of them; it rather depends on the size of your project.

You then break these two or three products down in detail, normally using a Work Breakdown Structure, until you again have 15–30. For these you draw a Work Flow Diagram and then go on to show the greater detail of activities in your Activity Network and Gantt Chart. You can find full detail of all these techniques in Chapters 5 to 7.

### Developing a Work Plan

Of the 15–30 stage-level products, a Work Package to be given to a team leader may comprise two or three of them or just a single product. If the products are complex and the product and activity plans at stage level don't go into enough detail, the team leader can put the Work Package products at the top of a Work Breakdown Structure, break them down to 15–30 sub-products, draw a Work Flow Diagram and then do activity planning (see Chapter 6). It's exactly the same planning sequence all over again, but this time at an even lower level of detail.

### Planning for resource and budget

In exactly the same way as the product and activity plans show more detail at stage and then Work Package levels, you now go into more detail in your resource planning, including for financial resource. Figure 9-3 shows this graphically.

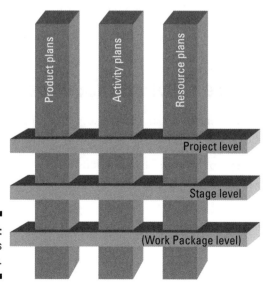

**Figure 9-3:**
Plan types
and levels.

Figure 9-4 summarises what plans you'll be producing during the life of your project and when.

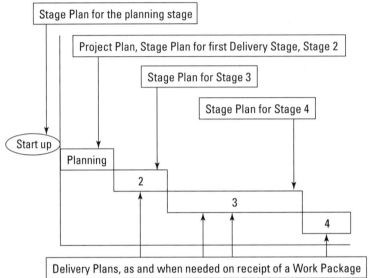

# Keeping higher level plans up to date

When lower-level plans are produced, it is common to find some things that weren't seen on the higher-level ones and to come up with better information such as on activity durations. Each higher-level plan should be updated as necessary from what is discovered when doing the lower-level planning.

# Planning at more than one level at once

Just occasionally, you may want go against the 'just in time' approach to planning in which you plan just before that plan is required; you draw up a Stage Plan towards the end of the previous stage. For example, in larger projects, you may ask suppliers to draw up Delivery Plans for their parts of the work in a forthcoming stage, and then build the Stage Plan from the Delivery Plans.

As in all areas of project planning, be flexible and do what's best for the project. The important thing is always doing what's best to get the job done.

Wellington attributed his success against Napoleon to flexibility. He said that Napoleon's battle plans were made of gold and fine jewels. Napoleon thought through and planned battles very carefully in advance. If the battle went the way he had envisaged, things generally went well for him, but if not he was in trouble. Wellington described his battle plans as being made of rope. If something snapped, he just tied a knot and carried on.

# Chapter 10

# Venturing into the Unknown: Dealing with Risk and Uncertainty

• • • • • • • • • • • • • • • • • • • • • • • • • • • • • • • • • • • • • • • • • • • • •

## *In This Chapter*

▶ Coming to terms with risk and risk management

▶ Taking a closer look at risk – risk analysis

▶ Deciding how to handle risks and taking action – risk management

▶ Drafting a risk management plan

▶ Getting some tools to help with a few risk management techniques

• • • • • • • • • • • • • • • • • • • • • • • • • • • • • • • • • • • • • • • • • • • • • •

*I*t's sad to hear about good projects that have failed – but it happens. It's even sadder when you find out a bit more and see that a project was killed off by a problem that the Project Manager could easily have foreseen, controlled or even prevented. Don't let your project be unnecessarily damaged or even destroyed by something that with a bit of effort – and sometimes not that much effort – you can get a handle on. This is the realm of risk management. The good news is that the basics aren't that difficult; in fact, you do risk management nearly all the time just to get through the day.

All projects need risk management, even the very small ones. However, some projects are clearly higher risk than others and justify more effort. Often the larger, more complex and longer your project is, the more risk management you need, but that doesn't let small projects off the hook. The highest-commercial-risk project Nick Graham has ever encountered was also one of the smallest: a six-week project with just two staff in a finance company in the City of London. If that project had failed, it would have seriously damaged the company's reputation in the City and threatened its whole business.

This chapter discusses risk when you're deciding whether you'll undertake your project and are simply evaluating the main risks, when you're developing your Project Plan, and while you're performing your project's work. We show you how to identify and assess the impact of project risks, and we explore strategies for minimising their consequences. We also offer pointers for preparing a risk management plan, and outline a few risk techniques.

# Understanding Risks and Risk Management

*Risk* is the possibility that you may not achieve some or all of your objectives because something unexpected occurs or something planned doesn't occur. All projects have some degree of risk because predicting the future with certainty is impossible. However, project risk is generally greater:

- The longer your project lasts
- The more unusual and groundbreaking the project is
- The less experience you, your organisation or your team members have with the type of project
- The more vulnerable the project is to things happening outside (such as in the wider business or due to change of government policy, change in the marketplace, activity of competitors or dependency on other projects)
- The newer your project's technology is

The current professional view of risk in projects is that it's about uncertainty, and that individual risks can be either positive or negative:

- *Negative risks*, also referred to as *downside risks* or *threats*, potentially have a detrimental effect on one or more of the project objectives, such as causing you to miss a deadline.
- *Positive risks*, also referred to as *upside risk* or *opportunities*, potentially have a beneficial effect on project objectives, such as allowing you to complete a task with fewer staff than you originally planned.

In other words, anything that can cause you either to fall short of or to exceed your established project targets, if it occurs, is considered a risk. Some approaches for analysing and responding to both types of risk are similar, but this chapter mostly focuses on approaches for identifying, evaluating and managing negative risks, because most (and maybe all) of your project risks will be negative.

## Seeing why you need risk management

Risk in projects is mostly negative: things that can go wrong. That's in line with dictionary definitions of risk, of which one is: 'The adverse consequences of future events.'

It's a no-brainer that wherever you can, you want to try to stop things going wrong and thereby increase the chances of success. The difference between project risk management and most of the risk management you do as part of daily life, like when crossing a road, is that you think out project risk management up front and handle it in a methodical way. Don't worry about a methodical approach here, and please don't confuse method with bureaucracy. We just mean that you need to think about the handling of the risk, consider all the possibilities for dealing with it, plan and carry out actions, and then check that the actions have indeed been carried out. It may well be that the chosen action for a particular risk is to not do anything about it, but even that's a considered decision that you should normally record.

Risk management can get complicated in high-risk projects, but for most it isn't going to be that difficult, and for many it's straightforward. The important thing is that you must manage risks unless you want to open the project to the possibility of costly damage and even failure, when you might have been able to take a simple action to control it. The right question isn't 'Should we do risk management?' but rather 'How much risk management should we do?'

On low risk projects, the answer may be that you don't do very much risk management at all, but you should always do some. For some projects, that may just mean gathering one or two people together for 20 minutes around a flip chart to look at what could go wrong with the project and how that might be controlled.

Watch out for small projects and don't assume you don't really need to risk manage them. In some respects, small projects are inherently high risk. Take staffing, for example. If someone leaves your project and you have 200 people, the impact is about 0.5 per cent (it may be more or less depending on how important that person's job is). If there's just you and one other person on a very small project and the other person leaves, the impact is magnified: it's 50 per cent.

## *Managing, not necessarily avoiding, risk*

It's important to take on board the exact wording of the subject area of this chapter, which is risk *management*. Managing risk doesn't necessarily mean avoiding it. Clearly, a positive risk (an upside risk) is something that you want to happen, and your management action includes making it more likely. However, even negative risk may be a good option in the project.

Have you ever done a bungee jump or a parachute jump? If not, would you like to? Some people would, and do, but isn't that rather strange when these sports are known to be risky? Well, the risk is controlled with safety devices and procedures, but a degree of risk remains. The people who decide to jump off bridges with an elastic band around their ankles or leap out of perfectly good aeroplanes do so because they like the thrill. They accept the risk, because in their eyes a very low probability of having a problem exists and it's worth jumping for the buzz.

In the project setting, a negative risk may be very high but worth taking, not for the buzz but for the business advantage. So, running the project very quickly and missing out some parts that are normally seen as essential could lead to more mistakes and higher costs. However, it's worth taking the risk in order to get to market faster and beat a competitor that you know is developing a similar new product.

Risk management, then, doesn't mean risk avoidance. In fact, if you have good risk management in place, you can afford to take more risks in the project, because you're exercising a degree of control. If you have no risk management, you can't afford to take many risks at all, because you have no control.

## *Keeping people informed*

Throughout the project, and whatever part of the risk cycle you're in (see the later section 'Working Through the Risk Cycle', you need to keep people informed about risks involved with your project. You'll probably need to adjust your Communications Management Plan (see Chapter 15 for more on this plan), if you're using one, as a reminder. As you consider who you need to keep up to speed with risk on your project, think about:

- ✔ **Corporate management,** including organisational risk systems or your organisation's risk manager, if you have one

- ✔ **Other projects** inside and outside your own organisation that need to know because they may be affected by the risk happening on your project or because a newly discovered risk may also need recording and managing on those projects

- ✔ **Programme management** if your project is one of a group of projects in a programme

- ✔ **Project sponsor** or steering committee members who need to know about new risks and changes in status to existing risks because they're authorising the countermeasures, including any finance needed for those countermeasures

- ✔ **Team leaders and team members,** so they know what to look for as they do their work, and can report relevant things that affect the risks

- ✔ **Statutory bodies** that need to know of a problem, when reporting an incident may be mandatory

People often share information about project risks ineffectually or not at all. As a result, their projects suffer unnecessary problems and setbacks that may have avoided with proper communication.

You may be reluctant to talk too much about risk, because it looks like you're identifying excuses for failure rather than ways to succeed. Some organisations have a strange reaction to risk and think it's all very negative. 'We're a can-do company' may be a bit of management-speak imprinted on your brain from frequent repetition, and imprinted all the more deeply if your manager is about to start work on your annual report. Risk management isn't negative, though: it's positive. It's giving the project the very best chance of success by taking control of things that may cause problems. It's worth some effort to get people to understand that perspective.

Communicate about project risks from the beginning and regularly. In particular, share information at the following points in your project (see Chapter 2 for more about these project life-cycle stages):

- ✔ **Starting the Project:** To support the process of deciding whether to undertake the project

- ✔ **Organising and Preparing:** To guide the development of all aspects of your Project Plan

- ✔ **Carrying Out the Work:**
  - • To allow team members to discuss potential risks and to encourage them to recognise and address problems as soon as they occur
  - • To deal with any risks discovered during the delivery stages
  - • To reassess risks in the light of changing circumstances and if necessary modify parts of the current approved Project Plan

You can improve your risk-related communications with your project teams and stakeholders by:

- ✔ Explaining the nature of a risk, how it may affect your project and how you estimated the likelihood of its occurrence

- ✔ Telling people the current chances that certain risks will occur, how you're minimising the chances of problems, and how people can reduce the chances of negative consequences

- ✔ Encouraging people to think and talk about risks, always with an eye towards minimising the negative effects of those risks

- ✔ Documenting information about the risks and making it available so others can see it to keep up to date with the risk position

You can discuss this information at regularly scheduled team meetings, in regularly scheduled progress reports and upper-management reviews, and in special meetings to address issues that arise. (See Chapter 15 for more on sharing project information.)

## Don't put all your eggs in one basket

Stan Portny once met a man who was starting a large project that was a top priority for an organisation. His project's success depended heavily on one person who would work on the project full time for six months and perform all the technical development tasks. Stan asked whether the Project Manager had considered the consequences of this person leaving the project before it was finished. The Project Manager said he didn't have to worry about that risk, because he simply wouldn't allow the man to leave.

The Project Manager's approach for dealing with risk is similar to somebody cancelling her travel insurance because she's not planning to have any problems on her extensive overseas travel next year. The Project Manager may have got agreement from senior managers that the person would have no other assignments for the duration of his project. However, he still couldn't guarantee that the person wouldn't get ill or decide to leave the organisation.

# *Keeping risk in focus throughout the project*

Risk management is ongoing, not just something you do at the start of the project. Here's a summary of the main stages in a project and what risk work you do at each of them (see Chapter 1 for a detailed discussion of these stages):

- **Starting the Project:** Here you look at any large and obvious risks to help decide whether it's even worth taking the project idea on to planning. If the benefits of the proposed project are quite low, but the risk is huge, it's probably not worth going any further.

- **Organising and Preparing:** Here you do the main risk analysis and planning work. If you didn't open a Risk Register (see the section 'Identifying risk') when you were doing the start-up stage, you'll open it now to record the risks and the action you intend to take to control them.

- **Carrying Out the Work:** In the delivery stages, you carry out risk actions and monitor known risks, but you also deal with any new risks that you find or that others report to you in the project.

- **Closing the Project:** At the end of the project, you pass on any ongoing risk management actions that affect products in their working life, such as actions relating to dangerous machinery. You also evaluate how the risk management went on the project in order to learn and pass on any lessons for future projects.

# *Working Through the Risk Cycle*

Different approaches to risk management offer different cycles, but the example in Figure 10-1 is from Inspirandum's publication *The Project Techniques Toolbox,* by Nick Graham.

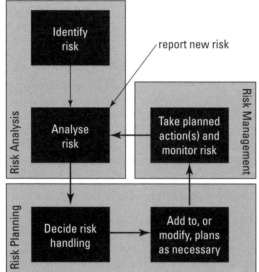

**Figure 10-1:**
A risk cycle example.

A cycle provides a framework to show how you analyse, decide actions and then manage the risks that may affect your project. As shown in Figure 10-1, the steps after the initial identification of a risk go on continually, with regular review, right through the project. Clearly, if something about the risk has changed, such as it has become more severe, you may need to make changes in the way that you're handling that risk. It could be that a course of action that wasn't justified when the risk was low severity is now fully justified because the risk has become high severity.

Here's an outline of the steps:

### 1. Identify risks.

Determine what the risks are that may affect your project. You want to look at things within the project but also things that can come in from outside, such as changes in the marketplace or new laws. During the project, in particular, some new risks may also be reported to you by other people involved in the project.

**2. Analyse risks.**

This is where you get to grips with each risk to make sure you really understand it and how it may affect your project. You normally put some measures on each risk at this point, such as the probability of the risk happening and the impact if it does.

**3. Decide risk handling.**

This is where you think what to do and how you can protect your project from negative risk while trying to take advantage of positive risks. It may be that for some risks you decide not to take any action at all, but that's still a decision.

**4. Add to or modify plans as necessary.**

Having decided what to do, if action is needed you're going to have to build that into the plan. For example, there may be risk actions that you'll need to include in the activity plans (see Chapter 6 for more on activity planning). Because this step is part of the cycle, you may already have some management actions planned for a particular risk, so in this step you adjust the action to reflect any changes you've decided on to manage that risk.

**5. Take planned action(s) and monitor risk.**

There's no point in planning actions if you don't take them, so this step is to take action, either as an ongoing action or as a response if the risk happens. You also monitor each risk to see whether it's changing and to check that any action is effective. If the action is proving insufficient or the risk has changed, the cycle goes back to step 2 to re-analyse the risk, and then on around the cycle again to decide how the risk handling should be changed.

The following sections look at each step in more detail.

## *Identifying risk*

The first step in your risk assessment is to identify the specific risks that may affect your project. You should record these in a *Risk Register*, which is simply a set of forms, each one describing a risk. Don't think of having a Risk Register as bureaucratic, because you've got to be able to refer back to the information, and you can't do that if you don't record it.

Although you only identify a risk once, so it isn't a repeatable part of the cycle, remember that in the project you check for new risks periodically. This may be at the end of each stage, when you're planning the next stage, or even, in a higher risk project, at regular timed intervals.

The good thing about risk management generally is that there are lots of techniques out there, so you will find plenty to help (including Inspirandum's *The Project Techniques Toolbox*). You can also find an explanation of a couple of techniques – the Risk Checklist and Ishikawa Diagram – in the 'Getting Some Help from Techniques' section at the end of this chapter. Both techniques are great for risk identification.

For each risk, you need to note basic information about it but you need to be a bit balanced. If you're in a risk workshop setting, for example, and people are coming up with a lot of risks, if you stop to carefully record all of the detail about each risk, you will break the flow and possibly end up missing some of the risks. It's usually better to record just the basic information and then later come back and fill in the gaps as you think more about each risk.

### Introducing some structure

You can just think of risks at random, but you may find it helpful to bring in some structure and think through the project in a more focused and systematic way. For example, you may think about risks in terms of the type of impact, such as:

- **Business risk:** Things coming from outside the project; for example, lower company profits this year or government cutbacks could lead to your project budget being reduced

- **Product risk:** For example, the risk that the technology may not produce the desired results

- **Resource risk:** For example, if the development turns out to be more complicated than you anticipated, existing facilities and equipment may not be adequate

- **Schedule risk:** For example, the risk that because staff are unfamiliar with the new technology, tasks may take longer than you anticipate

As part of the information you are holding about each risk, you may want to include a risk category. Categories can be helpful in two ways:

- They can help indicate how a risk should be handled and who should be involved in managing it. For example, business risks may all need to be 'owned' by the project sponsor who is primarily responsible for monitoring them.

- You can make use of categories to give structure to risk identification, by taking each category heading in turn and asking what risks may affect the project in that area.

---

# Risk categories

Some sets of risk category are quite long and complicated, and others relate to specific business areas such as insurance or construction. Here are a couple of simple category sets that are widely used in organisational risk management but that you can also use in projects.

| PESTLE | BPEST |
| --- | --- |
| Political | Business |
| Economic | Political |
| Social | Economic |
| Technological | Social |
| Legal | Technological |
| Environmental | |

---

Different organisations and project and risk approaches use different sets of risk categories, and you can look on the Internet to find a few. You'll find two simple examples, PESTLE and BPEST, in the nearby sidebar 'Risk categories'.

## *Looking around for help*

Don't think you always have to do everything yourself. With risk in particular, it really helps to get some different viewpoints, because different people will spot risks that you don't.

Here are a few ideas on finding help to get you started:

- ✔ **Review past records of problems encountered in similar situations.** If a risk materialised on a similar project in the past, you definitely want to be prepared for it this time.

- ✔ **Brainstorm with experts and other people who have related experiences.** The more sources of expert opinion you consult, the less chance you have of overlooking something important. This is where a risk workshop can be very effective.

- ✔ **Use a Risk Checklist.** You'll find more on this technique in the later section 'Risk Checklist', but basically it's a standard list of risks that you can look through. See whether any of the risks on the list could affect your project.

- ✔ **Look on the Internet.** It's surprising what a quick surf can turn up.

## Differentiating between risks and impacts

When looking for risks, it's really easy to confuse risks and impacts. For example, a common entry in Risk Registers is: 'RISK 99 – Project will be delayed'. However, delay isn't a risk, it's an impact. What you need to ask is what could go wrong in the project that would result in the project being delayed. So, a major machinery breakdown in the factory during your project could lead to the impact of project delay, because the engineers on your team will be taken off their project work to deal with the breakdown, and will only come back when it's sorted out.

Equally, overspending isn't a risk. Overspending is an impact, and you need to identify any risks that would cause overspending.

Impacts can be useful as another means of structuring risk identification work. Using the Ishikawa (Fishbone) Diagram (see the later section on this), you can put the impact of 'Overspending' as the effect or impact, and then with the fish bones look at all the risks that could cause it. Using the diagrams, you can systematically work through a range of impacts.

## *Analysing risk*

The second step in the risk cycle is analysis, when you get to really understand a risk. You need to know:

- What can cause the risk – it may have more than one trigger
- How the risk is likely to behave
- What impact or impacts the risk may have
- Whether the risk is related to any other risks

It's common in projects that people think about individual risks but fail to consider the possibility of relationships between them. For example, a single event may fire off several risks at once, or there can be a chain reaction when one risk happening has an impact that fires off another risk, and when that happens it fires off a third.

As part of your analysis, it's really helpful to assess the scale of the risk and when it can happen. In turn, that helps you think how much management of the risk you need to do, which is important because risk management will itself take time in the project and possibly cost money. The scales are normally in two dimensions – probability and impact – and you can use a Probability–Impact (P-I) Grid diagram to help (see Figure 10-2 for an example).

The P-I Grid is valuable to see where individual risks are, but also to spot patterns. You might see, for example, that although you have a lot of risks, they are mostly low probability but high impact, or that the risks are evenly scattered across the grid.

TIP

If you normally think about risk measures in terms of high, medium and low values, you may be surprised to see that on the P-I Grid there's a five-point scale. It's recommended that you use a scale of at least five, even if you don't use numbers (you can use very high, high, medium, low and very low). Risk experts advise that you're just not thinking hard enough if you only use a three-point scale. On the other hand, don't go for a scale of more than ten, or you start to get into difficulties about whether the risk is a 678 or if it tips the balance and really justifies a 679 on your 1,000-point scale.

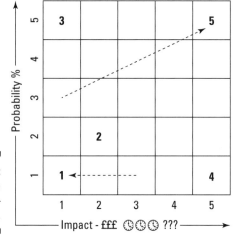

VH, H, M, L, VL
or numbers 1-5 or 1-10

Risk 1: 1 x 1 = 1
Risk 2: 2 x 2 = 4
Risk 3: 1 x 5 = 5
Risk 4: 5 x 1 = 5
Risk 5: 5 x 5 = not good at all!

**Figure 10-2:**
The
Probability–
Impact Grid.

When you have the position of each risk worked out, you can use this to help determine what action you need to take. Generally, the more you go towards the top right of the grid, the more action you need to consider. However, this isn't a numbers game, so be careful – particularly in the top left and bottom right of the grid. In Figure 10-2, Risk 3 is very low impact but very high probability. Because it's very high probability, you need to take action, even though its overall score, multiplying the impact scale by the probability scale, is only 5 ($1 \times 5$). Equally, Risk 4 probably justifies action. It's only got a severity rating of 5 ($5 \times 1$) but while it's very low probability, its impact would be devastating. For example, if you work in a large building, it will have smoke detectors, a fire alarm system, fire exit routes and fire hoses and extinguishers. With modern electrical equipment and a ban on people smoking, the probability of a fire is extremely low, but risk management action is justified because the impact is so high – life threatening – if a fire does break out.

The grid is also useful for regular risk reporting, and you can show any movement of a risk since the last reporting point with dotted lines. In Figure 10-2, you can see that Risks 1 and 5 have changed since the last reporting point, but the others still have the same evaluation of impact and probability.

### *Gauging probability*

Probability can be expressed as a number between 0 and 1, with 0.0 signifying that a situation will never happen, and 1.0 signifying that it will always occur. (You may also express probability as a percentage, with 100 per cent meaning the situation will always occur.)

You don't have to use the P-I Grid for recording probability and impact though. For probability, you can simply list risks in particular orders to indicate the degree of action you need to take:

- ✓ **Category ranking:** Classify risks into categories that represent their likelihood. You can use *very high*, *high, medium, low* and *very low* or *always, often, sometimes, rarely* and *never*.

- ✓ **Ordinal ranking:** Order the risks so the first is the most likely to occur, the second is the next most likely, and so on.

- ✓ **Relative likelihood of occurrence:** If you have two possible risks, you can express how much more likely one is to occur than the other. For example, you can declare that the first risk is *twice as likely* to occur as the second.

If you have objective data on the number of times a risk has occurred in similar situations in the past, you can use it to help determine the likelihood that the risk will occur again in the future. However, don't be surprised if you don't have such information, because most risk probability estimates just aren't like that. The lack of data makes the probability estimating difficult; it's been described as the Achilles heel of risk management.

Where you don't have objective data available, you can use personal judgements to estimate the likelihood that particular risks will occur. One technique that can help is the Delphi technique, described at the end of Chapter 6 in the context of estimating activity durations. Try also to get the opinions of experts and people who've worked on similar projects in the past.

When using objective data, you can estimate the probability of a risk occurring by considering the number of times the risk actually occurred on similar projects. Suppose, for example, that you designed 20 computer-generated reports over the past year for new clients. Eight times, when you submitted your design for final approval, new clients wanted at least one change. If you're planning to design a computer-generated report for another new client, you may conclude that the chance that you'll have to make a change in the design you submit is 40 per cent – (8 ÷ 20) × 100.

When using objective information such as past project reports to determine the likelihood of different risks:

- ✔ Consider previous experience with similar projects.
- ✔ Consider as many similar situations as possible.
- ✔ Keep in mind that the more similar situations you consider, the more confidence you can have in your conclusions.

Some computer-based risk-management tools give very precise results, but be careful because precision is different from accuracy. *Precision* refers to the detail of a number. *Accuracy* refers to how correct the number is. The computer may calculate the likelihood of a particular risk to be 67.23 per cent. However, that figure will have been determined from your answers to the questions posed by the software. If you just didn't know and entered wild guesses, don't expect the output to be accurate, even though it's very precise.

### Estimating the impact

After you identify the likelihood that a particular risk will affect your project, be sure to determine the impact if the risk does occur. That magnitude directly influences how you will decide to deal with the risk. Determine the specific effect that each risk may have on your project's product, schedule and resource performance. When evaluating these effects, do the following:

- ✔ **Consider the effect of a risk on the total project, not only a part of it.** Taking one week longer than you planned to complete an activity may cause you to miss intermediate milestones (and cause the people waiting for the results of that activity to sit idle). However, the effect on the project is even greater if the delayed activity is on your project's critical path (see Chapter 6), which means the week-long delay on that one activity also causes a week-long delay for your entire project.

- ✔ **Consider the combined effect of related risks.** The likelihood that your schedule will slip is greater if three activities on the critical path have a significant risk of delay, rather than just one.

### Being specific

Be sure to describe risks and their associated consequences as specifically as possible. For example, suppose a key piece of equipment you ordered for your project may arrive later than expected. You can describe that risk as *the delivery may be late,* or as *the delivery may be delayed by two weeks.* Just stating that the delivery may be late doesn't give you enough information to assess the likely effect of that delay on the overall project. It also makes estimating the probability of that risk's occurrence more difficult. Are you talking about a delay of one day? One month? Stating that the delivery may be delayed by two weeks allows you to determine more precisely the likely effect that the delay will have on the overall schedule and resources. It also allows you to decide how much you're willing to spend to avoid that delay.

# Areas of impact

When thinking about impact, you need to think widely about all the areas that could be affected; don't just focus on time and cost, important though they are. Consider these areas (some of which interact), but add more of your own to a checklist for your own projects:

✔ Business Case and the level of business benefits

✔ Cost

✔ Corporate targets

✔ Other projects (inter-project dependencies)

✔ Reputation damage (often underestimated)

✔ Resource scheduling

✔ Time

## Deciding on an impact scale

The scale for impact in particular is one that you or your organisation as a whole must decide, because it's relative to the organisation. For example, take an impact of a loss of £1 million. Is that a problem? Well, to a small business with just three employees, that isn't just 'very high' – it's a company killer and off the scale completely. However, Nick Graham has run project training courses for a multinational company based in the UK that has an annual turnover in excess of £20 billion. What's the impact of a £1 million loss to that company? An embarrassment and an irritation perhaps, but certainly not high up the scale in terms of the financial impact.

## Considering proximity

A third useful measure for each risk, after probability and impact, is the *proximity*: how soon it can happen. Proximity information is, obviously enough, very useful in planning. Three types of proximity exist:

✔ **Immediate:** Some risks always have a proximity of *now*, because they can happen at any time during the project with no notice at all. An easy example is with a key team member going sick. She may walk up to you in five minutes' time and say that she's feeling dreadful and needs to go home, or that could happen in five weeks' time or in five months' time.

✔ **Fixed date:** Some risks are pegged to a point in time. The new rocket can't fail to launch until it's time to launch it. The team can't find that a product is more complicated to build than they thought, and so will take longer, until they get to grips with the product as they start to build it.

✔ **Fixed period:** Some risks will always happen a certain time ahead. Today the proximity of a particular risk is four weeks, but in five months' time the proximity of the risk will still be four weeks. That sounds weird until you consider the simple example of someone resigning from your organisation and so leaving your project. If that person resigns today, she'll leave in four weeks' time, after she's worked her four-week notice period. If she resigns in five months' time, she'll leave four weeks after that. You just hope that she doesn't have four weeks' holiday owing and a fixed period turns into now! You might even decide to check that out.

# Deciding risk handling

Recognising and evaluating risks that pose a threat to your project are the first steps towards controlling them. But you can't stop there. You also have to develop specific plans for reducing their potential negative effects on your project. You start by deciding what options you have for dealing with each one, and then you select the option or set of options that are most suitable.

### Handling all risks

As you look at the risks, be clear on the point that you're going to manage all of them, even if your choice of action for some may be to do nothing. That may sound more than a little strange until you think back to the risk cycle. As the risk goes into the management part of the cycle, you monitor it to check for changes. It may be that a risk where you decided to take no action has now changed and now does justify action. So you're still managing a 'do nothing' risk because you will continue to monitor it.

For example, in London you identify a risk to your project: you won't be able to recruit enough bricklayers when you get to the construction phase of your large new headquarters building on the banks of the River Thames. However, you decide that you don't need to take action, because there's no reported shortage of bricklayers in London and you've budgeted for the going rate of pay. Then, after the project starts and the initial design work is going on, you hear that London has won the bid for the 2012 Olympics and a huge amount of early construction work will be kicking off on the Olympic sites just as you'll be approaching the brickwork part of your project. The circumstances surrounding that risk have changed, and doing nothing is no longer a sensible way of dealing with the risk.

### Thinking wide

When considering what to do about each risk, it's very easy to bounce off at a superficial level, and Project Managers often come up with a single option: throw money at the risk. But often you can do a number of things to manage a risk, and some may not involve money at all, just some ingenuity. Allowing sufficient time for risk analysis and management is important, then, so that you don't just rush into the obvious management actions that may not be the cheapest or even the most effective. As you come to decide what action to take, you may pick just one of the options you've come up with or you may implement more than one action to get good control of the risk.

Record all the risk management options for each risk, albeit as concisely as possible, and include the reasons for choosing the actions that are being taken and the reasons for not selecting the others. That way, if circumstances change later on and it's necessary to review the decision, the information is still to hand. There may be some additional work to do if new options can be identified during that review, but at least, if you haven't discarded the results, it saves you repeating work that you've already done.

### Deciding on actions

When making a decision on what action(s) to take, first consider the likelihood of a risk *and* its potential effect on your project. If the potential effect of a risk is great, and if the chances it will occur are high, you probably want to develop plans to manage that risk. If both the impact and the probability are low (bottom left of the P-I Grid; see the section 'Analysing risk'), you may decide not to take control action.

When the potential impact is high but the likelihood is low, or vice versa (the top left and bottom right of the P-I Grid), you must consider the situation more carefully. In these more complex situations, you can use a more formal approach for considering the combined effect of likelihood of occurrence and potential consequence – the severity – by defining the *expected value of risk*, using exact numeric measures as follows:

> Expected value of risk = Quantitative measure of the effect if it occurs × Probability it will occur

Suppose you need to buy certain materials for a device you're planning to build. When you place your order, you think you have an 80 per cent chance of receiving the materials by the date promised. However, this means you have a 20 per cent chance that something will go wrong and that you'll have to pay a premium to get the materials from another supplier by the date you need them. You estimate that the materials normally cost £1,000 and that you'll have to pay an additional £500 to get them from another vendor at the last minute. Determine the expected value of this risk as follows:

> Expected value of risk = Additional cost incurred if you use another vendor at the last minute × Probability that you'll have to use this vendor
>
> Expected value of risk = £500 × 0.2 = £100

You may conclude from that calculation that spending more than £100 to reduce the chances of this risk isn't a wise financial decision.

So, after considering the risk, you decide whether a potential consequence is so unacceptable that you're not willing to take the chance, even if it's very unlikely to occur.

### Understanding action types

You can categorise options for handling risks in different ways, but here are five main alternatives:

- ✔ **Avoidance:** Act to stop the risk happening. An example is deciding not to use a new, untested procedure that you're concerned may not produce the desired project results.

- ✔ **Contingency:** This is allowing for the risk to happen, so that you can absorb the impact. Three sub-types of contingency exist:

  - • **Action contingency:** Have a plan B. If the risk is realised, take the pre-planned alternative action. If the flight to Edinburgh is cancelled because of volcanic dust from Iceland, I'll go by train.

  - • **Cost contingency:** Have some extra money in a risk budget. If the supply from the cheaper source fails, the relevant part of the risk budget is released and the item can be purchased from a better stocked but more expensive supplier.

  - • **Time contingency:** Allow some contingency time in your plan to allow for a few deliveries to be late.

- ✔ **Mitigation:** To reduce the probability that a risk will occur or to minimise the impact if it does occur. Two examples of risk mitigation are:

  - • **Minimise the probability.** Use only experienced staff on the project and so reduce the chance of serious mistakes being made.

  - • **Minimise the impact.** Have a spare engineer identified who, alongside her normal work, will attend all the project briefings and be copied in on project engineering documents. That way, if someone leaves the engineering team suddenly, this spare person can step in and join the project as a replacement. She'll still have a learning curve, but it's less steep than if she knew nothing about the project at all. She'll get up to speed faster, and the impact of the staff change will be reduced.

- ✔ **Taking no action:** This is a conscious, and recorded, decision not to take action on the risk; it isn't neglect. If the risk does occur, everyone knew what the impact would be. You might use this option if taking actions is very expensive or time consuming, and the low impact and very low probability of the risk occurring (in the present assessment of it) doesn't justify such cost or work effort.

✔ **Transfer:** Get someone else to take as much of the risk as possible. For example, take out insurance to cover the financial impact.

You can use the action types in combination. For example, you might choose to have some contingency in the plan to deal with a time delay, but also take out insurance (transfer) to cover the financial impact.

We don't recommend the following risk approaches, even though they are in widespread use – particularly by senior managers:

✔ **The denial approach:** Refusing to accept that any 'real' risks are associated with the project work

✔ **The ostrich approach:** Ignoring all risks, pretending they don't exist

✔ **The prayer approach:** Looking to a higher being to solve the problems and make the risks disappear

Positive risks, or opportunities, generally need the opposite action from negative risk. Instead of trying to reduce a risk, you need to take measures to increase the chances of the risk happening and improve the effects if it does. An exception is with taking no action. Even though a risk has a beneficial outcome, it may not be worth the extra effort trying to bring it about.

## Adding to or modifying plans as necessary

Having decided risk management actions after you've identified and analysed a risk, you need to build those actions into the Project Plan and Stage Plans (see Chapter 9) and treat them like any other project management work. Where something has changed on a risk that is already known about and for which actions are planned or are already being taken, you need to modify those actions, depending on the review of what's now needed.

Conceptually, this step is simple enough. But do be aware that putting in the risk actions may then affect the overall plan. You'll need to make allowances for risk activity when first drafting the plan out, but later in the project risk activity could even lead to a significant update of the plan. In particular the risk management actions may:

✔ **Increase costs:** Such as for team member time, as well as for financial contingency, for taking actions

✔ **Increase time:** Because of the work involved in managing the risks, but also to build time contingency into the plan

✔ **Have knock-on effects:** Clearly, if the project will take more time because of contingency allowances, for example, it could affect the schedule for delivery of products during the project, which may in turn affect other projects if they need those deliverables too because of an inter-project dependency

In addition to the work on individual risk actions, there is also work to be put on the plan for the Project Manager (and perhaps others too) in order to regularly review risks and keep the risk documentation up to date. How much work is involved and how often depends partly on the criticality of the project and partly on the number of risks involved. In a very high-risk project, review will be more frequent than in a low risk project.

## *Taking planned actions and monitoring risk*

At the start of this chapter we made the point that it's sad when a project fails because something nasty happens that could easily have been identified up front and which could have been controlled or even prevented. Okay, but now for something even sadder. That's when risks were identified, actions planned, but then the project dies because those actions were never taken. Risks happened with nothing to stop or control them and killed the project.

This final step of the risk cycle is essential, obviously, and to be sure that it is done, it can be included in regular health checks. You normally do this checking in a project audit function (please see Chapter 11). That check isn't merely on the Project Manager, though. If team members, or even the sponsor, are supposed to be taking risk-related action, project audit will check that they are and sound the alarm bells if it's being overlooked.

### *Taking action on risk*

Risk action may be continuous or it may be responsive if the risk actually happens. If the building catches fire, then someone is designated to call the fire brigade; that's a responsive action if the risk occurs. Other risks may need ongoing action, particularly but not solely actions to avoid or reduce risk. So every Friday you jump out of your seat in shock at midday, despite the reminder notice in the lift, because the fire alarm system is being tested to reduce the risk of it not functioning in an emergency.

### *Monitoring risks*

Risks should be monitored regularly and in two dimensions:

✓ **For change:** The first dimension is to check whether things are still the same. Has the risk increased in probability? In the light of the latest information available, is the impact greater or less than expected? Has the timing of the risk changed? Any change means that the risk needs to be re-assessed and, if necessary, the control actions changed. That's where this step cycles around to the analysing risk step.

✓ **For adequacy of the action(s):** Where actions are being taken, are they working? If not, the actions need to be re-considered, which in turn means that some re-analysis may be helpful because something may have been missed which led to the wrong actions being selected in the first place. Again, the cycle continues with a link back to analysing risk.

# Documenting Risk

Two key documents are involved with risk management, and in all but very small projects these are both necessary and important. Even a small project should have some means of risk recording, though. The two documents are a *risk management plan* and a *Risk Register*.

## Risk Management Plan

A *risk management plan* lays out the strategy for how risk will be managed in your project. Develop your risk management plan in the Organising and Preparing stage of your project, refine it as necessary at the end of each stage when planning the next stage, and continually update it where needed during stages (see Chapter 2 for more on these stages). Include the following in your risk-management plan:

✓ Communications and interfaces, such as with programme management or other projects that may be affected

✓ How risk actions will be monitored and audited

✓ Reporting mechanisms, such as how team members should report newly discovered risks and how they should say if they believe a risk is starting to happen

✓ Review points where risk will be re-assessed, such as at the end of each stage and at regular monthly intervals during each stage, unless it's getting near an end stage

✔ Scales to be used, such as the impact scale

✔ Your plan for keeping people informed about risks throughout the project

# Risk Register

You need a *Risk Register* or *Risk Log* in which to record risks, the action being taken on them and the responsibilities for managing each one.

The Risk Register holds the day-to-day control information for each risk that's been identified. You can adjust the contents to meet the exact needs of your project but, as always, try to keep things simple. At a minimum, you're likely to need the following information:

✔ **ID:** Usually a number

✔ **Risk title:** A short name to identify the risk quickly

✔ **Status:** Whether the risk is increasing, decreasing, under review or dead

✔ **Description:** A full description covering the characteristics of the risk and how it is likely to behave, such as whether it may happen gradually or instantly

✔ **Metrics:** Impact, probability and proximity information

✔ **Responsibilities:** Who's responsible for the risk, including taking any action on it

✔ **Notifier:** Who spotted the risk in the first place (that might be a good person to involve in the analysis of the risk) or who to consult if there are changes

✔ **Planned actions:** What actions will be taken to control the risk, or the fact that it has been decided not to take action

Make the Risk Register available so people can see it, and actively encourage project staff to keep an eye on it. If your teams and sponsor are aware of the risks, they're more likely to report relevant things that they see happening. If they aren't aware of a risk, they may not even notice tell-tale signs that a risk is starting to occur. That availability includes being open with outside supplier staff on the project. Try not to hide risk from them. It's better to get non-disclosure agreements than to hide risk. Of course, some risk can't be shared, such as things that affect commercial or personal confidentiality, but most of what gets hidden from supplier staff in projects needn't be. Hiding things unnecessarily is itself a risk.

# Getting Some Help from Techniques

The good thing about risk management is that there are lots of techniques to help. In this last section you'll find four basic ones to get you started.

## Ishikawa (fishbone) diagram

The fishbone diagram is useful when you want to work through risk identification in a structured way. You can do this using one impact at a time, such as 'delay' or 'overspending'. Using your chosen risk categories as the primary fish bones, enter the risks as the secondary bones. Figure 10-3 gives an example with a partially completed diagram.

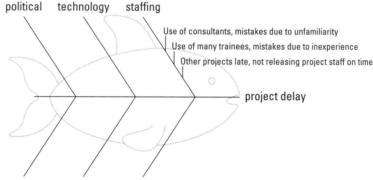

political    technology    staffing

Use of consultants, mistakes due to unfamiliarity
Use of many trainees, mistakes due to inexperience
Other projects late, not releasing project staff on time

project delay

**Figure 10-3:** The Ishikawa (fishbone) diagram.

## Work Flow Diagram

The Work Flow Diagram, explained in Chapter 5, shows all the project's products in sequence, including those coming into the project from outside. This gives a natural structure for part of the risk analysis. Simply go through the project products one at a time asking 'What could go wrong with producing this product or with this external supply?'

## Risk Checklist

The risk checklist is simply a standard list of known risks grouped by category. You can buy commercial ones, but making your own for your organisation is even better. You identify all the risks you can by using other techniques, and then use the Risk Checklist to see whether you have missed anything. Don't use the checklist first, or you're likely to get focused on it and so miss a new risk that's staring you in the face but isn't on the list.

# Decision Tree

A decision tree allows you to map options and cost them against the probability of them occurring. The result helps evaluate the best course of action. Figure 10-4 gives an example with two main choices of supplier. The actual cost for each then depends on whether that supplier delivers on time, early (in which case they get a bonus payment) or late (in which case there is a deduction from the cost for the inconvenience). The known history of the two suppliers allows estimation of the probability of each being early, on time or late.

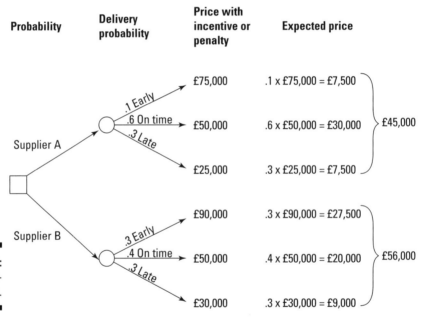

**Figure 10-4:**
The decision tree.

Multiplying the base price plus the performance incentive for early delivery by the probability of early delivery yields the expected value of the price you pay if delivery is early. You can calculate the total expected prices for suppliers A and B by totalling the expected prices if each is early, on time and late.

This analysis suggests that you can expect to pay vendor A £45,000 and have a 70 per cent chance she'll deliver on time or early. You can expect to pay vendor B £56,000 and have a 70 per cent chance she'll deliver on time or early. So you can see that vendor A is the better choice.

# Part III
# Putting Your Management Team Together

'I-NEED-A-BIGGER-BUDGET-FOR-MY-PROJECT!!'

## *In this part . . .*

*T*he key to successful projects is people – using their capabilities to the fullest, encouraging their mutually supportive work efforts and sustaining their ongoing commitment to your project's success.

This part looks at the organisational structure of a project, sets down clear roles and responsibilities, examines the impact of good and bad leadership and discusses how to get the best out of teams.

# Chapter 11

# Organising the Project

*I*n a project, clear organisation is vital. A commonly reported cause of project problems and project failure is unclear roles and responsibilities. This chapter helps you pin down very clear roles and responsibilities.

To get any job done involving more people than just you, some organisation is needed. You need to know who's doing what, who's in charge and who's responsible for different aspects of the work. It's normal for any group of people beginning a task ranging from pitching a tent to running a major corporate project to say, 'Right, let's get organised.'

In this chapter we explore project organisation, show some different options for it and give some hints and tips for getting it right. Getting the right organisation is important for your project for two reasons. First, if you have unclear roles and responsibilities, you're going to get communications breakdowns and misunderstandings. Second, if the structure doesn't fit the project properly – for example, if you have a big structure that requires an expensive meeting and lots of people to make a minor decision – you're likely to get delays and excessive overheads.

Then we move on to set the project organisation in the wider context of the organisational work environment and structure. Some organisations are becoming 'projectised', that is the structure of the organisation is being changed to fit around a project way of working. Some companies now have a dedicated projects department, while others have adopted something known as *Matrix Management*. The chapter will help you understand the organisational context of your project and will explain variants you may come across in the future, if you haven't already.

# Designing the Project Organisation Structure

In a small project, the organisation may be very simple with just a sponsor who's the manager who wants the project and is paying for it, a Project Manager who often does some of the project work alongside managing it, and then perhaps one or two more people who help with the work as team members. Figure 11-1 illustrates a simple organisation structure.

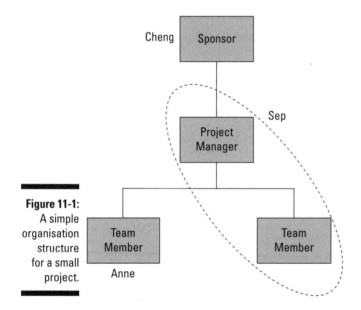

**Figure 11-1:** A simple organisation structure for a small project.

In Figure 11-1 only three people are involved in the project. Cheng is the manager in overall charge of the project and takes the role of sponsor. Sep is the Project Manager running the project day to day, but is also doing some of the project work himself so is also taking the role of a team member alongside his project management work. Anne is a technical specialist who's in the project as a team member, and she's working with Sep on the technical work.

In a bigger project, you may well have a project board or steering committee in overall charge, a Project Manager who is full time in that role, and then a number of teams from inside the organisation and some teams from outside suppliers, each with a team leader.

You may need to fight a bit – politely of course – to get an appropriate structure for your project. If your organisation has a standard organisation structure for its projects, geared to satisfy the needs of large projects, it's almost certainly going to be excessive if your project is small. It may take some effort to convince organisational managers that your project should have a simpler, smaller structure, but that effort will be repaid when you don't have to deal with an unwieldy structure right through the project. One way to help sell your argument is by showing that the project will have lower overheads.

## Understanding that organisation is about roles not jobs

People often talk about 'roles and responsibilities' without thinking too much about the phrase. In projects, though, the word *role* is very significant and also very helpful when you're designing the organisation of a particular project. The word is significant for three reasons:

- ✔ **One person (job) can have more than one role.** In smaller projects especially, one person's 'job' on the project could be made up of a couple of roles. An example is given in Figure 11-1 where Sep is the Project Manager but is also doing some of the work of the project. When he's doing technical project work, Sep is a team member. But when he's managing the project, he's a Project Manager. So Sep wears two hats: he's got two roles; for some of his time he's a Project Manager and for the rest of his time he's a team member.

- ✔ **Some roles can be shared by more than one person.** If there's a role on your steering committee for a user manager representative to make sure the project is delivering things that the user staff can operate, then that role can be split between two people. For example, if the project is delivering things that will affect staff in two operational departments, you may want a manager from each department to sit on the committee to make sure the deliverables are okay for each department's people. So two managers fill the one role of user representative.

- ✔ **Roles emphasise function and not status.** Project work isn't about status – how important someone is in the organisation – but function. Project organisation can turn normal reporting lines completely upside down. The Project Manager may be a relatively junior manager in the organisation, and one of the teams may have a very senior legal adviser on it. So in the project, a very senior manager may be accountable to someone who's much more junior in terms of grade.

Nick Graham has provided project training and consultancy advice to a number of UK police forces. UK police forces are very 'command and control' orientated, and in many cases more so than the military, so someone's rank is extremely important. One project involved significant change in force policy and, because of this, two of the team members were the deputy chief constable and the director of human resources (the most senior civilian grade in the force). The Project Manager was a police inspector (two hops up from the bottom grade: constable to sergeant to inspector). The normal reporting lines were turned completely upside down in the project, and a team member who was the deputy chief constable was accountable to the Project Manager who was an inspector. That's okay, though. Project roles are about function not status, and the police officers involved fully understood that.

## Getting to grips with project roles

Where your project is more than a very small one, you're going to need a more sophisticated organisation structure. Do be careful in your thinking when you do the work to set this up, though. Always keep the structure as simple as possible.

Figure 11-2 outlines the roles. You can have all of the roles filled with relatively few people if you need to. You can get models for project structure from many places, but this example comes from the PRIME project methodology (more on this in Chapter 2). Although you can see that this is more detailed than the simple example in Figure 11-1, it's also very flexible.

The PRIME approach is very flexible partly because it uses roles but also because it allows extra roles to be added to the organisation structure where you need them. In many methods, such as PRINCE2 (also see Chapter 2), the approach is presented in its full complexity in the manual, and you have to simplify it where you can. PRIME starts at the other end and sets out to keep things simple, which is fine for most projects, but where you need extra power for something more substantial, you can add in one or more PowerPacks. The PRIME PowerPacks provide more sophisticated content, such as for high-risk projects, and are relevant here because they can affect the roles. The High Risk PowerPack, for example, gives the option of adding a dedicated project risk manager into the top management of the project, and you see that in the 'optional power roles' box in Figure 11-2.

## Looking at the roles

This section explains the roles as set down in the example in Figure 11-1, but don't worry if you use a different method or none at all. The principles hold good whatever environment you're working in.

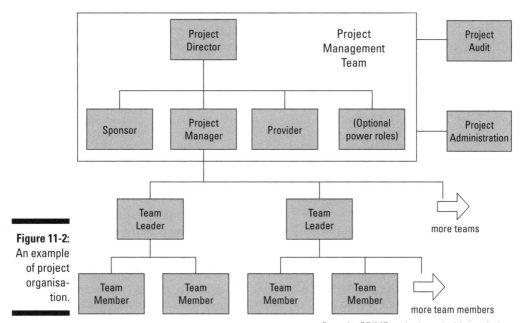

**Figure 11-2:**
An example
of project
organisa-
tion.

### Project management team

This is the top management team of the project. In a smaller project, you may have a single sponsor taking all the roles except Project Manager (see the later section about sponsors). You may know the top management group as a *project steering committee* or *project board*.

### Project director

If the project was a temporary department in the organisation, then this role would be the head of department. The *project director* is supported by other senior managers in the project management team, but is the manager ultimately responsible for the project. This position makes sense. Taking the analogy of a project as being like a temporary department, you have one person in overall charge of it.

This role can't be shared. Don't ever have a committee, for example, as project director. All members of the project management team are responsible for making sure that the project is viable, but the project director has specific, final and personal responsibility for it.

The project director needs to understand both projects and business, of course, but must also have sufficient authority to take decisions, and preferably some enthusiasm, charisma and leadership qualities to provide drive within the project. A bored and uninterested project director isn't going to inspire enthusiasm and hard work within the teams.

### Sponsor

The *sponsor* is the person who wants the project and whose staff will be using whatever the project is delivering. The sponsor is there to provide a strong link between the project and the staff in the operational area. The sponsor also provides any business staff who are needed on project teams to help specify what is needed, and perhaps to help test final products to make sure that they're okay for operational use.

PRIME uses the term *sponsor* to describe the person representing the business area that will use what the project is delivering. The person in overall charge is the project director. However, and confusingly when reading a book about project management, terms are not used consistently across organisations or even across project approaches. You may not have project directors in your organisation but have a single person who's both representing the user area and in overall charge of the project, who you refer to as the sponsor. That's very common and the usage through most of this book. PRIME is a bit more specific and so discriminates clearly between the two functions with two separate roles.

### Provider

The *provider* provides the technical staff resource for the project – the teams. The provider must have the authority to commit that resource, or get that authority from others. You don't want the Project Manager running around trying to persuade people to take part – especially if that Project Manager is you. Rather, you have a provider who has the organisational authority to commit resource. If the project involves a major outside supplier company working on the project alongside organisational staff, you'll probably want to have two people in the role. The provider from your own organisation will authorise internal staff resource, and the provider from the supplier company will authorise staff resource from that company.

### Project Manager

The *Project Manager* takes day-to-day responsibility for managing the project on behalf of the full project management team. The Project Manager has specific responsibilities to plan the project, control it and manage the staff resource. Normally a project has a number of teams, so the direct team management will be done by team leaders, but the Project Manager still has an important function to motivate and direct the project staff.

In addition to the main elements of planning and control, the Project Manager must also deal with problems and changes, referring to the full project management team anything that is beyond his delegated authority.

Only have one Project Manager – just one person in the role. Some organisations break that rule and have a 'business Project Manager' and a 'Technical Project Manager', for example. Splitting the role in two (or more) isn't a good idea though, because neither person is a 'project' manager by definition, because he doesn't have a view of the whole project, only a part of it. There's a danger of things dropping down the gap if neither person saw it or one person saw it but assumed that the other person was dealing with it. In really bad cases, the two Project Managers can come to loggerheads – and yes, it's been known! If you want a powerful analogy of this idea in another area of management, try a ship. Even huge passenger liners and oil tankers have only one captain when they're on a voyage, and for the same management reason as in a project: one person knows what's going on.

If you're using the PRINCE2 project management method, the Project Manager is not part of the senior management group in the project, which PRINCE2 calls the project board, although he will attend all of the meetings. PRIME takes the view that the Project Manager is an important part of the decision-making body for the project and, in a larger project, may even be a senior and influential manager in his own right as well as a project expert. PRIME therefore gives the Project Manager a recognised voice on the project management team alongside the provider and sponsor, although still under the overall authority of the project director. If you're not using a project method, you can make your own mind up.

Keep your project management team, steering committee or project board small; preferably with a maximum of six people. Big management groups don't ever meet – there's always someone unable to make the meeting and usually several. Big management groups tend to be a big problem in organisations using PRINCE2, and if you'd like advice on how to keep a PRINCE2 project board scaled down and working properly, it's worth investing in a copy of *PRINCE2 For Dummies* by Nick Graham (Wiley), in which you'll find a whole chapter on running project boards successfully.

### Project audit

It makes sense to have the project checked now and then to be sure that everything's okay. *Project audit* does that checking so that the project management team (and even the organisation) know that the project is being run well. That's no different in principle to a board of directors having an audit team who check things out for them and a financial audit team doing checks and reporting back to the finance director.

Unless the Project Manager is a devious and disreputable soul – so definitely not you then – he has nothing to fear from project audit, and actually the reverse. The Project Manager should be really pleased when project audit people appear in his office to do some checks. To draw a simple parallel, have you ever had a really tricky piece of work to do, and when you were finished you weren't too sure of it? Perhaps you asked an experienced colleague to cast an eye over the work for you. He did so and asked one or two questions. One question highlighted a mistake in your work, so you put it right. Then your colleague said, 'Well, other than that, it looks absolutely fine.' How did you feel then? Relieved? Grateful? Almost certainly both, and then you can add 'more confident' into the mix. Good project audit is like that and not to be confused with trouble-seeking nit-pickers whom you definitely don't want in the project audit role.

### Project administration

If your project is of any size, it usually makes sense to have a *project administrator*. In large organisations, senior staff often have a personal assistant who manages the diary, books travel and accommodation, answers the phone, takes messages, sorts email, answers basic enquiries, writes letters . . . well, you know the sort of stuff. Good personal assistants are invaluable and really earn their keep. So, too, in the project.

Project Managers can not only waste a lot of time doing admin, but also get distracted from running the project because they're too focused on admin stuff. It often makes sense, then, to have one or more than one project administrator who can do the admin work that's associated with all projects. Project administrators are normally of a lower grade than the Project Manager and so are cheaper for the project, but also, as very good administrators, they can probably do the work in half the time the Project Manager would take anyway.

Some organisations centralise project administration and have a project office that gives this support to all projects. That's great for economy of scale, for gaining experience and so doing things very well. Also, the project office can then offer help to smaller projects that can't justify their own full-time administrators.

### Team leader

Unless your project only has a single team, in which case the Project Manager often runs it, every team has a *team leader*. The number you have depends, obviously enough, on the number of teams working on the project at any one time. Teams are often formed mostly from inside your own organisation, but you may have supplier teams on your project as well. The supplier teams may be from outside your own organisation but they're inside the project and, if you're controlling the work, you need to include them in the same controls and reporting as for internal teams.

## If your project is in a programme . . .

If your project is part of a group of projects in a programme, headed by a programme director or equivalent, you may find that has an impact on project roles. Here are a few possible results:

✔ The programme director has already made all of the appointments to project management team roles as part of resourcing the programme.

✔ Someone from programme management may take a role in the project's organisation

so that a natural link is formed between the project and the programme.

✔ There may be an additional role on the project management team (see the 'optional power roles' box in the diagram in Figure 11-2), which is a programme liaison person.

✔ The same person may take a role in the project management team for several or even all projects in the programme to provide a natural horizontal communication between the management teams.

Many Project Managers maintain contact with team leaders both individually and by having regular team leader meetings where everyone can hear about progress across the project. The Project Manager can also use this meeting to collect information such as progress and time sheet information. The Project Manager can also push information out. Team leaders can go back and tell their team members so that information cascades. In bigger projects, that can be a very useful communication mechanism.

Team leaders often do low level detailed planning for their teams' work, but usually work with the Project Manager to help produce the plans at stage and even project level because they can provide valuable information on what work is needed in the project.

### Team members

*Team members* are the people doing most of the work of the project, so they're arguably the most important people of all in the project. The rest is just management. We say no more about team management in this chapter, and that's not because it's not relevant, but rather because it's so very important that you'll find two whole chapters – Chapters 12 and 13 – on the subject.

## Deciding or influencing the structure

If you're a Project Manager, the upper part of the structure can be a difficult area because the people involved are probably senior to you. You can't easily tell your managers what they should do and instruct them in their duties. In management, it's traditional that the more senior people tell the more junior people what to do. If you're asked about the structure, then that's great. If you're not asked, then you may need to persuade, and the logic behind the project organisation here may help. One thing's for sure: if your project management team or steering committee doesn't function well, it will be a significant problem in the project, and the Project Manager will have to do much more than is fair or reasonable.

Some steering committees are simply a disgrace and don't seem to regard projects as being in the same management environment as the rest of the business. Bad steering committees often delegate the whole project to the Project Manager and at the end take the credit if the project is a success or fire the Project Manager if it isn't. This management style has been nick-named 'Turkish slipper management': they turn up at the end! If ever that seems sensible to anyone, he should think of a department in an organisation. Would it be okay for the top managers to go on holiday for a year and put their feet up, and then come back at the end to see whether the department has been successful or not? No! Those senior managers are appointed to make sure that the department functions effectively and do everything possible to help their staff achieve success. So too in the project.

# Defining Three Organisational Environments

The project organisation can be influenced by the project method or approach that you're using, but it's also influenced by how the organisation itself is structured. Over the years, projects have evolved from organisational afterthoughts to major vehicles for conducting business and developing future capabilities. Naturally, the approaches for organising and managing projects have evolved as well.

This section explains how projects are handled in the traditional functional structure, the project-focused projectised structure and the extensively used matrix structure, which combines aspects of both the functional and projectised structures.

## The functional structure

The *functional organisation structure* (Figure 11-3 gives an example) brings together people who perform similar tasks or who use the same kinds of skills and knowledge in *functional groups*. In this structure, people are managed through clear lines of authority that extend through each group to the head of the group and, ultimately, to a single person at the top. In Figure 11-3, you see that all people who perform human resources functions for the organisation (such as recruiting, training and benefits management) are located in the human resources group, which reports to the chief executive.

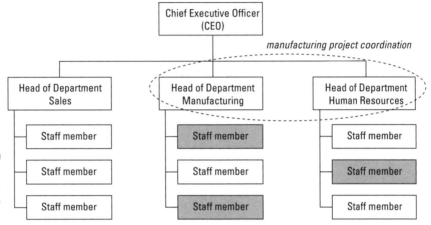

**Figure 11-3:**
A functional structure for administering projects.

Shaded boxes indicate the staff working on a manufacturing project

Depending on the nature of the project and the skills and knowledge required for it, a project in the functional structure may be handled completely by staff within a particular functional group. However, as illustrated in Figure 11-3, if the manufacturing group is performing a project that requires the expertise of a person from the human resources group, the head of manufacturing must make a formal agreement with the head of human resources to make the necessary human resources staff available to work on the project. The head of human resources must then manage this person for his project work.

The Project Manager has limited authority over project team members in the functional structure, because the functional managers maintain all authority over the project team members.

## Advantages of the functional structure

The functional structure has some advantages. Departments:

- ✔ Are natural reservoirs of skills and knowledge
- ✔ Have well-established communications and decision-making procedures
- ✔ Provide a focused and supportive job environment

### Disadvantages of the functional structure

The functional structure has the following drawbacks:

- ✔ It makes collaboration between different functions more difficult.
- ✔ Staff usually prioritise work in their departments rather than the project.
- ✔ The project may have difficulty getting buy-in from other departments.

## The projectised structure

The *projectised organisation structure* brings together all staff working on a particular project. Project team members are often located together and under the direct authority of the Project Manager for the duration of the project. As an example, you see in Figure 11-4 that a design engineer, an IT specialist and a test engineer all work on Project A, while a different design engineer and a different test engineer work on Project B.

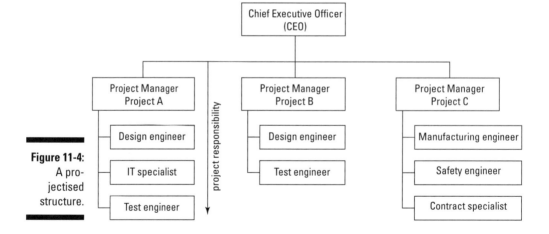

**Figure 11-4:** A projectised structure.

The Project Manager has almost total authority over the members of his team in the projectised structure. He makes assignments and directs team members' task efforts, he conducts team members' performance assessments and approves team members' raises and bonuses, and he approves annual leave.

### Advantages of the projectised structure

The projectised structure has the following advantages:

✔ All members of a project team report directly to the Project Manager.

✔ Team members can more easily develop a shared identity, resulting in a stronger commitment to one another and to the success of the project.

✔ Everyone on the project shares the same management processes.

## *Disadvantages of the projectised structure*

The projectised structure has the following disadvantages:

✔ Higher staff costs if the work leads to duplication of skills across projects and creates slack time

✔ Reduced technical interchange between projects

✔ Reduced career continuity, opportunities and sense of job security: team members may have no guarantee that the organisation will need their services when their current project comes to an end.

Some organisations have become partly projectised in that they have a projects department but then take staff temporarily from other departments for the duration of the project (see Figure 11-5). This can be easier than it looks, because the head of department for the projects department reports directly to the CEO. If the CEO backs this project and requires cooperation from other departments, then life is easier because CEO authority is behind the project.

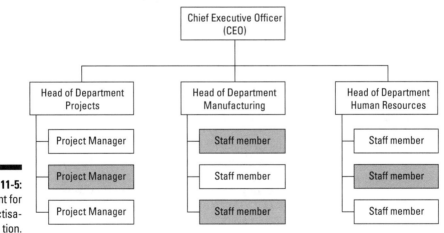

**Figure 11-5:**
A variant for projectisa-tion.

Shaded boxes indicate the staff working on a manufacturing project

With the form of projectisation illustrated in Figure 11-5, the organisation must decide how staff will be managed in terms of annual reporting, salary recommendations and so on. In turn, those decisions may depend on how long someone is assigned to a project. If a person is assigned for two years, then it makes sense to pass the management responsibility on to the Project Manager for that time, but if the person is working on the project for only two months, then clearly responsibility should remain in the staff member's home department.

## *The matrix structure*

With increasing frequency, projects today involve and affect many functional areas within an organisation. As a result, staff from these different areas must work together to successfully accomplish the project work. The *matrix organisation structure* combines elements of both the functional and projectised structures to facilitate the responsive and effective participation of people from different parts of the organisation on projects that need their specialised expertise. This section is a bit bigger than the two previous ones, and that's for two reasons. First, Matrix Management is increasingly common, and second, you need to understand it fully because it can sometimes make life rather more difficult when getting a project team to function well together.

Some organisations, and not least some UK government departments, like Matrix Management because staff time can be allocated in smaller units so staff are 'fully utilised'. That looks really good from a senior management perspective, but it can be a smokescreen because a big difference exists between allocation and achievement. If staff are constantly flitting from one project to another – an hour here, two hours there – how committed and motivated are they going to be? Someone may be fully allocated but it doesn't mean he's fully productive. Staff who are permanently on a team, who identify with the project and who are committed to each other and to the success of the project are going to perform much better than staff who are flitting between projects. It may be that full-time project staff who spend 20 per cent of their time playing computer games while they're waiting for the next job to come up are more productive than staff who are 'fully utilised'. To read more on this, take a look at the book *Peopleware* by Tom DeMarco and Timothy Lister (Dorset House Publishing Company). The authors calculate that well-motivated staff in good organisations work 11 times faster than staff in poor organisations doing similar work. In the light of statistics like that, full utilisation seems rather less significant, and motivation and performance seem rather more important.

As Figure 11-6 illustrates, in a matrix organisation structure, people from different areas of the organisation are assigned to lead or work on projects. At first glance, this diagram may look similar to Figure 11-5, which shows an organisation with a projects department, and indeed that form of projectised organisation is a variant of Matrix Management known as *strong matrix* (there's more on the strength of the matrix later in this section).

In Matrix Management, Project Managers guide the performance of project activities, while people's direct supervisors (from groups such as finance, manufacturing and sales, as in Figure 11-6) perform administrative tasks like formally appraising people's performance and approving promotions, salary increases or requests for leave. Because an individual can be on a project for less than 100 per cent of his time, he may work on more than one project at a time.

A matrix environment is classified as *weak*, *strong* or *balanced*, depending on the amount of authority the Project Managers have over their teams. So you get the full picture, here's a little more about each of these classifications:

- **Weak matrix:** Project team members receive most of their direction from their functional managers. Project Managers have little if any direct authority over team members and actually function more like project coordinators than managers.

- **Strong matrix:** Companies with strong matrix structures choose Project Managers for new projects from a pool of people whose only job is to manage projects. The companies never ask these people to serve as team members. Often, these Project Managers form a single organisational unit that has its own head of department, so it's a way that the organisation can be projectised (see the previous section). In addition to directing and guiding project work, these Project Managers have certain administrative authority over the team members, such as the right to participate in their performance appraisals.

- **Balanced matrix:** This type of matrix environment is a blend of the weak and strong environments. People are assigned to lead projects or serve as team members based on the projects' needs rather than on their job descriptions. Although the Project Manager may have some administrative authority over team members (such as approving leave requests), for the most part the Project Manager guides, coordinates and facilitates the project.

Check out the later section 'Working successfully in a matrix environment' for more information on the matrix structure.

### Advantages of the matrix structure

A matrix environment offers many benefits, including the following:

- Teams can assemble more rapidly. Because you have a larger resource pool from which to choose your project team, you may not have to wait as long for a skill to be available.

- Specialised expertise can be available for several different projects.

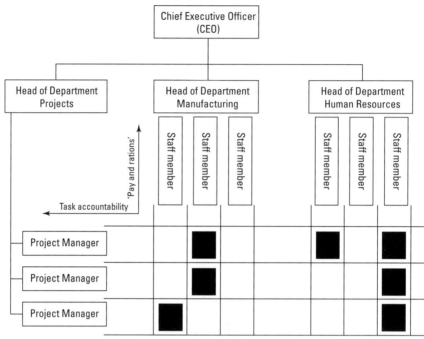

**Figure 11-6:** The general matrix organisation structure.

Shaded squares show staff allocation to projects

### Disadvantages of the matrix structure

A matrix environment introduces a number of challenges which the Project Manager must successfully address. For example, team members:

- ✔ Are accountable to multiple managers who often have conflicting priorities
- ✔ May not be as familiar with each team's way of working
- ✔ May not be as committed to or productive in any one project, because they're constantly moving from one project to another
- ✔ May focus more on their individual assignments than project goals

### Working successfully in a matrix environment

To be successful in a matrix environment, you need to align and coordinate the people who are involved in your project, deflecting any forces that pull those people in different directions. This section can help you, as a Project Manager, to get the highest-quality work from your team members in a matrix environment, along with timely and effective support from the functional and senior managers.

*Team* in this context means all the people working to build the project's products. In practice, you may have a number of teams, each with a team leader, so your work here is to get cohesion across the project as well as within individual teams.

To get a project 'feel' and identity, and then to encourage team members to function well:

✔ Clarify the project vision and working relationships.

✔ Make it clear how the group(s) will work, and communicate so people aren't working across each other, bringing procedures from different parts of the organisation.

✔ Clarify each person's authority and how the project organisation fits together.

✔ Be aware of and attend to how people are functioning – in inter-personal relationships, not just work performance.

✔ Be sure everyone appreciates that they are important, no matter how junior. Take the military maxim on board of 'we, not me'.

✔ Build commitment wherever and whenever you can by forging close links between the team members and the goal, and making sure everyone knows the significance of the work they are doing.

✔ Recognise good performance and actions which help the team. Just noticing and expressing appreciation can have a huge impact.

In Matrix ManagementMatrix Management, you're also going to need functional managers on side to release staff resource. This is primarily the responsibility of the project management team or steering committee, but in practice you need to keep a close eye on it too and work with the other members of the management team in the project to build good relationships. That relationship-building includes:

✔ Asking for functional managers' support. In some projects, support isn't forthcoming because it was never asked for in the first place.

✔ Heading off problems in advance, such as agreeing how work conflicts will be resolved before you get to the point where you have work conflicts.

✔ Planning in sufficient detail so that you can tell functional managers what resource you need and when, and you don't understate it.

✔ Being open in communications so you develop a reputation as someone who isn't trying to hide things or manipulate people.

✔ Encouraging your steering committee or project management team to maintain strong links with top management. A functional manager may be more willing to release staff if the CEO appreciates that some departmental targets may not be met because of heavy staff involvement in a business-critical project that's vital for the future of the whole organisation.

# Chapter 12

# Working With Teams and Specialists

. . . . . . . . . . . . . . . . . . . . . . . . . . . . . . . . . . . . . . . . . . . . . . . .

. . . . . . . . . . . . . . . . . . . . . . . . . . . . . . . . . . . . . . . . . . . . . . . .

*P*rojects usually involve working with people with different skill sets, from different areas within the organisation and possibly from outside it and who are used to working in different ways. You may not have worked extensively with your project team members before, so getting everyone working together well is something that you usually need to address early on. Just to make it more fun, your project probably has a tight time schedule, so you'll need to move fast, and of course you need to get it pretty much right first time. It's much harder if things go wrong and you have to try to start all over with people later on. No pressure then.

If you're working in a medium to large project, then as a Project Manager you'll probably be dealing with Team Leaders who in turn directly manage the teams. This can obviously make your work easier, but it can also make it harder because you need to be careful to provide encouragement and support but not tread on toes and bypass your Team Managers.

Success in this kind of environment needs agreement on how to work to maximise contributions and minimise wasted time and mistakes. Those mistakes include misunderstandings that range from the annoying to the project destroying. The project needs an approach that gives everyone confidence that team members will live up to their commitments. The Project Manager, any Team Leaders and every team member must understand and be comfortable with their planned roles.

This chapter explains how to distinguish between the different degrees of involvement, make key assignments, encourage people to give their best and keep their commitments to the plan, and present an overall picture of team members' roles and responsibilities. Finally, looking up the chain of command, we offer a bit of advice on how to handle a micromanager.

# Working With Others

Unless your project is very small indeed and only needs you, you're going to be involved with other people. Those people may be above you in the project organisation, so you are accountable to them, and also below you, so they are accountable to you. The following sections focus on your management of the teams and Team Leaders, and then in the final section, 'Dealing with Micromanagement', we give some advice on dealing with a common problem in relationships with those higher up the chain of command.

## Treading carefully

It's probably not necessary to point out that good management relationships in a project are vital – but there, it's said anyway. As a manager, you need to tread a careful path to get and keep people on side without being overbearing or lax to the point that the job doesn't get done. It's a whole lot easier if you know the people, because you already have some working relationship with them, but the chances are that at least some of the people in the project will be new to you, and you to them.

In managing the project, you need a balance in your communications. On the one hand, if you start explaining the obvious to team members, then they're going to get annoyed and feel that you don't trust them to get on and do the job that they're fully qualified and able to do. On the other hand, if you're not clear or detailed enough in your communication, you run the very real danger of misunderstanding, not getting what you wanted and then wasting time – and probably money – while people put things right.

Before getting involved in project management, Nick Graham was a user representative on a large UK government computer project. The project was time critical because it was geared to dates set down in legislation and public announcements. The whole project nearly came to grief over the word *current*. The organisation involved with building the system, and which was then going to run it for the Government, understood *current* to mean any record that was held on the system and not yet archived. However, the Government use of the word was in the legal sense where *current* means something is still in force. A record could still be on the system, but not be current. Happily a later discussion confirming the processing that was needed for current records revealed the two interpretations, and everything was put right – but only just in time to prevent a very serious problem.

# *Working with external suppliers*

Before getting too deep into the chapter, it's worth thinking about the place of external suppliers. Remember that if you have teams working on your project but they're from outside your own organisation, they're nevertheless inside your project. The way that some UK organisations work with suppliers is more than worrying, and to read the way some agreements are set up, you'd be forgiven for thinking that the supplier is the enemy.

## *Supporting supplier teams*

Some projects give very little help or support to supplier staff and then fast-forward to an aggressive position, invoking clauses in the contract if those staff don't do so well. Poor work from suppliers cannot be excused for a single moment, but a key point here is that supplier staff in the project need support too. To help hammer the point home, have a look at this quotation from the American space agency NASA's 'One Hundred Rules for NASA Project Managers':

> *In award fee situations, the government personnel should be making every effort possible to make sure the contractor gets a high score (i.e., be on schedule and produce good work). Contractors don't fail, NASA does and that is why one must be proactive in support.*

So, the supplier staff don't fail, you do. It's in your interest to help supplier staff as well as organisational staff, because if the suppliers succeed, you succeed. Obvious really, but you wouldn't think so when you see some projects.

Beware of accountants who don't understand projects and who assure you that it's okay to go with a cheap supplier because they'll protect the project with a 'penalty clause' in the contract. For a start, under UK law you can't have a penalty clause, only liquidated damages, which means that you'll be awarded money in line with what the court (not you) thinks is the extent of the damage you've suffered. However, if you have such a clause, you'd better not need to invoke it because if you do, you just lost. If you invoke the clause, then you haven't got what you needed. You may get your money back, but if you wanted the money, you wouldn't have gone out for the supply in the first place. You wanted the project and now you haven't got it. So much for the penalty clause protecting the project then.

## *Choosing suppliers carefully*

Given that if your project needs external supplier resource, your success will partly depend on those staff, it pays to choose your suppliers carefully. Suppliers need to make money to stay in business, so of course they pay attention to making a profit on the job. However, dangers occur when suppliers are concerned only about making a profit. This problem isn't unique to some large consultancy companies, but it's certainly very visible in them when their staff are focused on 'selling in' more days to their clients rather than being focused on their client's project. Strangely, although smaller suppliers also need to watch their profit margins, they're often more focused on the client because each client is proportionately more important to them, rather than just being 'an account' – a line item in a monthly sales target. You need suppliers who, while making a profit, will work well on the project and integrate with other project staff.

### Thinking time, not just costs

How much are you willing to pay for supplier resource? If two suppliers can both do a job, do you go for the one whose bid is the cheapest? Project mathematics is often a bit strange, and nowhere more than here. Suppose one supplier can do a job in three months for £100,000, and another can do the same job in two months for £200,000; which is actually the cheapest? Well, if your project is due to save £500,000 a month after it's finished, and using the second supplier means you'll get to the point of delivery a month earlier, the mathematics shows that the more expensive supplier is actually £400,000 cheaper. But that's only if you see the work in its full business context rather than in the narrow confines of the bid. If you use contract staff in your organisation who are used to normal procurement and not projects, you may need to sit them down and explain the bigger picture rather s l o w l y!

# Understanding Teams

A project entails performing specific pieces of work, making decisions and coordinating the activities of others. To accomplish the project with a minimum of time and resources, each piece of work must be done in the correct order, and each person must work at peak efficiency, being sure not to repeat unnecessarily work that others have already done. The more complex the project and the greater the number of people working on it, the more difficult it is to ensure that people don't step on each other's toes along the way.

The people doing the work are your *project teams*. In the context of planning, a team may be a group of people, probably with a team leader, or just an individual – a team of one.

To help you start thinking through and then coordinating people's efforts on the project, this section defines three different areas of responsibility that team members can fulfil when working on a project activity, and takes a look at their similarities and differences.

# Distinguishing between authority, responsibility and accountability

The following concepts can help you define and clarify how team members should relate to each other and to their assigned tasks:

- **Authority:** The ability to make binding decisions about your project's products, schedule, resources and activities. Examples include signing purchase orders that don't exceed £5,000 and making a change to a scheduled date of no more than two weeks.

- **Responsibility:** The commitment to achieve specific results. An example is a promise to have a draft report ready by 1 March.

- **Accountability:** Bringing consequences to bear in response to people's performance, such as your boss noting in your annual performance appraisal that you solved a tough manufacturing problem.

   Unfortunately, many people think accountability means only paying the price when you foul up. This fear of having to be accountable for their mistakes often leads people to avoid situations in which they would be accountable for their performance. Paying a price when you foul up is certainly half of the concept, but the other half is being rewarded for doing a good job. So positive reinforcement is far more effective than negative reinforcement for encouraging high quality results.

Your immediate reaction may be that you need to stay in control of your project and you don't want to delegate authority downwards, or at least not to team member level. But bear in mind these reasons to delegate:

- Some decisions, including technical decisions, may best be taken at team member level. You probably aren't quite as well placed as the senior radio engineer on the team to say if a change to the 6.6–6.7 gigahertz range is okay to fit in with the rest of the installation and avoid undue inter-modulation products on the point-to-point ultra-high-frequency links.

- If a lot of decisions are to be made, you're going to end up as a project control bottleneck if you don't delegate some authority.

- Not letting anyone else make any decisions is disempowering and conveys mistrust. Remember when you were more junior than you are now? How would you have felt if nobody 'trusted' you ever to make any decision about anything? Given that motivation and morale are key to your project, this is a rather important point.

- Part of your objective is to 'grow' your staff to be more and more useful through successive projects. If they can never make decisions and face the consequences of them, how can they possibly learn and develop?

You can find more on delegation in the later section 'Delving into delegation', and more on motivation and team performance in Chapter 13.

# Comparing authority and responsibility

Both authority and responsibility are upfront agreements. Before you start your project, you agree who can make which decisions and who'll ensure particular results. However, authority focuses on processes, and responsibility focuses on outcomes:

- ✔ **Authority** defines the decisions you can make but doesn't mention the results you have to achieve.

- ✔ **Responsibility** addresses the results you must accomplish but doesn't mention the decisions you can make to reach those results.

Remember, too, that you can transfer the authority to make decisions to another person, but you can't transfer the responsibility for the results of those decisions. (For more about delegating authority and sharing responsibility, check out the next section.)

Suppose you have the authority to issue purchase orders up to £5,000 for your project. Assume no policy or instructions specifically prevent you from giving some or all of this authority to someone else, so you give Mary, a team member, authority to sign purchase orders not to exceed £2,000 for your project. However, if Mary mistakenly issues a £1,000 purchase order for 50 reams of specialised paper instead of a £500 purchase order for the 25 reams that the project really needs, you're still responsible for her error.

You can always take back authority that you gave to someone else, but you can't blame the person for exercising that authority while she has it.

# Making Project Assignments

Effectively eliciting the help and support of others in the work you do is essential to get the most out of all team members. This section focuses specifically on what you need to know about deciding what can and cannot be delegated, assigning authority with confidence, sharing responsibility and holding everyone accountable.

## Delving into delegation

*Delegating* is giving away something you have. (Other definitions of delegating exist, but to keep it simple: *to delegate* is to give away.) The following sections help you decide what to delegate and to understand different degrees of delegation, and then how to support your delegations and achieve the best results possible.

You can delegate authority, but you can only share responsibility. You can completely transfer your decision-making power to someone else so that she can make the decisions with no involvement or approval from you. However, when another person agrees to assume a responsibility of yours, you're still obliged to ensure that she achieves the desired results. See the later section 'Sharing responsibility' for more details.

Although the potential benefits of delegating can be significant, not every task can or should be delegated. Consider the following guidelines when deciding which tasks are appropriate candidates for delegation, and to avoid the problem of failing to delegate what you should:

- ✔ **Focus on things that you should do, not just like to do.** A common problem facing all managers, not just Project Managers, is that they don't leave their old jobs behind; they still want to be *hands on*. That's okay if the person who's Project Manager is also taking a team role, but it's not okay if that involvement undermines the team members working on an activity – 'Oh, you're doing it like that! Well, the way I always used to do it . . . actually, let me borrow your pen, move your chair over and I'll show you.' Neither is it okay if the team work becomes too absorbing and the Project Manager neglects her role, causing the project to fail.

- ✔ **Recognise and accept that you may be able to do a job better.** Strangely perhaps, a problem in organisations is that people get promoted because they're very good! If you're project managing in an area where you 'learned your trade', you may be frustrated to see team members not doing work as well as you could do it. Don't let that tempt you to cut back on delegation and try to do everything yourself. Instead, expect that in many cases you can indeed do things better; that's why you got promoted.

- ✔ **Assign yourself to the tasks that you do best.** Suppose you're the best lawyer in town and there's more demand for your services at a fee of £300 per hour than you can meet. Suppose also that you can type twice as fast as the next fastest typist in town, who charges £100 per hour. Should you type all your own legal briefs? Clearly not; this concept is referred to as the *law of comparative advantage*. That law applies to tasks such as project administration as well as to any technical work.

- ✔ **If possible, assign yourself to tasks that aren't on a project's critical path.** (See Chapter 6 for a discussion of critical paths.) A delay on any activity on a project's critical path pushes back the estimated date for project completion. Therefore, when you have to stop working on a technical task that's on your project's critical path to deal with a project management problem, you immediately delay the entire project.

- ✔ **Don't assign other people to work on a task that you can't clearly describe.** The time you save by not working on the task is more than offset by the time you spend answering questions and continually redirecting the person to whom you've assigned the unclear task.

### Understanding degrees of delegation

Delegation doesn't have to be an all-or-nothing proposition in which you either make all decisions yourself or you withdraw from the situation entirely. Consider the following six degrees of delegation, each of which builds on and extends the ones that come before it:

- ✔ **Get in the know.** Get the facts and bring them to me for further action.

- ✔ **Show me the way to go.** Develop alternative actions to take, based on the facts you've found, and then bring them to me along with the facts.

- ✔ **Go when I say so.** Prepare one or more of the actions you've proposed, but don't do anything until I confirm it's okay.

- ✔ **Go unless I say *no*.** Tell me what you propose to do and when, and take your recommended actions unless I tell you otherwise.

- ✔ **How'd it go?** Analyse the situation, develop a course of action, take action and let me know the results.

- ✔ **Just go!** Here's a situation; deal with it.

Each level of delegation entails some degree of independent authority. For example, when your manager asks you to find the facts about a situation, you choose what information sources to consult, which information to share and which to discard. The primary difference between the levels of delegation is the degree of checking with the manager before taking action.

### Supporting your delegations of authority

You must reinforce and support your delegations of authority, or you can find yourself doing the task you thought you'd assigned to someone else.

Suppose you've been a manager of a project for the past two months, and Mary, who has been your assistant, has been dealing with people's technical issues. When someone comes to Mary with a technical problem, Mary analyses the problem, decides how to address it and passes the problem and her proposed solution by you. If you agree with her solution, you ask her to implement it. If you don't, you help her develop a more acceptable one.

Yesterday, you told Mary that, from now on, she doesn't have to pass her proposed solutions by you before implementing them. After discussing this with her, you told the other team members about the new procedure.

This morning Joe came to Mary to discuss a problem he was having with a contractor, and after listening to the problem, Mary gave Joe very specific instructions for how to deal with it. When Joe left Mary's office, he called you, recounted the problem he had discussed with Mary and her proposed solution, and asked you whether you agreed with Mary's approach.

You now have a dilemma. On the one hand, you want to support Mary's newly delegated authority. On the other hand, you want to ensure that your project goes smoothly and successfully. What should you do?

The only response you can make to Joe that supports your delegation of authority to Mary is: 'Do whatever Mary told you to do.'

Responding to Joe with, 'Yes, Mary's solution sounds good to me,' doesn't work because, by declaring that you like Mary's solution, you undercut Mary's authority to make the decision on her own! Perhaps you intend your words to assure Joe that you have full confidence in Mary's ability to develop an appropriate solution and that the one she proposed is an example of her good judgement. In reality, your response suggests to Joe that you're still in the approval process because you gave your approval to Mary's *decision* rather than to her exercising her *authority to make the decision*.

You want to support your delegation, but you also want to ensure your project's success. So how do you deal with the following situations?

> ✔ **You don't agree with Mary's recommendation.** If you fear that following Mary's recommendation will have catastrophic consequences, you must suggest to Joe that he wait until you can discuss the issue with Mary. In this instance, protecting your project and your organisation is more important than supporting your delegation of authority.
>
> In all other instances, though, you need to tell Joe to follow Mary's suggestion because she has the authority to make that decision. Here are several reasons to follow Mary's recommendation even if you don't agree with her choice:
>
> > • She may know more about the situation than Joe told you.
> >
> > • Maybe she's right and you're wrong.
> >
> > • If Mary believes that you'll jump in to save her every time she makes a bad decision, she'll be less concerned about making the correct decision the first time.
>
> You can always ask Mary later to explain to you privately the rationale for her decision, and you can offer your thoughts and opinions when you feel they're necessary.
>
> ✔ **Joe's call indicates a more general problem with the team's procedures and working relationships.**
>
> > • Perhaps you weren't clear when you explained the new working procedures with Mary to your team. Explain and reinforce the new procedures to Joe and the other team members.
> >
> > • Perhaps Joe didn't like Mary's answer and is trying to go behind her back to get his way. Again, you must reinforce that the decision is Mary's to make.

- Perhaps Mary didn't adequately explain to Joe why she recommended what she did. Suggest to Mary that she discuss with Joe the reasons behind her solutions and that she verifies that he understands and is comfortable with the information she shares.

- Perhaps some interpersonal conflict exists between Joe and Mary. Talk with both of them to determine whether such a conflict exists and, if it does, how it came about. Work with Joe and Mary to help them address and resolve the conflict.

### Delegating to achieve results

Delegation always involves some risk – you have to live with the consequences of someone else's decisions. However, you can take the following steps to improve the person's chances for successful performance:

1. **Clarify what you want to delegate.**

   Describe in unambiguous terms the activity you want the other person to perform and the results you want her to achieve. If necessary, also explain what you *don't* want the person to do.

2. **Choose the right person.**

   Determine the skills and knowledge you feel a person must have to perform the task successfully, and don't delegate the task to a person who lacks the skills and knowledge. (See Chapter 7 for more on describing the skills and knowledge people need to do different jobs.)

3. **Make the delegation correctly.**

   Explain the activity to be performed, the effort you expect the person to expend and the date she should have the activity completed. Put this information in writing for clarity and future reference.

4. **Be available to answer questions.**

   Maintaining contact while the person performs the task allows you to ensure that any ambiguities and unexpected situations encountered are resolved promptly and to your satisfaction. It also conveys to the person that the task is important to you.

5. **Monitor performance.**

   Set up frequent well-defined checkpoints at which you can monitor the person's performance. Then keep to that schedule.

6. **Promptly address problems that arise.**

   If you feel the person's performance isn't satisfactory, discuss your concerns and develop steps to bring it back on track.

# Sharing responsibility

The decision to delegate authority is unilateral; it doesn't require the agreement of both parties. You can choose to give someone the authority to make a decision, whether or not she wants it. After you give your authority to another person, she's free to pass it on to someone else (if you haven't specifically told her not to).

Responsibility is a two-way agreement. Say you ask a team member, Bob, to respond to a customer enquiry, and Bob agrees that he will. Because you and Bob agree that he'll handle the enquiry, Bob can't decide to give the assignment to someone else and then not worry about whether he'll handle it. Bob committed to you that the he would address enquiry; the only way Bob can free himself from this responsibility is to ask you to agree to change your original understanding.

# Holding people accountable when they don't report to you

People who make promises, fail to keep them and then suffer no consequences create some of the worst frustrations in a project environment. Observe these guidelines to encourage people to honour commitments to you:

- ✔ **If you're responsible, you should be held accountable.** In other words, if you make a promise, you should always experience consequences based on how well you keep your promise.

- ✔ **If you're not responsible, you shouldn't be held accountable.** When something goes wrong but you weren't responsible for ensuring that it was handled correctly, you shouldn't face negative consequences. (Of course, you shouldn't receive accolades when it goes well, either.)

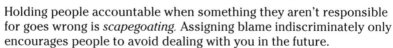

Holding people accountable when something they aren't responsible for goes wrong is *scapegoating*. Assigning blame indiscriminately only encourages people to avoid dealing with you in the future.

When a person who doesn't report to you administratively promises to do something for you, holding her accountable can be a touchy issue. You may not try to hold her accountable, because you think it's inappropriate (after all, you're not her boss) or because you don't know how to do so. But remember: holding people accountable is appropriate and necessary when they've accepted a responsibility. Accountability helps people know that they're on the right track, and it enables you to acknowledge when they've completed the promised assignments. You don't need authority to hold people accountable; the people just have to have accepted the responsibility.

Use the following approaches to hold people accountable when you don't have direct authority over them:

- **Find out who has direct authority over the person and bring that supervisor into the process.** Consider soliciting the approval of the person's boss when you ask the person to accept responsibility for a task. When you do so correctly and at the right time, you can improve the chances of success. If a person's boss is unaware that her staff member agreed to perform a task for you, your chances of getting the boss's help when the person fails to perform as promised are small. However, if the boss supported her staff member's offer to help you when it was made, the boss and her staff member shouldn't be surprised if you solicit the boss's help when the staff member doesn't do the task.

- **Put your agreement in writing.** Have you ever noticed how strangely people react when you put an informal agreement in writing? All of a sudden, they act as if you don't trust them. Don't let this reaction deter you. Put your agreement in writing to confirm it, to clarify the terms and to serve as a reminder to both you and the person agreeing to do the task. If the person asks whether you want to have a written agreement because you don't trust that she'll do what she promises, explain to her that if you didn't trust her, you wouldn't want to work with her!

- **Be specific.** The more clearly you make your request, the easier it is for the person to estimate the effort she needs to make to respond to the request and to produce the right result the first time. You may feel that being too specific is inappropriate because you have no direct authority over her. But recognise that putting a request in writing doesn't make it an order; it just clarifies the specifics and makes it easier for the person to perform the task.

- **Follow up.** Negotiate a schedule to monitor the person's performance and to address any issues or questions that arise. Be sure to agree a follow-up schedule at the outset of the agreement. If you call unannounced at random times, you appear to be checking up because you don't trust the person.

- **Get commitment.** When a person indicates that she'll help you out, be sure to get a firm, specific commitment that the desired result will be achieved by a specific time and for a specific cost. Beware of vague declarations like 'I'll give it my best effort' or 'You can count on me.'

- **Create a sense of urgency and importance.** You may want to minimise any pressure the person feels by offering to *understand* if she can't perform to your expectations because of one reason or another. Unfortunately, this approach can suggest that the work you're asking her to do isn't really that important, and actually increases the chance that she won't complete it. Instead, let the person know how her work influences other activities and people on the project. Let her know why she needs to perform to expectations and what the consequences will be – to the project and the organisation – if she doesn't.

# Showing Roles with a Responsibility Assignment Matrix

Defining and sharing team roles and responsibilities up front can help you improve performance and identify and head off potential difficulties during a project. One way you can display team roles and responsibilities is in a *Responsibility Assignment Matrix* (RAM) – also called a *Linear Responsibility Chart.* This section helps you understand the elements of a RAM, effectively read one, develop your own chart and improve your chart to meet your own needs. Your only limit is your creativity!

A *RACI Chart or Matrix* is a particular type of RAM. The RACI Chart derives its name from the first letters of the four roles most commonly used in the chart: **R**esponsible, **A**ccountable, **C**onsult and **I**nform.

## Introducing the elements of a Responsibility Assignment Matrix (RAM)

The RAM is a table that depicts each project participant's place in the performance of different project activities (see Chapter 11 for more on project roles). The format is as follows (see Figure 12-1, which illustrates a portion of a RAM for designing and conducting a customer needs survey):

- ✔ Project deliverables are in the left-hand column.
- ✔ Project audiences are in the top row.
- ✔ The role a particular audience will play in performing the work to produce a deliverable is shown at each intersection of a row and column.

| Products | | Team Leader | Designer | Team Member | Sales Director |
|---|---|---|---|---|---|
| Prod code | Title | | | | |
| 2.3 | Questionnaire design | | P | S | A |
| 2.4 | Mailing list | A | | P | |
| 2.5 | Questionnaire order | A | | P | |
| 2.6 | Questionnaire results | S | | P | A |

P = Primary responsibility   S = Secondary responsibility   A = Approval

**Figure 12-1:** A RAM displays project roles.

The RAM in Figure 12-1 indicates which of the following three roles people can have in this project's activities:

- ✔ **Primary responsibility (P):** You'll ensure the results are achieved.

- ✔ **Secondary responsibility (S):** You'll ensure some portion of the results is achieved.

- ✔ **Approval (A):** You're not actually working on the deliverable, but you approve the results produced by others who are.

The RAM is just a format; for each project, you define and assign the roles you think are appropriate. You may, for example, decide to use the following roles in addition to the three already defined:

- ✔ **Input (I):** You provide input for the activity work.

- ✔ **Output (O):** You receive products from the activity.

- ✔ **Review (R):** You review and comment on the results of an activity, but your formal approval isn't required.

## Reading a RAM

To illustrate how you read the RAM, consider the deliverable *questionnaire design* in Figure 12-1. The chart suggests that three people work together on this activity as follows:

- ✔ The designer has primary responsibility for the questionnaire's content, format and layout.

- ✔ A team member performs selected parts of the questionnaire design under the general direction and coordination of the designer.

- ✔ The sales director must approve the entire questionnaire, even though she isn't doing any of the actual design or layout herself.

You can analyse any RAM vertically by role and horizontally by activity for situations that may give rise to problems. For an example, have a look at Table 12-1, which notes two observations about the assignments displayed in Figure 12-1 and issues they may suggest. After you identify these situations, you can decide how to address them.

| Table 12-1 | Situations and Issues Suggested in Figure 12-1 |
|---|---|
| *Situation* | *Possible Issues* |
| The sales director is heavily committed. | The sales director won't have time for a thorough review of the questionnaire design. |
| The team member is involved with work on a large number of other, higher priority, projects simultaneously with this one. | The team member won't be able to give the amount of assistance anticipated to the designer and there could be delays in finalising the mailing list, placing the order for the questionnaire printing and collating results. |
| The team leader doesn't get involved until she is asked to approve the funds for printing the questionnaires. | The team leader may slow down the approval process by asking questions about the layout and suitability of the questionnaire. She is being asked to approve funds for the questionnaire, so may feel duty bound to check it out before committing to the spend, despite not having a RAM responsibility for product construction. |

## Ensuring your RAM is accurate

For complex projects, the RAM can be quite large. And keeping the chart current and consulting throughout the project with all the people identified can be time consuming. However, having a chart with incorrect information can result in duplicated efforts and overlooked activities.

Including 50 or more activities on the same RAM can be cumbersome, so consider developing a series of nested charts for larger projects. Prepare a high-level chart that identifies responsibilities for higher-level components in your Project Plan, and then develop separate charts that detail responsibilities for lower-level deliverables in Stage Plans and Delivery Plans. Chapter 9 has more on the planning levels.

# Dealing with Micromanagement

So far, this chapter has looked at working relationships between the Project Manager and those doing the work of the project – the team members – even though that may involve some senior people. This final section looks at the relationship between the Project Manager and sponsor, and focuses on a particular problem that's very common: that of micromanagement from above.

You may be tempted to scream, 'For goodness sake, give me some space and let me get the job done!' However, because that isn't normally a very acceptable way of dealing with your boss, this section unpacks the problem and provides some ideas you can use to help deal with the situation, or at least minimise its effects.

*Micromanagement* is a person's excessive, inappropriate and unnecessary involvement in the details of a task that she asks another person to perform. Micromanagement can lead to inefficient use of personal time and energy, as well as to tension and low morale.

## *Realising why a person micromanages*

Unfortunately, no simple rules define when a person is micromanaging. If you think your boss is getting a little too close for comfort, let her know that you feel that her oversight is a bit excessive. Try to give her some objective indicators to explain why you feel the way you do.

If the person doesn't change, you need to understand why she continues to micromanage you. Think about whether one or more of the following explanations may be the reason, and try the suggested approaches:

✔ **The person is interested in and enjoys the work.** Set up times to discuss interesting technical issues with the person.

✔ **The person is a technical expert and thinks that she can do the job best.** Review your technical work frequently with the person; give the person opportunities to share her technical insights with you.

✔ **The person may think that she didn't explain the assignment clearly or that unexpected situations may crop up.** Set up a schedule to discuss and review your progress frequently so that the micromanager can promptly uncover any mistakes and help you correct them.

✔ **The person is looking for ways to stay involved with you and the team.** Set up scheduled times to discuss project activities. Provide the micromanager with periodic reports of project progress, and make a point of stopping by to say hello periodically.

✔ **The person feels threatened because you have more technical knowledge than she does.** When talking about your project in front of others, always credit the micromanager for her guidance and insights. Share key technical information with the person on a regular basis.

✔ **The person doesn't have a clear understanding of how she should be spending her time.** Discuss with the person the roles she would like you to assume on project activities. Explain how the person can provide useful support as you perform the work.

✔ **The person feels that she has to stay up to date on the work you're doing in case anyone else asks about it.** Discuss with the person what type of information she needs and how frequently she needs it. Develop a schedule to provide progress reports that include this information.

# Helping a micromanager trust you

Your boss may be micromanaging you because she doesn't yet have full confidence in your ability to perform. Instead of being angry or resentful, try one or more of the following steps to help your boss develop that confidence:

✔ **Don't be defensive or resentful when the person asks you questions.** Doing so makes you appear like you're hiding something, which only makes the person worry more. Instead, willingly provide all the information the person asks for.

✔ **Thank the micromanager for her interest, time and technical guidance.** Complaining about what you perceive to be excessive oversight strains your relationship and increases the person's fears and insecurities. After you explain that you value and will incorporate her input, you can try to develop a more acceptable working relationship.

✔ **Offer to explain how you approach your tasks.** Seeing that you perform your work using appropriate, high-quality techniques increases your manager's confidence that you'll successfully complete the assignment she gave you.

✔ **Work with the person to develop a scheme for sharing progress and accomplishments.** Develop meaningful and frequent checkpoints. Frequent monitoring early in your work reassures both of you that you're performing the assignments successfully.

# Working well with a micromanager

You can reduce or even eliminate most micromanagement by improving your communication and strengthening your interpersonal relationships.

Consider the following tips as you work with a micromanager:

✔ **Don't assume.** Don't jump to conclusions. Examine the situation and try to understand the motivations of the person who's micromanaging you.

✔ **Listen.** Listen to the micromanager's questions and comments; see whether patterns emerge. Try to understand her real interests and concerns.

✔ **Observe the person's behavior with others.** If the person micromanages others, the micromanagement likely stems from her feelings rather than from your actions. Try to find ways to address the person's real interests and concerns.

✔ **If at first you don't succeed, try, try again.** If your first attempts to address the situation are unsuccessful, develop an alternative strategy. Keep at it until you succeed.

# Chapter 13

# Being an Effective Leader

*A*fter intense work on a tight schedule, you submit your Project Charter (the document that integrates and consolidates your project's Scope Statement, roles and responsibilities, product and activity plans, resource plans, budget, and all the other control elements; see Chapter 2) for review and approval. A few days later, your boss comes to you and says:

> 'I have some good news and some bad news. Which would you like to hear first?'

> 'Tell me the good news,' you respond.

> 'Your charter's been approved.'

> 'So, what's the bad news?' you ask.

> 'Now you have to do the project!'

Suddenly, it's like everything flashes from two dimensions to three and gets very real. Planning the work is something that, although you consult with other people, you do a lot on your own. Now you're working with others and your success from this point on will depend on their success from this point on! You move from being just a planner to a leader.

This chapter gives you some ideas about leadership in the context of a project and how to get the best out of your team. Doing so isn't just selfish either. Yes, good leadership helps you get your project delivered successfully, but if you do it right, then you also make team members' work enjoyable and allow them to develop and achieve.

# Practising Management and Leadership

Managing is mostly concerned with controlling the work of others and yourself, but leadership throws in a whole new dimension. *Leadership* involves being in front and inspiring others, not just throwing work at them.

Make no mistake: if you're a Project Manager, leadership is a vital part of your role. You can do all of the planning you like, but if the teams don't work well, then you're going to have problems.

The good news is that team members (with a few exceptions) want to do a good job, so you will be working with them, not against them. You know yourself that you are the most satisfied when you have achieved something and done it very well. Your team members feel the same, and there lies one of the keys to effective management: your team members are like you. Too many people go through a strange metamorphosis when they're appointed to a management position, a bit like Jekyll and Hyde or Harry Enfield's sketch of Kevin's 13th birthday when he turns into a teenager.

## Understanding what makes a good leader

To be effective yourself, it helps to stand back a bit and analyse what makes someone a good leader and manager, and also what makes for a bad one. Although this section goes on to spell out the factors, you probably already know most if not all of them from your own experience of being managed.

### Thinking back to your own managers

So, think back to those who've managed you. Who did you like working for? Who managed you so that you could give your very best, and what were the characteristics of their management styles? Then think about managers who weren't so good, who closed you down and made life difficult. What was it about those poor managers that made them poor? We provide a few characteristics in the nearby sidebar 'Management characteristics', but you can add more. Faces will probably come to mind as you consider each characteristic.

'How do I become a good manager?' you might ask. On one level the answer's easy. You emulate the things that you've seen in good managers and avoid the things that you've seen in bad managers. You know the things that helped you give your best, and when you really wanted to do that because you enjoyed what you did, and you also know the sorts of things that closed you down and made you want to give up and go home early.

Just as your managers have had a huge impact (positive and negative) on the volume and quality of your work in the past, so too you can expect to have a huge impact on the work of your staff.

# Management characteristics

Good managers:

✔ Are cool headed and rational when problems crop up

✔ Are supportive and available

✔ Give opportunities and challenges

✔ Have a clear sense of direction and communicate objectives well

✔ Have a sense of proportion so minor problems aren't treated as crises

✔ Plan well so their staff aren't forever racing to meet unrealistic deadlines

✔ Recognise and show appreciation of good work and extra effort

✔ Respect their staff

✔ Trust and give responsibility

✔ Value the views of the staff, even if the manager finally disagrees sometimes

Bad managers:

✔ Are control freaks and micromanagers

✔ Are emotional, including regularly getting angry and having emotional highs and lows

✔ Are power hungry and play power games

✔ Don't listen to their staff

✔ Focus on the task only – at the expense of the staff

✔ Find fault and apportion blame if things go wrong, and even if they don't

✔ Take all the credit for achievements

## *Leading in the hard times too*

Some people think that leadership is great and people will follow if you're going somewhere nice and the journey there will be pleasant. That's not true, however, and leaders can inspire people to follow them and endure even hardship. One of the best examples has to be Winston Churchill, who on being appointed Prime Minister in a time of war said to the House of Commons: 'We have before us an ordeal of the most grievous kind.' That statement was immediately preceded by his famous words, 'I would say to the House, as I said to those who have joined the Government: I have nothing to offer but blood, toil, tears and sweat.' Churchill was an inspiring leader, and although not many people are gifted to that extent, you can still provide good leadership on tough tasks as well as easier ones.

## *Leading team members who are older and/or more senior than you*

It can be difficult to lead if team members are senior to you in experience and also in age. It may help to remember that projects are all about roles. Your role is to manage. That doesn't mean that you're inferior or superior to any team member, just that your role is different. Chapter 11 is all about project roles and their significance.

One of the characteristics listed for good managers in the sidebar 'Management characteristics' is having respect for team members. You can respect someone's knowledge, age and experience, and indeed you should. But that doesn't mean you can't project-manage the person. You've been appointed to the post, so get on and manage with skill and confidence, irrespective of the seniority or otherwise of those on your teams.

# Developing personal power and influence

To get a job done you need authority, and it will help you in the project if you think through just where that authority comes from. In turn, authority gives you a sense of personal power in the best sense. Not a power that rides roughshod over others, but a power that gives you a calm confidence. Some people have that naturally, the sort of people for whom everyone looks up when they enter a room. Others need to develop that air of leadership. Although this book is not primarily about management and leadership, the next two sections give you a couple of pointers that may help you with leadership within the project.

### Understanding why people will do as you ask

The very title *Project Manager* gives authority and everyone knows that the Project Manager has day-to-day responsibility for the project. A natural respect and compliance follows from Team Leaders and team members who can see from the project organisation structure, even if they haven't already realised, that they're accountable to you. Unless you give the teams reason to challenge that inbuilt authority, then you can expect it to stand. Reasons why the teams may challenge your authority are if you lead badly and give instructions that they can't follow, or if you incite them to rebellion! However, if you plan carefully, consult fully and are open to hearing views and ideas from your teams, then you're unlikely to be opposed in such a way.

Because personal power is the ability to influence and guide the actions of others, the first step in developing this power is understanding why people choose to do what you ask in the first place. People respond to your requests and directions for many reasons, including the following:

- **Rewards:** People do what you ask because they want the benefits you can give them. Examples of rewards include pay rises and recognition.

- **Punishments:** People do what you ask because they *don't* want what you can give them. Examples of punishments include poor performance appraisals and negative feedback to line managers.

- **What you stand for:** People do what you ask because they agree with your goals. They know that your requests and actions are attempts to achieve the same results they want to achieve.

✔ **Who you are:** People listen to you because they appreciate and respect who you are, as reflected by your sensitivity, your loyalty to others, your sense of humour or other positive characteristics of your attitudes and behaviours.

✔ **Your expertise:** People listen to you because they respect the skills and knowledge that you bring to your job. They listen to you because they believe you're probably right.

✔ **Your position:** People take your requests more seriously because they think the Project Manager should direct team members. You can lose this power if you behave inappropriately, but you have it initially.

You don't have to be the technical expert on your project to command the respect of your team members and effectively lead your project. But you do have to be an expert in the skills and knowledge that your job demands on the project. Because you're the Project Manager, these skills and knowledge include your abilities to plan and control the project, encourage effective communication, encourage a positive and productive work environment, and understand the political environment in your overall organisation.

Of course, your technical expertise can be a significant asset if you use it correctly. Your praise for a job well done means a lot more to your team members than praise from someone who's less qualified to assess the work.

Take note that being both the technical expert and the Project Manager on your project can work against you. If you're not careful, you can discourage others from accepting responsibilities and performing their work independently, for one or more of the following reasons:

✔ They feel that their work can never be as good as yours.

✔ You keep the more challenging and important assignments for yourself, because you like the work and think you can do it better.

✔ You resist approaches that differ from the ones you normally take.

✔ You tend to want people to perform assignments just as you would.

Although many factors can contribute to your ability to influence people, your power over your team members is generally one of the following:

✔ **Achieved:** You earn the respect and allegiance of other people.

✔ **Ascribed:** Someone gives you authority.

Achieved power is far more effective and longer lasting than ascribed power. People who act in response to your ascribed power usually do the least amount of work necessary to get the rewards they want or to avoid the consequences they fear. On the other hand, people motivated by your achieved power work to accomplish the highest possible quality of results because they've decided that doing so is in their best interests (and yours).

### Understanding the base of your authority

As the captain of the ship (see Chapter 11 on project organisation), you have initial authority on two grounds:

- ✔ **Appointment:** Unless your project is very small and in your own area of work, more senior managers will have appointed you to the role of Project Manager. That appointment itself displays their confidence in you and reflects an authority within the organisation.

- ✔ **Delegation:** This project is being run for the organisation, not your own ends, and was commissioned by a sponsor or perhaps even a more senior group such as a management board. You're running the project on behalf of those who commissioned it, and therefore you have their authority, not just your own.

Both of these grounds add to your confidence in your position because you're backed by authority that is higher than your current position. That point should help too when you come to manage more senior people who are working on your project.

# Knowing What Motivates, and also What Demotivates

To have a healthy project that stays on schedule, you need motivated staff who will work well in terms of the quantity of work they do in a given period and the quality of it. Remember, if the quality is poor, that affects the project schedule as well as the end product, because of all the correction and re-testing. So what makes for good motivation on teams and within the project as a whole?

## Taking a lesson from Fred Herzberg

There have been many books and theories on motivation over the years, but one of the simplest and most powerful models is from Fred Herzberg (1923–2000), an American psychologist who became a leading light in management practice. Fred Herzberg's model is great for management, and is highly relevant for creating productive project teams.

Herzberg says that people will normally give an average performance – something he calls *the potter line*, where people potter along doing what they think is a fair day's work for a fair day's pay. Things like money, good working conditions and company cars, he argues, won't motivate people to give more than an average performance.

You may know yourself, if you have a company car, for example, that when you first got it you were delighted. But very quickly it became part of your normal environment and now you jump into the car and rarely think about when you didn't have it. It's the same with any pay rise you had a year ago – that level of pay has now become normal. Fred Herzberg called things like fair pay, good working conditions and company benefits *hygiene factors.*

Where Herzberg differs from many management experts is where he says you can't neglect these hygiene factors or you drag performance down below the potter line. You need to have good working conditions for your teams, so fight hard to get them if you need to. Try to make sure that team members are paid properly for the work they do. However, important though these things are, they don't motivate.

Herzberg argues that the *motivators* are things like achievement, recognition, doing sensible and worthwhile work, having responsibility, moving on in a career with promotion, and having opportunity for personal growth. It's those things that make people, including you, perform above the potter line.

Clearly, then, if you want good team performance you need to build opportunities for achievement and personal growth into the way that you allocate your project work. If you always give someone boring, meaningless work that provides no interest or challenge, don't be surprised if your project performance indicators show that person pottering along and not having the drive and productivity you're really looking for. If he's paid poorly and sitting on a broken chair in a drab, beaten-up office as well, then you can confidently look forward to productivity well below the potter line.

Look out for interesting work that isn't on your project's critical path and so has some slack time (see Chapter 6 for full details on the critical path). This work is ideal for giving someone a new challenge, because if they take a bit longer than someone already experienced in the task, it won't damage the project schedule. If you do that you don't get win–win, but win– win–win! Your team members develop and they enjoy their work; they're more motivated overall, so you get better performance and the organisation gets staff with a wider skill set and more experience, which will benefit future projects. A secondary level of benefit is that your team members see that you're looking out for them, not just focusing on the project with no thought for them.

## *Understanding points of demotivation*

Predictable points of demotivation exist. Just like Hertzberg's motivators (see the previous section), this information is valuable indeed when planning work and can prevent real problems with team performance. Figure 13-1 shows a demotivation model, which has three elements:

> ✔ Doing the work
>
> ✔ Seeing the result
>
> ✔ Getting recognition and also reward

A break between any of those three components leads to demotivation.

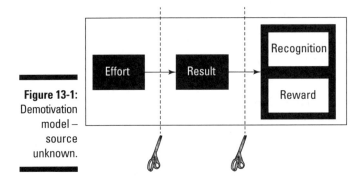

**Figure 13-1:**
Demotivation
model –
source
unknown.

Working hard but not seeing a result is demotivating. Taking the opposite perspective, a research scientist who keeps on experimenting but doesn't see any result for some years has to be very highly motivated to keep going. Or, someone puts in the effort, sees the result and then . . . nothing. Nobody notices and nobody offers any reward for all of that effort – that's demotivating and is highly likely to affect performance adversely on future tasks.

As a Project Manager you can do something about both break points and so do much to avoid demotivation. First, considering Herzberg's point in the last section about meaningful work, try to design tasks on your project so that team members see an end result. Then, when that result is forthcoming, give recognition and, if it's within your power, reward. You can at least recognise achievements, even if you can't influence reward. The earlier sidebar 'Management characteristics' listed recognising and showing appreciation of work and extra effort as attributes of a good manager.

## *Ensuring that others are on board*

Other people may also play a role in your project's success, even though they may not officially be members of a project team. Two such groups fall within the stakeholder category (see Chapter 4 for more on stakeholder management), and you can think of them as *drivers* (people who have a say in defining the results of your project) and *supporters* (people who will perform a service or provide resources for your project).

Contact your stakeholders to:

- ✔ Inform them that your project has been approved and when work will start.

- ✔ Reaffirm your project's objectives.

- ✔ Let them know, at regular intervals, about progress and achievements to date.

- ✔ Confirm the resources you need from them, and the dates when you will need them. If there are slight changes (perhaps the project is a bit ahead of schedule), consult to see whether their provision of resource can be changed to be earlier too, so as to maintain the lead.

- ✔ Confirm the project completion date as you get towards the end of the project, particularly if one or more of your stakeholders needs to make preparations for that.

Some people will be interested in your project but won't define its planned results or directly support your efforts. Identify these *observers*, as they're often called – the individuals you want to keep informed of your progress throughout the project – and plan how you'll communicate with them.

# Developing Your Teams

Merely assigning people to tasks doesn't create a project team. A *team* is a collection of people who are committed to common goals and who depend on one another to do their jobs. Project teams consist of members who can and must make a valuable and unique contribution to the project.

Just how much involvement you will have in creating effective teams depends on the nature and particularly the size of your project. If you're in a large project, you will have Team Leaders who are primarily responsible for the teambuilding aspects. However, even then, you have a role in establishing a project identity and encouraging Team Leaders in their teambuilding work. You may even get involved in assisting with the teambuilding such as by going along to give project briefings. If you do have Team Leaders, your leadership role must tread the normal careful path in management of being supportive and engaged on the one hand but not interfering or undermining Team Leader authority on the other. In a smaller project, you may be running the team, and in that case the teambuilding work falls entirely to you.

A team is different from other associations of people who work together. For example:

- ✔ A *group* consists of people who work individually to accomplish their particular assignments on a common task.

✔ A *committee* consists of people who come together to review and critique issues, propose recommendations for action and, on occasion, implement those recommendations.

## Defining your project operating processes

Develop the procedures that you and your teams will use to support the day-to-day work. Having these procedures in place allows people to effectively and efficiently perform their tasks, and to know how to communicate. In turn, that clarity will help avoid misunderstanding and conflict and will contribute to a positive atmosphere in the project. At a minimum, develop procedures for the following:

✔ **Communication:** These processes involve sharing project-related information in writing and verbally. Communication procedures may include:

- How to address special issues that arise, such as on technical matters involved with the development

- How to set up regularly scheduled reports and meetings to record and review progress, warn of problems and newly identified risks, and communicate suggestions and ideas

- When and how to document informal discussions

- When and how to use email to share project information

- Which types of information should be in writing, and what can be reported or discussed verbally

✔ **Conflict resolution:** These processes involve resolving differences of opinion between teams regarding project work. You can develop the following conflict-resolution procedures:

- *Standard approaches* (normal steps that teams take to find a solution)

- *Escalation procedures* (steps to take if the people involved can't readily resolve their differences)

✔ **Decision making:** These processes involve deciding among alternative approaches and actions. Develop guidelines for choosing the most appropriate approach for a situation, including consensus, majority rule, unanimous agreement and decision by technical expert. Also develop escalation procedures – the steps you take when the normal decision-making approaches get bogged down.

Think long and very hard to keep written information to the minimum. Written communications all contribute to project overheads and also sap your team members' energies if they're forever having to complete project documentation instead of getting on with the job. Turn to Chapter 15 for more on the whole area of project communications.

Government figures in 2010 showed that UK police officers spent, on average, 20 per cent of their time filling in forms and only 14 per cent actually out on patrol, their key front-line activity. Be careful and monitor how much of your own time and that of your project staff is consumed in project overheads rather than in delivering the project's products.

## Helping your teams become smooth-functioning units

When team members trust each other, have confidence in each other's abilities, can count on each other's promises and communicate openly, they can devote all their efforts to performing their project work instead of spending time dealing with interpersonal frustrations. One approach to help teams achieve this high-performance level of functioning is guiding them through the following commonly used phases:

- **Forming:** This phase involves meeting team members and discussing project objectives, work assignments and so forth. Share the Project Plan, introduce people to each other, and discuss each person's background, organisational responsibilities and areas of expertise. Unless your project involves a lot of people, forming is something you may want to do project-wide, not just within each team.

- **Storming:** This stage involves raising and resolving personal conflicts about the project or other team members. As part of the storming stage, do the following:

    - Encourage people to discuss any concerns they have about the Project Plan's feasibility, and be sure you address those concerns.

    - Encourage people to discuss any reservations they may have about working in the team and with others in the team. For example, a junior team member may feel nervous being surrounded by highly qualified specialists who clearly know exactly what they're doing.

    - Focus these discussions on ways to ensure successful task performance.

You can initially speak privately with people about issues if they're uncomfortable about bringing them up in front of the entire team. Eventually, though, you must discuss their concerns with the entire team to achieve a sense of mutual honesty and trust.

- **Norming:** This stage involves developing the standards and operating guidelines that govern team members' behaviour. Encourage members to establish these team norms instead of relying on the procedures and practices they use in their functional areas. Examples of these norms include the following:

- **How people present and discuss different points of view:** Some people present points of view politely to the point of understating them, and others enthusiastically debate with their opponents to the point of appearing aggressive as they work to resolve points.

- **Participation in meetings:** Some people sit back and observe, and others actively participate and share their ideas. The norm will be to encourage active participation – why have a meeting when you could have sent an email?

- **Timeliness of meeting attendance:** Some people always show up for meetings on time, but others are habitually 15 minutes late. Set the norm for this project, which of course will normally be that people show up on time, or everyone's time is wasted.

At a team meeting, encourage people to discuss how team members should behave in different situations. Address the concerns people express, and encourage the group to adopt team norms.

✔ **Performing:** This stage involves doing project work, monitoring schedules and budgets, making necessary changes and keeping people informed.

As you guide your team through these developmental stages, keep in mind the following guidelines:

✔ **Teams won't automatically pass through these stages; they have to be guided.** Left on their own, teams often fail to move beyond the forming stage. Many people don't like to confront thorny interpersonal issues, for example, so they simply ignore them. The Team Leader's job is to make sure that team members address what needs to be addressed and become a smooth-functioning team.

✔ **Your involvement as Project Manager needs to be heavier in the early stages and lighter in the later ones.** During the forming phase, if you're responsible for the team, you need to take the lead as new people join. Then, in the storming stage, you take a strong facilitative role as you guide and encourage people to share their feelings and concerns. Although you can help guide the team as it develops its standards and norms during the norming stage, your main emphasis is to ensure that everyone participates in the process. Finally, if you've navigated the first three stages successfully, you can step back in the performing stage and offer your support as the team demonstrates its ability to function as a high-performing unit.

✔ **On occasion, you may have to revisit a stage you thought the team had completed.** For example, a new person may join the team, or a major aspect of the project may change.

✔ **If everything goes smoothly on your project, it doesn't matter whether the team has successfully gone through the forming, storming and norming stages.** But if the project runs into problems, your teams may become dysfunctional if they haven't progressed successfully through each phase. Suppose, for example, that the team misses a major project deadline. If team members haven't developed trust for one another, they're more likely to spend time searching for someone to blame than working together to fix the situation.

✔ **As the Project Manager, you need to periodically assess how the teams feel they're performing.** Again, if you're working with Team Leaders then you may want to do this mostly through them by checking things out at a Team Leaders' meeting. But nothing is as good as a first-hand view, so schedule time to go and see how each team is getting on – adopt the MBWA style, which is *management by walking about.* You don't have to say much except to encourage and show interest, but you can observe. Here are a few pointers:

- Are the team members upbeat and cheerful, or are they downcast and gloomy?

- Do the team members show an active interest in the work when you ask them about it, or are there signs of disengagement and just 'going through the motions'?

- Are they working together, or is everyone isolated and working on their own, even where they are supposed to be building products together?

- Is the work area organised and tidy, or cluttered and disorganised?

- How do team members seem to relate to the Team Leader? Is it happily as a colleague or are there signs of reluctant obedience or even disrespect? For example, if you see the Team Leader speak to a team member, perhaps to ask something, what does the team member do when the Team Leader turns away? (Watch out of the corner of your eye – don't look directly.) Does the team member simply get on with the work, or does he look across at another team member and raise his eyes to the sky?

If your organisation works a standard day, try calling into a team room at the normal finish time. Is everyone keen to get out on the dot or just before, or are they still working to finish a job, showing commitment to the task? Be careful with this check, though, because it doesn't work in all countries. In some cultures, people stick very much to standard work hours out of respect for family life, and this doesn't indicate any lack of commitment to the project. In those same cultures, out-of-hours social events for project staff aren't welcomed either, and for the same reason.

## *Harnessing conflict*

It's a common mistake to think of conflict as always being something bad. If conflict is destructive, then certainly it's negative, but positive conflict also exists. *Positive conflict* is where two team members disagree and fight it out, but both thoroughly respect the other's view, and often both have great fun arguing the point through. This sort of conflict drives analysis deep, and when the outcome is finally agreed, both team members are fully confident in it.

Strangely, people who get on together too easily, who tend to see things the same way or who cave in at the first hint of an opposing view can end up with a superficial result that hasn't been properly thought through or challenged. However, the conflict is time consuming, so who you put on a task depends on the importance of that task, how soon you want it finished, and how important it is for the outcome to be right. A critical design product may justify putting staff on to the work who are going to see things differently and who are strong characters; they'll go deep. Deciding in which order to paint the three inner walls of the stationery cupboard probably doesn't justify too much in the way of conflict and deep discussion. So, yet another dimension for your resource planning – there's a lot to project management, isn't there?

If you don't have team members who see things differently, you can engineer the situation by getting one to play devil's advocate. This is where one person deliberately throws everything he can think of against a product, such as a design, to see whether the other person can counter the arguments. Or you can get everyone to take on the negative stance to try to spot the problems with an idea or a design product. For more on the negative stance, you might like to read about the *black hat* thinking style in Edward de Bono's book *Six Thinking Hats*, published by Penguin, or check out Edward de Bono's website for a short explanation.

# Stoking the Boilers

A final word about leadership and motivation is a reminder to keep your teams well motivated and encouraged throughout the project, not just build them up at the start. Particular points to watch out for aren't when things are very busy and lots of products are being delivered, but rather the quieter times when a lot of work is being done but there isn't much to show for it yet. That's a key time to go around encouraging and showing appreciation.

## Letting people know how they're doing

Getting your team members to appreciate your project's value and feasibility helps you build initial enthusiasm. However, if the project lasts longer than a couple of weeks, the team's initial momentum can die without continual reinforcement from you. In general, people working on a particular task need to know how they're doing over time for three reasons:

✔ Achieving intermediate milestones provides personal and group satisfaction.

✔ Recognising their successes confirms to people that they're on the right track and motivates them.

✔ Successfully completing intermediate steps reinforces people's belief that they can accomplish the final goals.

To keep people abreast of their progress:

✔ Use frequent milestones to show progress. Chapter 5 on product planning gives you a particularly powerful and visual way of showing progress.

✔ Continually assess how people are doing.

✔ Frequently share information with people about their performance.

✔ Continually reinforce the project's potential benefits.

## Motivating people when they leave

Rewarding and recognising team members' work through the project confirms to them that they're achieving the desired results. It also reassures them that team members and managers recognise and appreciate their contributions.

You should also give recognition and reward at the end of the project. This is really sensible for three reasons:

✔ **The team members deserve it.** They've been part of the project's success and deserve the recognition and reward that comes with that.

✔ **Recognition makes it more likely that team members will welcome the opportunity to participate in future projects.** If you really build staff up as they leave, just imagine the positive attitude they'll have if they come into one of your future projects.

✔ **You gain a reputation for being an appreciative manager.** That way even people who have never worked with you before will have a positive attitude when they join one of your future projects, and your initial work to build enthusiasm will be half done already.

To make sure that the recognition and rewards you offer are effective:

✔ Be sure your acknowledgment and appreciation is honest and sincere.

✔ Note the specific contribution that each team member has made.

✔ Respect the person's personal style and preferences when giving a reward:

- Some people enjoy receiving acknowledgements in front of their co-workers; others prefer receiving them in private.

- Some people appreciate receiving an individual award; others appreciate receiving an award presented to the entire team.

## Keeping your finger on the pulse

It's important to build a trusting relationship with your Team Leaders so that they know that you won't be undermining their authority as you go round to see what teams are doing. If you spot problems, take them to the Team Leader and be very careful not to start giving instructions to individual team members that run counter to what a Team Leader has said to do. With that normal management stance in place, you can then go and talk to individual team members without Team Leaders thinking that they're being bypassed or that their authority is being undermined.

Ongoing contact with individual team members does a lot to keep cohesion and a sense of belonging in a project, and avoid the Project Manager seeming to be some superior being who never comes near the real work of the project. But the communication is a two-way street. You can also keep your finger on the pulse and see for yourself how the teams are doing, which may or may not align with the hard data in the teams' progress reports.

# Part IV
# Steering the Project to Success

'We thought by giving you a special uniform to wear as project manager, Ponsonby, would give you more authority with your team.'

## *In this part . . .*

*I*t's one thing planning out a project and printing it off in full colour for everyone to admire. It's quite another when the project starts and things begin to go a little differently, where other people get involved and somebody decides they want a change . . . or two.

Project control is essential to keep the project on track and heading towards successful delivery. This part covers ways of monitoring progress and keeping in control, dealing with change and the vital area of communications – keeping information flowing through the project – and then bringing the project to an orderly close.

# Chapter 14

# Tracking Progress and Staying in Control

## In This Chapter

▶ Monitoring progress against the plan

▶ Checking up on spending against the plan

▶ Making corrections to keep on track

▶ Controlling change

*H*aving planned your project and started it off, you now need to keep your eye on the ball and keep it on track. All projects experience problems, but far too many Project Managers don't detect that things are off the plan until the deviation is severe. At that point it's much harder, and sometimes impossible, to put right. It's a bit like walking across some open moorland. If you go a couple of degrees off course and you detect this quickly, you need take only a few steps to get back on track. If you don't find out for several hours that you deviated by two degrees . . . well, you get the picture. When you run your project, you can be very sure of one thing: it won't go exactly to plan. That makes it all the more important to identify deviations from the plan promptly so that you can react quickly and make the necessary corrections.

The really good news is that if you've followed the approach to planning set down in this book, you have an easy but particularly clear progress-monitoring tool available to you. Chapter 5 covers this rather different start to project planning, which is *product based*; it begins the plan with a focus on what's to be *produced* or delivered. In turn, the product-based planning approach opens the door to very effective progress control.

In this chapter, then, look forward to see how you can track progress quickly and effectively, and look at your options when things don't quite go to plan. You can also expect some very real help in controlling change in the project and avoiding that common project killer, scope creep. If you put into practice what you read in this chapter, you may not eliminate scope creep, but you'll certainly go a long way towards it.

# Understanding What Underpins Effective Progress Control

There are three key underpinning elements for effective progress control. Those key things are having a good plan, having clear and frequent milestones and then putting in place an effective progress-reporting mechanism. This section covers each element in turn.

## Having a reliable plan

Knowing that projects just about always go off track could lead the less well informed – and organisational managers anxious for project teams to get on with the 'real work' – to think that it's not worth spending much time on planning. As you almost certainly realise, though, the complete opposite is true. The fact that the project is going to go off plan means that the plan is even more important; in fact, planning is essential.

When a large ship sets out on a voyage, it has a sail plan that shows the planned course to the destination port. However, this course is the one route the ship is guaranteed not to follow. Winds and water currents will push the ship off course. However, the planned course is all the more important because that's what the ship will constantly correct to in order to ensure that it arrives safely at its destination. So, too, with a project: you need a plan in order to exercise control and make corrections.

You need a plan, then, but not just any plan; it's got to be reliable. If the plan itself is unrealistic, incomplete and superficial, then clearly it's going to be next to useless for control. The plan isn't just some luxury that, in an ideal world, projects really should have if they have the time to create them. In addition to establishing what the project is about, when it will deliver and what it will cost, the plan is also fundamental to effective control.

The plan must also be up to date, within a few days at least. If something is reported as off track, then you need to be able to assess the impact and work out your options. If you last updated the plan seven weeks ago, it isn't going to be a lot of help in planning where to go from here, because you won't know where 'here' is. Get into the discipline of updating your plan once a week with 'actuals' of what has been delivered, the timings of those deliveries and what resource, including staff time, has been expended.

# *Having clear and frequent milestones*

To know for sure where you are, you need milestones – and it helps to have a lot of them. Having a lot of milestones means that you have a superb early warning system if things do start going off track. The deliverables or products in each stage form natural milestones and so provide an excellent foundation for progress control. Chapter 5 of this book, on product-based planning, advises you to have 15–30 defined products for project, broken down into more detail in the Stage Plans to give 15–30 at the stage level of detail. (More on stages in Chapter 9.) The importance of having frequent milestones becomes increasingly clear as you read on in this chapter.

Other sources of project advice have different things to say about milestones. One approach devised by a major management consultancy advises having four or five milestones in your project. The 2009 edition of the PRINCE2 project method manual advises not having every product as a milestone. If you come across that sort of advice, just smile to yourself, nod knowingly . . . and then ignore it. If you do only have four or five milestones in the whole project, an awful lot can go wrong before you get to find out for sure where you are. You can only project-manage what's ahead of you. You can't project-manage what's behind: it's gone and it's too late. With frequent milestones, if something slips, you know quickly. Now, if the milestones represented a lot of work, then the advice to have only a few of them might almost have been worth listening to. In fact, with the approach set down in this book with products used as milestones, you have the huge advantage that the milestones are virtually no work at all.

Where you are using a computer-based project management tool to maintain a Project Plan, it will almost certainly track progress using *percentage complete* for each activity. You'll see in Figure 14-1 that the percentage complete is shown with the solid bar in the middle of the activity bar filling up like a thermometer. So, with the project in Figure 14-1 it looks like things are a bit ahead, if you believe the percentage complete. You can find more on percentage complete and its drawbacks later in the chapter.

**Milestone/activities**

**12. Initial design**
　12.1 Interview staff
　12.2 Review requirements
　12.3 Draw up Initial design

**13. Final design**
　13.1 Collect comments
　13.2 Amend Initial Design
　13.3 Circulate Final Design
　13.4 Sign off Final Design

**Figure 14-1:** Product delivery and percentage complete shown in combination.

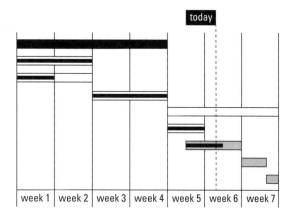

When you do use a computer tool, you can use it in combination with having products as milestones. Figure 14-1 illustrates one way of showing the products. Here the products are the numbered headings, and the activities to build the products are grouped below each one.

## Having an effective reporting mechanism

Clearly, you aren't going to have good progress control without an effective reporting mechanism accompanying it to show you when the project reaches milestones. If you aren't using products, despite the approach in this book, then you'll need regular estimates of progress from those doing the work. If you use products as milestones, then you need a mechanism to advise when products are delivered and so the milestones are achieved.

By the way, a product is only *complete* when it's been quality checked and signed off. If a product hasn't passed the test yet, it isn't complete.

# Harnessing Product Power for Progress Control

The progress-tracking mechanism of percentage complete on activities does have some problems. The mechanism is known to be unreliable because at best it's based on an estimate and at worst team members exaggerate the progress they've made. Using products as a progress measure avoids the problems of estimation for progress reports. With products, progress isn't a matter of estimation but a matter of factual reporting. Which products are complete (quality checked and signed off) and which aren't? That gives you – and the project sponsor or steering committee – an accurate, factual statement of exactly where you are in the stage and in the project.

## Compiling a Work Checklist

A *Work Checklist*, sometimes known as a *Product Checklist*, is an extraordinarily simple device, but a very powerful one. It's just a list of products to be produced in a stage, together with the products' target delivery dates and then, when they are complete, their actual delivery dates. You can also add a column for the variance between the two. Table 14-1 gives an example.

| Table 14-1 | The Work Checklist | | |
|---|---|---|---|
| *Work Checklist – Stage 6 – Position at 7 July* | | | |
| *Product* | *Target Delivery* | *Actual Delivery* | *Days +/–* |
| Inner gears | 12 June | 15 June | –3 |
| Power and fuse housing | 20 June | 20 June | 0 |
| Feeder tubes | 3 July | 3 July | 0 |
| Control panel | 8 July | 6 July | +2 |
| Conveyor mechanism | 12 July | | |
| Assembled rotor unit | 20 July | | |

Even if, surprisingly, you don't have intimate engineering knowledge of inner gears or rotor units, you can nevertheless see at a glance where this stage is. The checklist shows clearly what has been delivered, when, and how the date compares with that on the plan. At the moment, things are looking good because it seems the work is a couple of days ahead after being a bit behind plan at the start of the stage. Remember, a completed product is one that has been quality checked and signed off, so with the Work Checklist you know that products have been confirmed as meeting their specified quality requirements; it's not that they have been thrown together and finished in a hurry to meet a deadline.

Most experienced Project Managers agree that the first sign of trouble on a project isn't overspending, as many assume, but rather slippage on delivery. In that context of delivery, the Work Checklist gives even more value as a monitoring tool.

## Getting visual with the Work Flow Diagram

Chapter 5 on product planning shows how to create an extremely useful diagram, the Work Flow Diagram. You can use this diagram in all sorts of ways in the project, but it's relevant here because you can adapt it to form a very simple and highly visual progress report. The idea came from Philipp Straehl, co-author of the PRIME project management method (more on this in Chapter 2), who first used it on a £15 million project and with great success.

The Work Flow Diagram shows the products to be produced in the order that they'll be created. Philipp had the idea of including Work Checklist information in the Work Flow Diagram and then colour-coding the symbols. Flip back to Chapter 5 and have a look at Figure 5-5 to see an example of the Work Flow Diagram showing the product status with shading.

Now you've seen the Work Checklist and the progress-annotated Work Flow Diagram, you can fully understand why frequent milestones are a great idea and why all products should be milestones. It isn't onerous jotting down the date of delivery of a product and altering the colour of its symbol on the Work Flow, and in return you have extraordinarily precise progress-tracking information based on factual reporting of products states (not-complete or complete), not on someone's guess of percentage complete on an activity.

## Monitoring at project, stage and Work Package levels

Monitoring and reporting progress is often at stage level. However, sometimes project sponsors, steering committee members and others in the organisation such as a management board like to see project-level progress – the big picture. That's no problem, and you can colour-code the Work Flow Diagram (see the previous section) in the project-level plan as well as the stage-level diagrams.

Equally, if a team is working on a complex *Work Package* – a work assignment to build a product or a group of related products – the Team Manager may well have drawn up a more detailed plan. This lower level plan will include a Work Flow Diagram at a more detailed level still than the stage-level plan. If there is a lower-level Work Flow Diagram, this too can be used for progress monitoring where the Project Manager is keeping tabs on the progress of individual Work Packages.

# Taking Action When Things Go Off Track

And yes, the word *when* and not *if* appears in the title of this section. Projects are always going into the unknown to some extent, and we can almost guarantee that your project won't go exactly the way you thought. So, that's some important good news for you! If your project doesn't go exactly to plan, don't panic: that's normal.

When the project does go off track, you need to follow these five steps:

1. **Find out why the project is off track.**

2. **Look at all the things you could do to bring the project back on track.**

3. **Decide which action or actions you're going to take.**

4. **Take the action you have decided on.**

5. **Monitor to see whether the actions are working. If the steps are not working, go back to step 1 to find out why, and then follow the other steps through again.**

The rest of this section will explore these steps in more detail.

In a panic, Project Managers often leave out the first two steps and jump into step 3, but that's a big mistake. It's all too easy to rush into an action when actually that action isn't the easiest, cheapest or most effective. Knee-jerk reactions are rarely the best ones when dealing with project problems.

Nick Graham has a small project management training and consultancy company, but he boasts he has a boardroom that's bigger than those in even the largest multinational companies. It's Chesil Beach in Dorset, which is 12 miles long with the sea on one side and the Fleet, a marine lagoon, on the other! When he wants to think something through, he walks along the beach, well beyond where anyone else is, and sits on the pebbles looking at the waves rippling across the blue sea, the sun shining overhead and the seagulls circling. He can think there. You need a 'Chesil Beach' to retreat to when you need to think carefully before springing into action.

## *Finding out why the project is off track*

When you hit a problem, first look for the underlying causes and try to understand the characteristics of the problem. This may well involve talking to a Team Leader or two and perhaps some team members and external supplier specialists. In the case of a problem affecting the overall running of the project, perhaps it would be good to have an informal chat with the sponsor or one or two members of the project steering committee as well.

It's only when you properly understand both the characteristics and the causes of deviations from the plan that you can come up with sensible corrective actions.

If your project goes off track, it probably isn't anybody's fault. It's simply that the project isn't going in exactly the same way as you anticipated on the plan. You need your team members on board to keep the project momentum going and probably to help solve the problem. If you're disappointed – or even worried – about a problem, try not to translate that into a negative approach to your team. If you do show irritation or even anger, for example to a supplier who's let you down and doesn't seem very bothered about it, let that be as a considered action. Deliberately showing anger should be an ultimate tool to communicate the importance of a failure and to help prevent recurrence. It shouldn't be an ill-considered outburst, driven by frustration, that will probably only serve to make things worse.

When your project is going off track, you need to both identify the causes and understand the characteristics of the problem. When doing your initial analysis, consider the following (they're in no particular order):

- ✔ Is the project going off track or is it that the project is 'right' but the plan is unrealistic? You may need to adjust the plans for the rest of the project in the light of this experience.

- ✔ Is this a problem with planned work, or has extra necessary work been discovered that wasn't anticipated on the plan? This problem is made less likely if you have done the 'bottom up' checks on the Work Flow Diagram described in Chapter 5. The problem is more likely if you have only done activity planning (see Chapter 6).

- ✔ Is there a problem because the work requires more effort than expected, or is the work estimate right and the problem that the team members haven't been able to put in the planned time? For example, have team members been called away repeatedly to do unforeseen operational, non-project, work?

- ✔ Are the team members going more slowly than expected because of unfamiliarity and inexperience? Would it help to ask for more experienced staff, or would the learning curve of new staff getting to understand the project only make things worse still?

- ✔ Have the teams been held up because necessary equipment isn't available? For example, have delays in other projects held up the release of equipment needed for this one?

- ✔ Is the problem because something is more complicated than anticipated? Does that mean that other products will also be more complicated?

- ✔ Is this problem a one-off problem that affects only this part of the work? Or is the problem the first sign that everything is going to take longer than expected; in other words, are the estimates understated through the whole of the project?

- ✔ Is the cause of the problem something you can control or is it, by its very nature, outside your control, such as higher than normal sickness levels due to a particularly nasty bug circulating?

- ✔ Is the activity on a critical path? Delayed activities on a critical path will delay your overall project schedule (see Chapter 6 for a detailed discussion of critical paths). If the activity is on the critical path, you'll need to take more extensive control action than if it has spare time that can absorb some or all of the delay.

- ✔ Is the activity on a path that's close to being critical? Activities on non-critical paths can have some delays before their paths become critical. The maximum delay for non-critical activities is called *slack time* or *float* (see Chapter 6). If an activity's float is very short, a small delay can cause that path to go critical.

✔ Has the work already been identified as involving risk? If so, have you got some management actions planned already and set down in your Risk Register? (See Chapter 10 for more on the Risk Register.)

✔ Have you already encountered problems with this activity? Unless new factors have arisen, the recurring problem suggests that previous control actions aren't proving adequate.

## Thinking about what you can do to get back on track

It's important to 'think wide' when considering possible actions to get a project back on track. A common knee-jerk reaction is to throw more staff resource or money at the problem, but that isn't always the best thing to do. Indeed, for some problems putting more people onto the work just makes matters worse.

A great help is to bring in the team leader and possibly team members to talk about the problem. It's often the case that team members themselves can see solutions, especially if they're technical experts and have 'been there, done it and got the t-shirt'.

One course of action that you may identify is . . . do nothing! Don't forget that you have the plan available to you, so don't fall into the trap of trying to decide what to do about something without having the plan in front of you. If something has taken a week longer than expected so far, and the team now anticipates that it will finally be delivered two weeks late, you may just say 'fine'. Your plan shows that the team isn't working on anything else in the two weeks, you have three weeks' float on the activity, and you're currently below budget – so you can be cool about it and absorb the overrun without any action.

When considering your options for bringing the project back on track, include the following in your thinking:

✔ **Use contingency to absorb an overrun if no float exists.** If the activity is something that you can't put extra people on, just accept the fact – it's what contingency is there for. However, if you're unhappy that it's taken up too much of your contingency for this point in the project, you may be able to buy back some contingency time by putting more staff on a later activity and so shortening its duration.

✔ **Split the work.** It may be that part of the work must be done now, and although it was preferable that the whole job was completed, in fact some of it can be done later in parallel with other things.

## Deciding what you'll do

Having considered a range of options for action, now's the time to make your mind up on what action or actions you're going to take. Your decision is likely to hinge around three factors:

- ✔ What you think will be the most effective
- ✔ What the cost is likely to be in terms of money and staff time
- ✔ What the impact on other project work will be

For the last of these factors, your plan needs to be up to date – repeating the important point from the earlier section 'Having a reliable plan'. Computer tools can really come into their own when looking at impacts, because you can do 'what if' projections using the tool. Remember to save a copy first before you start playing about with the plans, though.

As with identifying options for corrective action, you may also consult others to help establish which options would be the most effective. If the decision is within your authority as Project Manager, you can make the final call, but if it's outside your authority, you may now need to go to your sponsor or steering committee if you haven't already involved them.

## Taking action

Having reached a decision on what to do, now you must adjust your plans to include those actions and then adjust the work in line with the revised plans. The implementation may involve talking with others in the project, including individual team members, to explain the problem, what you're doing about it and how it will affect their work. If you do that, you can also get project staff on board to help with the next step of monitoring to see whether the solution is working and, if it isn't, to let you know.

## Monitoring the effectiveness of the action

In some cases, after the control action is put into effect, that's the end of the matter. But in many cases you need to check whether your actions are proving effective. If the actions are working, that's all well and good, but if not, you'll need to look at why that is, see what range of actions are now possible in the light of this new information, choose what to do . . . Yes, go through all the steps again. Then monitor again. If the new actions aren't working too well either, then you go back around the steps for a third time.

# Monitoring Work Effort and Costs

Progress monitoring is very important to be sure that you deliver on time. However, progress isn't the only thing to watch. You also need to keep an eye on work effort and costs – which, of course, are related.

## Keeping an eye on work effort

It may be that products are being delivered on time but are taking more work effort than expected. Comparing work effort expended with work effort planned can highlight when people are:

- ✔ Cutting corners on quality

- ✔ Encountering unexpected difficulties performing the work

- ✔ Incorrectly expanding or reducing the scope of an activity

- ✔ In danger of using up allocated work effort before the project ends

- ✔ More or less qualified than anticipated

To monitor work effort, you need to collect data on the actual effort spent on each activity to build each product. The following sections give a steer on what data to collect, how to collect it, how to improve its accuracy and how to analyse it.

### Analysing work effort expended

You can evaluate your project's work hours by comparing the actual hours with those forecast in the plan. Figure 14-2 gives an example of a report showing the planned and actual work to produce a design for a questionnaire. The following initial information comes from the Project Plan:

- ✔ The activity identifiers and names

- ✔ The total hours budgeted for each team member to spend on each activity

- ✔ The hours budgeted for each team member to spend on each activity each week

You obtain the actual time spent by team members from their time sheets, and then you can calculate the variance:

- ✔ The number of hours each team member spent on each activity

- ✔ The number of hours left for each team member to spend on each work package

- ✔ The difference between the number of hours in the plan and the number of hours each team member actually spent on each Work Package

| WBS Code | Description | Employee | | Budget | Work Effort Expended (Person-hours) | | | | |
|---|---|---|---|---|---|---|---|---|---|
| | | | | | Week 1 | Week 2 | Week 3 | Week 4 | ... |
| 3.1.2 | Design questionnaire | H. Jones | Planned | 130 | 20 | 40 | 50 | 30 | ... |
| | | | Actual | 0 | 10 | 30 | 35 | 25 | ... |
| | | | Remaining | 130 | 120 | 90 | 55 | 30 | ... |
| | | | Difference | 0 | +10 | +20 | +35 | +40 | ... |
| | | F. Smith | Planned | 70 | 0 | 20 | 20 | 15 | ... |
| | | | Actual | 0 | 0 | 25 | 10 | 15 | ... |
| | | | Remaining | 70 | 70 | 45 | 35 | 20 | ... |
| | | | Difference | 0 | 0 | -5 | +5 | +5 | ... |

**Figure 14-2:**
A staff
resource
report.

REMEMBER

Actual staff hours rarely agree 100 per cent with the planned amounts. (In fact, if the number of hours for each task each month is identical to the number in your plan for several months, you may wonder whether people are copying the numbers from the plan onto their time sheets! See the next section for more on time sheets.) Typically, variances of up to 10 per cent above or below the expected numbers in any month are normal.

Consider the work-effort expenditures for the two team members in the resource report in Figure 14-2. Fred Smith appears to be working in accordance with the plan. He charged more hours in Week 2 than planned, fewer than planned in Week 3, and the same as planned in Week 4. Hilary Jones's situation is very different. Each week, Hilary spends less time on the project than planned, and the total shortfall of her hours increases steadily. Whether this shortfall indicates a problem isn't clear from the report, but the systematic undercharging does need further investigation.

### Collecting work-effort data

Asking your team members to complete time sheets is the most effective way to collect work-effort data. You need to include the following information on each time sheet (see Figure 14-3 for an example of a typical time sheet):

✔ The list of activities that the team member is known to be working on currently, or which are slightly in the future but are included because work may have started on them early

✔ The number of days or hours' work logged against each activity on previous time sheets

✔ The number of days or hours a team member worked on each activity in the current week

✔ The time the team member estimates she will need to complete the activity

| ProjectAlpha – Timesheet | | | | |
|---|---|---|---|---|
| Staff member: Fred Smith | | Week commencing: 3 September | | |
| **Activities** | Planned (days) | Booked previously | Time this week | Estimated time to complete |
| Design flange unit | 15 | 14 | 0.5 | 0 |
| Consult specialists | 5 | 4 | 1 | 1 |
| Adjust flange unit design | 4 | 1 | 2 | 1 |
| Design safety mechanism | 12 | 2 | 1 | 7 |
| Design box assembly | 8 | 0 | 0 | 8 |

**Figure 14-3:** A typical weekly time sheet.

If you're logging hours rather than days, recording work on activities to the nearest half hour is sufficient.

Good computer tools often produce time sheets at the click of an icon, and in fact Figure 14-3 is based on a tool where the software has entered the first two columns of figures. If you think about it, the tool already knows who's working on the project, what work they're scheduled to do and how much time is estimated for each activity. If you use the computer to print out the time sheets, you make life easy for your team members who just need to fill in the remaining information each week. They'll be much more open to providing information for you if, in turn, you've made the reporting as easy as possible for them.

## Asking for the Estimated Time to Complete

*Estimated Time to Complete* provides an excellent early warning system for unexpectedly early or late completion. For example, an activity may have been planned to take 20 days, the team member has so far spent a total of 10 days on it but now expects to finish the job in another 5. In other words, she's expecting to come in five days early. Knowing that may be really useful when doing forward 'what if' projections on the plan. You'll be looking to see whether you can exploit that early finish to make it even more beneficial, perhaps by bringing forward other project work or reducing the hire period for that very expensive piece of equipment, and so save money.

You can see a couple of examples of the value of Estimated Time to Complete in Figure 14-3. Having done three days work so far on designing the safety mechanism, team member Fred now thinks he can complete the job in a further seven days and so bring in the work two days early. In contrast, having spent five days consulting specialists on the design of the flange unit, Fred is warning that the consultation isn't quite complete and he'll need another day on it, taking the activity to a total of six days against the originally estimated five days.

### *Improving the accuracy of your work-effort data*

Just as with schedule performance data, the more accurate your work-effort expenditure data are, the more meaningful your analyses will be.

The following steps can help increase the accuracy of the work-effort expenditure data you collect:

- ✔ **Explain to people that you're using their staff hours information to help you manage the project, not to spy on them.** When you ask people to detail the hours they spend on specific assignments, they often fear that you'll criticise them for not spending time exactly in accordance with the plan – no matter what the reason – or for not spending enough hours on project work as opposed to other duties. Unfortunately, if people believe criticism is your motive, they'll allocate their work-hours among activities to reflect what they think you want to see instead of what they're really doing.

- ✔ **Ask project staff to record the actual hours they work instead of making their total hours equal 37.5 hours per week.** If people must record a total of 37.5 hours per week and they work overtime, they'll omit hours here and there or try to reduce them proportionately. You want team members to record accurate data.

- ✔ **Include categories for time on non-project activities, such as 'unallocated', 'administrative overhead' and so on.** If you want people to record their time expenditures honestly, you must provide them with appropriate categories. An alternative is not to expect the time sheets to cover all the hours in the week but rather just the hours spent on your project. In the time-sheet example in Figure 14-3, you may have noticed that Fred's work on the project totalled four and a half days not five.

- ✔ **Make sure people to fill out their own time sheets – daily.** Some people ask a third person such as a secretary or personal assistant, if they're senior enough, to fill out time sheets for them. But people have a hard enough time remembering what they themselves did the past day or the past week; expecting someone else to accurately remember it for them is totally unrealistic. Encourage your project staff to fill in their time each day – it only takes a few moments. Otherwise, when it comes around to Friday, it can be guessing time as to what they did on Monday and Tuesday, because they can't clearly remember. You need to monitor progress based on factual information not guesswork.

- ✔ **Collect time sheets weekly.** If people do wait until the time sheet is due before they complete it, you limit their recall to the current week. If you collect sheets once a month, those people will be sitting there at the end of the month trying to remember whether they were even in the office four weeks ago! Besides which, you need to have the plan up to date in order to control the project. If a problem comes up, it's no good trying to work out what to do using a plan that was last updated almost a month ago.

✔ **Don't ask people to submit their time sheets before the period is over.**
On occasions, managers ask staff to submit time sheets on Thursday
for the week ending on Friday. But this practice immediately reduces
the accuracy of the data because a team member can't be certain what
she'll do tomorrow. More importantly, though, this practice suggests to
project staff that, if guessing at Friday's allocation is acceptable, maybe
they don't have to be too concerned with the accuracy of the rest of the
week's data either.

*Earned Value Management* (EVM) is a great technique for calculating – from
resource expenditures alone – whether you're over or under budget and
whether you're ahead of or behind schedule. On complex projects, Earned
Value Management is a useful way to identify areas you should investigate for
possible current problems or potential future problems. See Chapter 19 for an
explanation of Earned Value Management.

### Choosing a system to support your work-effort tracking

If your organisation already has a time-recording system, this may be fine for
your project too if you can get access to set up your project activity codes
and then have access to the information that's been input. However, you'll
often find that organisational systems just don't have the level of detail
needed for project control. If you do need more detailed information, you're
going to have to ask your staff to complete two time sheets: the organisational one and the project one.

When asking for additional data, explain clearly why you need the more
detailed data and make it as easy as possible for staff to log it and return it, so
minimising the extra work you're asking them to do.

You can make life easier for yourself too if you use a computer tool for
recording time information, such as:

✔ Database software such as Microsoft Access or Open Office Base

✔ Dedicated time-recording tools – some are available for free

✔ Project management software like Microsoft Project

✔ Spreadsheet software such as Microsoft Excel and Apple iWork Numbers

See Chapter 18 for a discussion of the potential uses and benefits of software
to support your project management.

When you ask team members to supply information, you're making work for
them. So only ask for information that you know you'll need. It will be damaging to your credibility, as well as being poor management practice, if team
members find that they have spent time and effort giving you accurate information but you never actually needed it and didn't ever use it.

If you decide to use *per cent completed* alongside product delivery to monitor progress, because it's included in your software package, be careful. It's not a reliable way to indicate progress, and Chapter 5 explains why. But even looking at an individual activity, problems exist with using per cent complete. For example, saying that your new product design is 30 per cent complete is virtually meaningless, because you can't determine objectively *how much* of the thinking and creating is actually done. Suggesting that you have completed 30 per cent of your design because you have expended 30 of the 100 hours budgeted for the task, or because three of the ten days allotted for its performance have passed is equally incorrect. The first indicator is a measure of *resource* use, and the second is a measure of *time* elapsed. Neither measure indicates the amount of substantive *work* completed.

## Follow the money: Monitoring expenditure

Alongside tracking progress, you must monitor your project's spending to verify that it's in line with the plans and, if it's not, to address any deviations. You may think that you can determine project funds used to date and funds remaining just by reading the balance in your project's financial account. However, if you're working in an organisation of any size, spending project funds usually involves several steps before an item is actually paid for. Monitoring just what stage the spending has reached for each item is important for your financial reporting, because your accounts department is going to want to know. It follows that you'll probably need to set up your financial plan and records to show the same steps in the process, so that you can report the financial position quickly and easily, as well as use the information for checking the actual spending against the planned spending.

### Tracking spending against the plan

To keep control of project spending, you need to compare the amounts it was planned to spend with the amounts that were actually spent. There's usually no need to get complicated about it, and you can set up a simple report format such as that shown in Figure 14-4.

The actual numbers for the period come from the data you obtain during that period. *Actual* in this illustration may mean the value of purchase requisitions, purchase orders, commitments, accounts payable and/or expenditures. Total remaining funds are the difference between the total budget and the actual amounts expended to date.

Clearly, the 'actuals' on the spending report can only be on spending to date. It's certainly important to know what has been spent in total to this point, but it's also important to compare that figure with what you planned to have spent by this point. If the plans shows that this eight-week stage is forecast to cost £102,000, and by Week 4 a report shows that the amount actually spent or committed is £51,000, it doesn't tell you very much and it certainly doesn't tell you whether the spending is on track, even though half the time is gone and half the money is spent. If, in Week 6, there was a planned expenditure of £80,000 for a new machine, you'd be more than a bit concerned at this point and you certainly wouldn't think that the spending was on track. So, to be clear, you need to compare *what has been spent at this point* with *what you planned to have spent at this point*.

# Spending steps

Few organisations allow you to just draw out cash and go spend it. Normally there are several steps to the process of buying goods and services, and usually you'll need to discriminate clearly between each of them:

✔ **Planning:** You'll plan finance with ballpark figures when first sketching out your project, then in increasing detail as you go through project planning and, later, stage planning (see Chapter 9 for more on levels of planning). The financial plan will need updating at each point as better information becomes available.

✔ **Getting approval:** What you want and what you get may be two very different things. Having planned your project expenditure, you will find that most organisations require you to get approval. Financial approval may be included when the Project Plan is agreed, or it may require a separate submission to a finance manager or some financial approval committee. Beyond that, for large expenditures in particular, you may need to obtain additional specific authority for each spend.

✔ **Placing the order:** When an order is placed, the money is committed, and that's of interest to the accounts department. They will want to know that funds have been committed, even though the money hasn't been spent yet and it's still sitting in the organisation's bank account. With large expenditures in particular, the finance staff will need to keep an eye on cashflow, but as a minimum for all expenditure they'll want to note what is being committed in each financial year. Toward the end of a financial year especially, commitment of funds can be very sensitive.

✔ **Receiving an invoice:** When goods are delivered, the invoice will shortly follow from the supplier. Receiving the invoice is significant, since the clock is now running to the point of actual payment. In many cases, there will be an agreed payment period, often 28 days, and you should make sure that payment is indeed made in this time. Unless you want to get a bad reputation with your suppliers and be very unfair to them, you need to ensure prompt payment. You've received the goods or services, and it's only right and proper that the supplier should get the money for them.

✔ **Authorising payment:** Often before an accounts department will make payment, some confirmation is needed that the goods or services have been received and are satisfactory. Be careful to keep track of invoices and don't delay payment and cause problems for your suppliers (and your accounts staff, who are having to deal with the suppliers chasing payments) because the invoices were buried in a pile of paperwork and you forgot to stamp and sign them.

✔ **Making payment:** This is when the funds actually go out. However, be careful even now because funds don't always go

*(continued)*

out immediately. If you work in a large organisation that pays electronically in batches, there may be a weekly, two-weekly or even monthly payment run, and the payment may be delayed by that period if it has just missed a batch submission.

If your organisation has fixed financial procedures that take time, such as a monthly payment run, you probably won't be able to do too much about that. However, what you can do is keep suppliers informed of when they will be paid. If suppliers know when the money is coming, that's not as bad as being completely in the dark. However, check your facts before mentioning payment dates. It leads to bad working relationships if there are a string of broken promises over payments. In the worst case it can mean you lose good suppliers. Small specialist companies in particular may be less inclined to work for your organisation in the future if they know that there are constant problems and expenses (phoning, sending chasing letters, even taking legal action) over getting paid.

**ProjectAlpha – Financial Report**

**Stage 5 spending**                                 Position as at 20 September

| Purchase items | Planned (£'000) | Actual (£'000) | Estimated remaining | Variance |
|---|---|---|---|---|
| Computers | 22 | 20 | 0 | –2 |
| Network equipment | 8 | 9 | 0 | 1 |
| Cabling | 4 | 4 | 0 | 0 |
| Contract cabling staff | 12 | 9 | 5 | 2 |
| Contract design staff | 8 | 0 | 8 | 0 |

Variance to date:  +1

**Figure 14-4:** A simple financial report.

You may spend more or less money on your project activities than you planned, for the following reasons:

- ✔ You receive the bills for goods or services later than you planned, so they're paid for later than you planned.

- ✔ You buy and take delivery of items early, or just prepay, to receive special discounts, 'buy one, get one free' offers or sale prices.

- ✔ You don't need certain goods or services that you budgeted for in your plan.

- ✔ You find you need goods or services that you didn't budget for in your plan.

### Differentiating between overspending and early spending

Even if spending is greater than planned for this point, it may still not be a problem. In exactly the same way that you need to ask why if a stage is going off the plan, you also need to ask why if the spending is different to the forecast. An important check is whether the spending is overspending or something has been bought in advance of what was originally planned, so it's early spending – the early purchasing mentioned in the second bullet point in the previous section. In the case of early spending, the stage (or project) will actually finish close to target, but in the case of overspending, then clearly it won't.

### Choosing a system to support your expenditure tracking

Before developing a way of monitoring the project's expenditures, first check the nature and capabilities of your organisation's financial tracking system. Most organisations have a financial system that maintains records of all expenditures. Often the system also maintains records of accounts payable. Unfortunately, many financial systems categorise expenses by cost centre but don't have the capacity to classify expenses by components within a project, and if that's true for your organisation, then you need to find something else to provide the additional detail you require.

Probably, you'll find that a spreadsheet is more than enough to give the tracking and reporting you want. Spreadsheets have the advantage that they are very clear and also powerful. However, you can use other software such as dedicated accounts packages or even the inbuilt functions of project-scheduling software such as Microsoft Project or Open Workbench. Check out Chapter 18 for more on using software to make your life easier. However, don't forget to make regular backups of your valuable financial information, or you may suddenly find that your life has become far from easy.

# Dealing with Change and Avoiding Scope Creep

Alongside progress and financial control, you'll also need to exercise change control if your project is not to experience problems. So look out, there's a project killer about, and its name is *scope creep*. Scope creep, as the name suggests, is a change to scope, but it's made up of small movements – and actually *small* is the problem. If a project was known to be just about achievable with the given budget, staff resource and time, and somebody came along and asked for a huge change with no increase of resource or timescale, then clearly you'd turn the change down flat. The problem comes with a small change. Imagine a year-long project and a small change that will *just* (people almost always use that word) take eight minutes and cost 37p. Now surely you can manage to absorb this tiny job as a goodwill gesture in a 12-month project with a £14 million budget? Well, perhaps not.

The management writer Charles Handy uses an example in his book *The Age of Unreason* (but please don't try it at home) that if you drop a live frog into boiling water, it will jump out very smartly. If, however, you put a live frog into cold water and very slowly heat the water up, the frog will allow itself to be boiled to death. Apparently, frogs can't detect incremental changes in temperature. Charles Handy has applied that illustration to companies that have a strong product and a leading position, but some years later go bankrupt. A huge shift in the market had occurred, but it happened very gradually and was made up of a large number of tiny changes. Had the changes been big, the companies would have seen them and reacted. It's because each change was small that the companies didn't notice the market shift until it was too late.

Projects can, and do, suffer the same fate as the frog and the companies Charles Handy describes. Each change that is asked for in the project is very small, but cumulatively the changes represent a very big change that the project can't absorb and that proves unmanageable and so fatal.

So what's the answer to scope creep? Simple: change control. Note the word *control*. We're not talking about change *prohibition*. In fact, prohibiting change in the project is usually damaging, but sometimes it's impossible anyway. The thing to try to eliminate then isn't change but *uncontrolled* change.

If you're not fully convinced that you want to allow changes in your project, consider the following:

- Changes in the project to reflect changes in the business environment
- Correction of mistakes
- Good ideas that will make things simpler or cheaper
- Legislative changes such as new electrical or safety standards
- New technology that's easier to use and cheaper to maintain

This section helps you set up a change control process to manage changes in your project. It provides some helpful steps to follow when considering and acting on a change request.

## *Understanding different types of change*

Different types of change are significant because you may fund them in different ways. Where something has been delivered by a supplier and it's wrong, then it needs to be changed to be put right. If the original specification is clear, then the cost of this corrective change will fall to the supplier. But when the change is because the project customer has had a change of mind or something has changed in the business environment, then the cost of that change will fall to the customer. When additional work falls to an external supplier as a result, there will normally be an additional charge.

Whatever the change, to control it you're going to need some procedures, albeit perhaps simple ones, and usually a change budget. Both need some careful thought.

### Setting up change procedures

To get a change, it has to be asked for, considered, approved (or not) and then implemented. By definition, if you want to avoid uncontrolled change, there needs to be control. You can do this very simply with the use of a Change Request form – but of course this can be electronic and sent by email, it doesn't have to be paper.

A *change request* should set down basic information, but that may be supplemented by the Project Manager after the request has been analysed. It should have basic information included on 'what' and 'why' as a minimum. In some cases, until some exploratory investigation has been done, it may not be possible to say exactly what's involved in making the change. Basic information includes:

✔ Name of the person asking for the change

✔ Date of the request

✔ Description of the change, including any products it affects

✔ Reason for the change, including advantages, or saying if the change is mandatory

✔ Impact of the change

This information may be recorded in a Change Log and then supplemented with more information and the eventual decision on the change request.

✔ Work needed to effect the change

✔ Decision taken, to agree the change or refuse it

✔ Date the change request is closed

Having a *Change Log* or *Issue Log* is really helpful in the project, because it gives you an overview of the change requests received and what is happening to each. You can use a spreadsheet for your log and then you have the advantage that it can be sorted in different ways. For example, you may normally keep it so that live changes are at the top and closed change requests that have now been dealt with are sorted to the bottom.

Do bear in mind that you may need to consult other people about a particular change request, such as technical experts on teams, or the sponsor or steering committee members if it's something that requires authority beyond your own delegated authority, such as the change being high cost. It follows that when planning resources in the project, you should schedule some time for team specialists to help examine change requests. The more the project is going into the unknown and the more change requests you anticipate, the more time you should allocate to deal with them.

### Budgeting for change

In the same way that you need to set aside some time in the project for dealing with changes, so too you're going to need some budget. If there's no change budget, then any change request will have to go to the sponsor because, by definition, it's not on the plan that the sponsor originally authorised.

How much there should be in a change budget depends on two main factors:

- The amount of change anticipated in the project. If it's rather unclear what will happen in the project, then you can expect more change than if things are very clear and definite and can be put on the plans.

- How much the sponsor wants to be involved with authorising changes and how much of this decision making the sponsor wants to delegate to the Project Manager.

The sponsor can set two dimensions on a change budget: a total amount and an item amount. So, for example, the Project Manager must go back to the sponsor if the total changes exceed a limit of £25,000 or for any single change that will cost £5,000 or more.

## Looking at impacts – the four dogs

Some people, and many senior business managers, live in a comfortable, rose-tinted world where project changes can be absorbed with no impact. Sadly perhaps, the rose-tinted world is imaginary and projects happen in a real world with some very real change dynamics.

Different project approaches identify different control factors. The Project Management Institute (PMI) recognises four, and that's realistic. Nick Graham was teaching project management to a group of police officers, and came up with the analogy of four dogs (in their case, police dogs) pulling on a piece of project 'canvas'. As illustrated in Figure 14-5, the four dogs are:

- Cost
- Quality
- Scope
- Time

The piece of project 'canvas' is very strong; it won't stretch and it won't tear. If one of the dogs pulls a corner of the canvas, something's got to give. Perhaps the canvas will pull sideways and just one other dog will get pulled along, or perhaps it will pull the other side and two dogs will get dragged, or perhaps all three will be taken in tow.

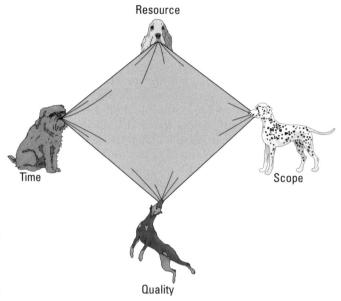

Resource

Time

Scope

Quality

**Figure 14-5:**
The four
control
dogs.

The dogs model shows the dynamic between the four control elements, and is so simple you can keep it in your head when you're thinking about a change. If the 'scope' dog pulls the canvas, then what action is available to you as a Project Manager? You could ask for an increase in resource to deal with the change, but keep the quality the same and maintain the delivery date. Or perhaps you could ask for extra staff resource, but allow a bit more time as well so that the project can take a bit longer to accommodate the extra work.

Sometimes one of the control points is fixed, as in the case of the rather stout-looking 'Time' dog in Figure 14-5. This project must be delivered by the end of the financial year, and that's not up for debate. The Time dog is sitting firmly on the ground, so if there is to be a decrease in resource (the 'Resource' dog pulls the canvas), you have only two dogs left to consider. Should you reduce quality and do less testing, or de-scope the project and leave something out, or both?

You may notice in Figure 14-5 that the 'Quality' dog looks a bit thin and weedy. It isn't fed on such good dog food as the other three dogs and is weaker. In many projects – not yours of course – the Quality dog is the first target because 'perhaps we'll get away with it if we only do the main tests'. Clearly, that's not a good general strategy, but it may sometimes be necessary to reduce quality if the pressure is on. However, that's a decision that you need to take both thoughtfully and cautiously.

Sometimes people think that a dog has pulled a corner of the canvas and nothing has happened – 'We got away with it' – but it's not true. A look behind the dogs will reveal claw marks in the turf where one or more has been dragged. A common example is where organisational managers have insisted that the scope of the project is extended but there will be no allowance made for extra time or cost, and the quality level is to stay the same. But if the project completes, claw marks in the turf may show that the 'Quality' dog was dragged and important testing was left out. Or perhaps the 'Time' dog was dragged and project staff put in all sorts of extra hours to complete the job within the original limits. If that situation extends into the next project and the one after (and organisational managers tend to make a habit of creating such pressures), then payback will come when valuable project staff start to leave the organisation. These staff get fed up with bailing out projects that bring constant pressure and long working hours because of bad management, and they move to jobs with better organised companies. And guess who finds it easiest to find a better job somewhere else – the best staff or the worst staff?

The control dog model in Figure 14-5 is useful in initial planning as well as in change control. It's a good acid test for the plan to ask whether the project 'canvas' is in the right tension. So you, and the sponsor, can ask, 'Can we deliver that scope, to that quality level, with that resource within that timescale? Is it realistic?' When looking at the plans of failed projects, it is often immediately identifiable that it was never possible to be successful with that particular balance of the control elements, and the project was doomed to failure from the very beginning.

## Responding to change requests

Whether you handle change requests formally or informally, always follow these steps:

1. **When you receive a request for change to some aspect of your project, clarify exactly what the request is asking you to do.**

2. **Unless your project is very informal, ask for the request in writing.**

   In a change control system, people must submit every request for change on a change request form. This provides a clear record of the request.

3. **Assess the change's potential effects on all aspects of your project.**

   Also consider what may happen if you don't make the change.

4. **Decide whether you'll implement the change.**

   If this change affects other people, involve them in the decision too.

5. **If you decide not to make the change, tell the requester and explain the reason(s).**

6. **If you decide to make the change, write down the necessary steps to implement the change.**

   In a formal change control system, all aspects of a change are detailed in a written change order.

7. **Update your project's plan to reflect any adjustments in schedules, outcomes or resource budgets as a result of the change.**

8. **Tell team members and other appropriate people (such as stakeholders) about the change and the effect you expect it to have on them and on the project as a whole.**

If you have an effective change control system, you can handle very big changes as well as the small ones. The key question is always 'Is the change justified?' If a big change would bring very substantial additional business benefit, then it may well be worth doing. In that case, the sponsor will make the decision to accept the change, and the Project Plan and Stage Plans can be adjusted to accommodate the additional work. In that way, the extra time and resource will be allocated and the project brought back into balance – as with the control dogs in Figure 14-5.

## *Eliminating scope creep – well, almost*

This section on change started with the warning that scope creep is a major project killer. In surveys of the causes of project failure, expect to see scope creep in the top five reasons, because it's nearly always there, and frequently it occupies the number one slot.

Two elements of project management help you almost eliminate scope creep:

- ✔ A change control procedure, as covered in this section
- ✔ Clear, precise and agreed definitions of project deliverables, as explained in Chapter 5 on product planning

There is a small area left where there can still be misunderstanding on what is included in the project: where a customer assumed something was included that a supplier assumed wasn't. Even with the Product Definitions in planning (see Chapter 5), you can't always spell out every last minor detail. But the potential for misunderstanding is small and therefore any misunderstanding is likely to cause only minimal difficulty if it does occur.

# Chapter 15

# Keeping Everyone Informed

· · · · · · · · · · · · · · · · · · · · · · · · · · · · · · · · · · · · · · · · · · · · · ·

## In This Chapter

▶ Identifying the underlying causes of communication problems

▶ Thinking through the communication needs in your project

▶ Establishing the most effective means of communicating

▶ Planning for communications coming into the project, happening within it and going out of it

· · · · · · · · · · · · · · · · · · · · · · · · · · · · · · · · · · · · · · · · · · · · · ·

*I*magine standing at one end of a large room filled with assorted sofas, chairs and tables. You've accepted a challenge to walk to the other end without bumping into any of the furniture. But as you set off, the lights go off and you now have to complete your trip in total darkness, with only your memory of the room's layout to guide you.

Surprisingly, many projects are just like that walk across the room. People plan how the project will work – who'll do what, by when and for how much – and they share this information with the team members and other people who'll support the project. But as soon as the project work begins, people receive no information about their progress, the work remaining or obstacles that may lie ahead; they have to walk in the dark.

In your project, you want things to be different from those 'walk in the dark' projects. In fact, effective communication – getting the right information to and from the right people in a timely manner – is a key to successful projects.

Communications are a major source of problems in projects and are a factor frequently cited as a common cause of project failure. Such failure is unnecessary, though, because having good communications just needs some thought up front. As with so much else in this book, you won't find this chapter difficult, but it is essential.

In this chapter we set the scene by looking at the underlying causes of communication problems, and then take a quick look at the dynamics of communications. Finally, we turn to the practicalities of planning exactly what communications you're going to need in your project and how best to carry them out.

# Looking Underneath Communications Failure

Communications are inherently difficult. You don't need to think for long about day-to-day life, let alone projects, to remember misunderstandings even over simple communications. Sometimes such misunderstandings can be funny, such as the Chinese whispers party game where a spoken message is passed around a circle of people and the final version – usually hilariously – bears no resemblance whatever to the original. The oft-quoted military example is where the message 'Send reinforcements – we're going to advance' is finally delivered as 'Send three and fourpence – we're going to a dance.' Funny at a party and as a joke perhaps, but communications problems are potentially extremely serious in a project.

## Communications breakdown – the big project killer

If you've read other chapters in this book before coming to this one, you may react with, 'Oh no, not another project killer.' We do indeed mention quite a few project killers in the book, and for the very good reason that quite a few project killers exist! Communications problems are particularly significant when you see the results of surveys into failed projects. Communications failure doesn't always take first place as the most common cause, but it's always in the top few and frequently it does occupy the number one slot.

Good communications need careful thought, and the emphasis must be on appropriate communication, carried out intelligently. In the 'old days', communication problems were related to not knowing what was going on, or having to wait weeks to find out. In the days of wooden ships, vital news could take months to arrive. The problems today are the opposite. Information travels in the blink of an eye, including details that people haven't had time to consider or correct. And far from not having enough information, you're bombarded with it to the point that it's hard to find what you want among the huge volume of redundant stuff clamouring for your attention. You may be thinking of your email inbox as you read this, and nodding.

Coming to the specifics of projects, what, then, are the particular underlying causes of communication problems? The following sections help you understand the causes so that you can then avoid the pitfalls when planning communications in your projects.

### Having unclear roles and responsibilities

A lot of communications problems result from unclear roles and responsibilities, where people involved in the project don't have a clear understanding of what they should be doing, and are even less clear on what other people in the project are supposed to be doing. Small wonder, then, that things drop down the gaps. Avoiding this problem is straightforward enough, and you can find help in Chapter 11 on project organisation. If project staff are absolutely clear on what they should be doing and exactly what they're responsible for, and are equally clear on the roles of others in the project, the potential for communication difficulties is immediately reduced.

### Being fuzzy on products

*'I've finished it. Here it is.'*
*'But that's not what I wanted at all! It's not even close.'*
*'But you said you wanted . . .'*
*'Yes, I did say that. But surely it was obvious that what I meant was . . .'*

Great misunderstanding arises in projects over what people are to deliver. It's all too easy for people to use similar words but have different ideas, or simply to make assumptions (see the next section too) that the other person is thinking along similar lines. This is a serious communications problem because misunderstanding over deliverables, or *products*, leads to confusion, wasted work, frustration and project delay.

Turn to Chapter 5 for some serious help in avoiding product confusion, hinged on the *product-based* approach to planning. Chapter 5 includes the *Product Definition*, which sets down exactly what the product is, what quality criteria it must satisfy and how it is to be tested. Simply make sure that the definition, while not going into unnecessary detail that team members don't need, carries enough detail to be unambiguous. You can also involve team managers in planning – perhaps in a workshop – to discuss and even help define the deliverables.

### Making assumptions

It's not the conscious assumptions that are the problem in communications, but rather the unconscious ones. You can record conscious assumptions so everyone can see them – for example: 'This plan is based on the assumption that the government grant will be authorised and the funds will be available at the start of the new financial year.' Unconscious assumptions are those that, by definition, you doesn't realise you're making. You just 'understand' something and don't realise that you've misunderstood. It's impossible to eliminate unconscious assumptions, but you can reduce the number you make.

You can help reduce assumptions by putting aside any thought of having a cool image as the Project Manager who knows everything. A cool image may be fine in a social setting to boost your street cred, but can be damaging in a project. A parallel is when you're new to an organisation and you've been asked to attend a meeting of senior managers. So, take a test. The senior managers are discussing their grave concerns over the state of HMRTs, of which too many are proving to be inaccurate. Now, do you . . .

- ✔ Nod knowingly and frown a bit, as if you're also deeply concerned about inaccuracies in the HMRTs.

- ✔ Keep your head down but surreptitiously make a note on your pad for action straight after the meeting to go and find someone in your department and ask what on earth an HMRT is.

- ✔ Interrupt the meeting and say that you're sorry but you're new and you don't know what an HMRT is. Please could someone briefly explain?

The correct answer for the meeting is, of course, the third. But so, too, it is the correct answer in a project when a junior team member is discussing something with you that you need to know about but don't understand. To do anything else but ask is to cause communications problems in which someone thinks you understand and are agreeing to something, whereas actually you don't and your nodding, or simply failure to say 'no', wasn't intended to convey agreement.

You'll do more damage to your image by pretending to have understanding when you don't than by swallowing your pride and being prepared to ask the dumb questions in order to have a successful project.

### Failing to feed back

When information is really important, it's helpful in a conversation to feed back to check your understanding. So many misunderstandings go undiscovered because people don't use the simple mechanism of feedback. It doesn't have to be difficult or embarrassing. You can simply say, 'That's really important. Now can I just go back through it to make sure I've got it absolutely right, and you can tell me if I've misunderstood anything?' That gives both opportunity and permission for the other person, even a very junior team member, to put you right if you have got something wrong.

Keep in mind the amusing words of author Robert McCloskey: 'I know you believe you understand what you think I said, but I'm not sure you realise that what you heard is not what I meant.'

# Communicating Effectively

The process of transmitting information includes the following components:

- ✔ **Message:** The thoughts or ideas being transmitted.

- ✔ **Sender:** The person transmitting the message.

- ✔ **The message:** The message translated into a language understandable to others. This language may consist of words, pictures or actions.

- **Medium:** The method used to convey the message (we cover different mediums in the section 'Choosing the Appropriate Medium', later in this chapter.)

- **Noise:** Anything that hinders successfully transmitting the message. Noise may include physical and visual noise – distraction – as well as 'internal' noise such as preconceived notions, biases, difficulty with the language used, personal feelings, nonverbal cues and emotions.

- **Receiver:** The person getting the message.

- **Decoded message:** The message translated back into thoughts or ideas.

Depending on the nature of a particular communication, any or all of these elements can affect the chances that a message is received as intended.

The expression *visual noise* in the previous bullet points may seem odd, but an excellent example of this happened at a university. Students were sitting in a lecture theatre, all listening with great interest to a distinguished professor who was a subject expert. In the middle of the lecture, a dog pushed its way in through the door and went from student to student wagging its tail and getting patted on the head. The professor went on with the lecture, totally immersed in his subject and completely unaware of the dog. But none of the students were now listening, despite the interesting subject; they were all looking at the dog. Sometimes in a project, you need to get someone out of the working environment and take him into a meeting room or even just a quiet corner to be as sure as you can that he will concentrate on what you're saying.

In your project, it helps to think through each element of the communication to understand it and then decide the best means of communication. For example, who's receiving the message? If you're communicating with technical staff, be careful not to talk down to them and explain matters when they have much more knowledge than you. On the other hand, if you're talking to trainee user staff, don't have unrealistic expectations about the amount of understanding they have of the business process you're dealing with in the project; obviously, you're going to have to spell things out and check to be quite sure they understand.

## *Distinguishing between one-way and two-way communication*

Some communications are one way, and others are two way:

- **One-way communication:** Going from the sender to the receiver with no opportunity for clarification or confirmation that the receiver got and correctly understood the intended message. This type of communication can be effective for presenting facts, confirming actions and sharing messages that have little chance of being misinterpreted.

One-way communications are either:

- **Push:** Proactively distributed to particular people; examples include memos, reports, letters, faxes and emails

- **Pull:** Available to people who must access the communications themselves; examples include Internet sites, knowledge repositories and bulletin boards

✔ **Two-way communication:** Going from the sender to the receiver and from the receiver back to the sender to help ensure that the intended audience received and correctly interpreted the intended message. Examples include face-to-face discussions, phone calls, in-person group meetings, interactive teleconferences and online instant messaging. Two-way communication is effective for ensuring that more complex content is correctly received and for conveying the sender's beliefs and feelings about the message.

## Can you hear me? Listening actively

The one skill that most strongly influences the quality of your communications is your ability to listen actively. Good listening skills are important to be sure that you're hearing correctly what others are saying to you, but are also important when you're checking the response of the other person to ensure that he's heard your message clearly.

Be especially careful to listen in those cases where you disagree with someone. It's fine to disagree and even to come into healthy conflict (see Chapter 13 on team dynamics). The danger of having even a healthy argument, though, is that you're so focused on getting your next point clear in your head that you fail to take on board what the other person is saying. Instead, slow down. Listen very carefully to what the other person is saying. Then don't be afraid even of leaving a short silence while you think about what the other person said before making your next point. Remember, it's no coincidence that God gave you two ears but only one mouth!

Listening is important to help you understand, but as a by-product it also has a powerful effect on those you're communicating with. Even if people disagree with you, they're much more likely to accept your authority and over-ruling of their points if they think that they have been heard. It is incredibly frustrating if you believe you have an important point but a key decision-maker hasn't taken the trouble to even listen to you. Going back to the argument in the last paragraph, you know that you would be impressed too if, when you are arguing with someone, he listens very carefully to each point that you make and stops to think about what you said before making his next contribution.

## Listening

When listening to project staff such as team members, you can learn a lot about how your project is going by paying attention to *how* things are being said, not merely what is said. Consider the following:

✔ What words are being used? Are they emotionally charged or neutral?

✔ How is the person standing or sitting? Does he appear to be actively involved in the communication, often shown by leaning forward, or is he passive, disinterested or defensive, sometimes shown by leaning back and folding his arms?

✔ Is the person maintaining good eye contact, or looking to the side or down? Is he trying to avoid the communication and, if so, is that likely to be an attempt to cover up some problem?

✔ Is the communication clear and to the point, or is the person showing signs of confusion, indicating misunderstanding or being in over his head in his project work?

If you have a number of teams working in your project, rather than just one that you're leading yourself, it's worth the effort to get along to team meetings from time to time. It demonstrates interest and gives you a chance to encourage a team in its work and express appreciation. But it's also invaluable to gauge how things are really going. Try to get to the meeting early and then watch how team members walk into the meeting room. Do they come in with a cheerful 'Good morning' and a smile and immediately start chatting about the project and the work they're doing, or do they slouch in with downcast eyes and go quietly to their places and sit silently waiting for the meeting to start? That sort of information never appears on progress reports.

# *Choosing the Appropriate Medium*

When deciding how to communicate with different people in and around your project, choosing the right medium is as important as deciding what information to share. Your choice of medium helps ensure that people get the information they need when they need it.

Project communications come in two forms:

✔ **Planned:** Planned communications will be conducted in a form that you have to think through, even if only briefly, in advance. Examples include weekly team meetings, stakeholder briefings and monthly progress reporting.

✔ **Ad hoc:** Ad-hoc communications occur as people think of information they want to share. These communications occur continuously in the normal course of business. Examples include brief conversations by the water cooler and spur-of-the-moment emails you dash off during the day.

Both planned and ad-hoc communications can be either written or oral.

*Beware of making an assumption that project communications all need to be written. Some communications may be carried out verbally, such as some of the reporting. Considerable project effort can be expended in documentation, so you don't want to do too much. For some things you may not need a full written report because a brief note of a phoned report may be sufficient. In the UK, the stock market used to work on the principle of 'my word is my bond'. In other words, when someone said something, they stuck to it. When that trusting culture can be developed in projects (and it has been done) then it's often accompanied by a considerable reduction in paperwork because a lot of documentation is defensive, to be able to prove what was said or agreed to. In some cases, documentation is important, but perhaps not for all communications.*

The following sections look at major communications options.

## *Writing reports*

Unlike informal oral communication, written reports enable you to present factual data efficiently, choose your words carefully to minimise misunderstandings, provide a historical record of the information you share, and share the same message with a wide audience.

Although written reports have quite a few benefits, they also have some drawbacks that you need to consider:

✔ They take time and effort to produce, so you need to think carefully about the frequency of regular reports.

✔ They don't allow your audience to ask questions to clarify the content, meaning and implication of your message.

✔ With written reports alone, you can't verify that your audience received and interpreted your message as you intended.

✔ They don't enable you to pick up nonverbal signals that suggest your audience's reactions to the message, and they don't support interactive discussion and brainstorming about your message.

✔ You may never know whether your audience reads the report!

Keep the following pointers in mind to improve the chances that people read and understand your written reports:

- **Prepare regularly scheduled reports in a standard format.** This consistency helps your audience find specific types of information quickly.

- **Stay focused.** Preparing several short reports to address different topics is better than combining several topics into one long report. People are more likely to pick up the important information about each topic.

- **Minimise the use of technical jargon and acronyms.** If a person is unfamiliar with the language in your report, he'll miss at least some of your messages.

- **Identify a contact person for further information.** A contact person can address any questions a recipient has about the information.

- **Clearly describe any actions you want people to take.** The more specifically you explain what you want people to do, the more likely they are to do it.

- **Keep your reports concise – one page if possible.** The longer your report, the less likely it is that people will read all of it. If the report is really long, people probably won't read more than the title. (For an example on the importance of brevity, check out the nearby sidebar 'Keep it short – and that means you!'.)

## Keep it short – and that means you!

Be careful of the *'yes, but'* syndrome – in which you think an idea sounds great for others, but your *special* situation requires a different approach. In a training programme a number of years ago, Stan Portny shared a suggestion to keep project reports to one page or less. Most people agreed that doing so made sense, but one participant rejected the notion. He proceeded to explain that his project was so important and so complex that he sent his boss monthly project reports that were a minimum of ten pages in length. 'And,' he added, 'my boss reads every word.'

A few weeks after the training session, Stan had the opportunity to speak with this participant's boss about a totally unrelated matter. In the course of the conversation, the boss happened to mention his frustration with a member of his staff who felt his project was so important that he had to submit monthly progress reports no fewer than ten pages long. He said that he usually read the first paragraph but he rarely had time to review the reports thoroughly. He added that he hoped this person had listened carefully to the suggestion that reports should be one page or less!

### Preparing progress reports

Progress reports are some of the most important reports you have in the project. Progress reports operate at two levels:

- **From Team Leaders** to inform the Project Manager of the progress being made on their current work assignments or *Work Packages*.

- **From the Project Manager** to inform the sponsor or steering committee members about the progress in the current stage and through the whole project. This report may be copied to others who have an interest, such as key stakeholders, management boards and other projects.

Progress reports can be a real problem if they're unwieldy or if the content is unclear, so it's important to think through and agree the content and the format at the start of the project. A good progress report should be short, and one way of achieving this is to use a dashboard layout (see the next section).

Typical information in a progress report will be:

- **Delivery:** Products that have been produced in the stage to date.

- **Schedule:** Whether the project is on time, behind or ahead of schedule. You might combine this with the delivery reporting – see the Work Checklist in Chapter 14.

- **Budgets:** What staff time and money has been used so far, and how that compares with what was planned to be spent by this point. You might also show the spending against the total for the stage. For example, saying that spending has reached the 40 per cent mark against the stage total.

- **Performance:** How teams are performing against estimates. Are things taking more time than expected, less or is performance on track?

- **Risk management:** Current status of key risks and brief information on any new ones.

- **Other information:** Such as on significant problems currently being addressed or any other information of which the recipient(s) of the report needs to be aware.

It can be really helpful to include a traffic light indicator:

- **Green** shows that everything is going pretty much to plan.

- **Amber** shows that there are problems and if they get any worse then the problem will need to be addressed by the Project Manager (in the case of a team leader's progress report) or the sponsor or steering committee (in the case of the Project Manager's progress report).

- **Red** means that the project is already off the plan and is currently subject to discussion on how, or even whether, to proceed.

Alternatively, you might use a traffic light indicator to show the state of individual products or activities. We include an example in the dashboard illustration in Figure 15-1 in the next section.

### Using a dashboard format for progress reporting

To make your written project-progress reports most effective, you want to include the greatest amount of information in the least amount of space, but also to make that information as easy to understand as possible. A *project dashboard* is an information display of key indicators of project performance in a format that resembles an instrument panel on a dashboard.

Figure 15-1 shows some types of display in a project dashboard.

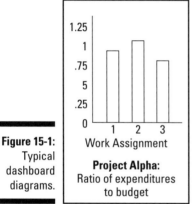

**Figure 15-1:**
Typical dashboard diagrams.

Work Assignment

**Project Alpha:**
Ratio of expenditures to budget

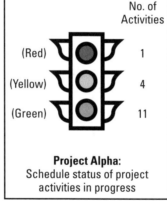

No. of Activities

(Red) 1

(Yellow) 4

(Green) 11

**Project Alpha:**
Schedule status of project activities in progress

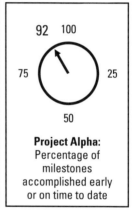

**Project Alpha:**
Percentage of milestones accomplished early or on time to date

When creating a dashboard for your project, be sure to:

✔ Work with the intended recipients of a report to establish the information they want to see.

✔ Always present *actual* indicator values alongside *planned* values.

✔ Keep the project dashboard report to one page or less.

# Meeting up

Few words elicit the same reactions of anger and frustration that the word *meeting* can provoke. People consider meetings to be everything from the last vestige of interpersonal contact in an increasingly technical society to the biggest time waster in business today.

You've probably been in meetings where you wanted to bang your head against the wall. Ever been to a meeting that didn't start on time? How about a meeting that didn't have an agenda or didn't stick to the agenda it did have? Or how about a meeting at which people discussed issues you thought were resolved at a previous meeting?

Meetings don't have to be painful experiences, though. If you plan and manage them well, meetings can be a highly effective and concise form of communication.

The Queen is reputed to have an interesting approach for meetings to make people communicate concisely and keep meetings short. There are no chairs, so everyone stands up!

You can improve your meetings by using the suggestions in the following sections. (In addition, be sure to check out the later section 'Holding project meetings' for information on different types of meetings.)

### Planning for a successful meeting

To have a good meeting, you need to do some pre-meeting planning. Keep these pointers in mind as you plan:

- ✔ **Clarify the purpose of the meeting.** This step helps you ensure that you invite the right people and allows attendees to prepare.

- ✔ **Decide who needs to attend and why.** If you need information, decide who has it, and make sure they attend the meeting. If you want to make decisions at the meeting, identify who has the necessary authority and who needs to be part of the decision making, and make sure those people attend.

- ✔ **Give plenty of advance notice of the meeting.** This step increases the chances that the people you want to attend will be able to do so.

- ✔ **Let the people who should attend the meeting know its purpose.** People are more likely to attend a meeting when they understand why their attendance is important.

- ✔ **Prepare a written list of topics.** This document helps people see why attending the meeting is in their interests. The list, or agenda, is also your guideline for running the meeting.

- ✔ **Circulate the written agenda and any background material in advance.** Doing so gives everyone time to suggest changes to the agenda and prepare for the meeting.

- ✔ **Keep meetings to one hour or less.** You can force people to sit in a room for hours, but you can't force them to keep their minds on the activities and information at hand for that long. If necessary, schedule several meetings of one hour or less to discuss complex issues or multiple topics.

## Conducting an efficient meeting

How you conduct the meeting can make or break it. The following tasks are essential for conducting a productive meeting:

- ✔ **Start on time, even if people are absent.** After people see that you wait for latecomers, everyone will come late!

- ✔ **Assign someone to take a written note of who attended, which items you discussed and what decisions and assignments the group made.** This procedure allows people to review and clarify the information, and serves as a reminder of actions to be taken after the meeting.

- ✔ **Keep a list of action items that need further exploration, and assign one person to be responsible for each entry.** This step helps ensure that when you meet to discuss these issues again, you have the right information and people present to resolve them.

- ✔ **If you don't have the right information or the right people to resolve an issue, stop your discussion and put it on the list of action items.** Discussing an issue without having the necessary information or the right people present is just wasting everyone's time.

- ✔ **End on time.** Your meeting attendees may have other commitments that begin when your meeting is supposed to end. Not ending on time causes these people to be late for their next commitments or to leave your meeting before it's over. If your project meetings have a reputation for over-running, people are also strongly motivated to find reasons not to attend the next one.

## Following up with the last details

Your meeting may be over, but your work isn't done. Make sure you complete the following post-meeting tasks to get the greatest benefit from the session:

- ✔ **Promptly distribute meeting notes to all attendees**. These notes allow people to check the information discussed at the meeting when it's still fresh in their minds, and notes quickly remind people of their follow-up tasks. Try to distribute the notes within 24 hours of the meeting, and ask recipients to let you know if they have any corrections or additions.

- ✔ **Monitor the status of all action items that are performed after the meeting.** Because each action is itself a mini-project, monitoring the progress of all actions increases the chances that people successfully complete them.

Don't just talk about these suggestions for making your meetings more effective. Discussing suggestions can't improve your meetings. Act on them!

### *Holding project meetings*

Meetings you may want to hold in the project include:

- ✔ **Ad-hoc team meetings:** To discuss a problem with something being developed and get everybody's ideas for the best way of dealing with it.

- ✔ **Project progress meetings:** With the sponsor or steering committee, often every two weeks or every four weeks, to talk about progress and the outlook for the next period.

- ✔ **Regular team meetings:** Often held weekly within a team to discuss progress during the week and talk about the work in the coming week.

- ✔ **Stakeholder meetings:** To keep stakeholders up to date with what's going on in the project and help maintain interest, enthusiasm and a positive outlook. Check out Chapter 4 for more on stakeholder management.

- ✔ **Workshops:** Perhaps to sort out technical details such as a specification, but also useful for project planning, such as holding a risk workshop.

## *Setting up a project website*

Do you ever get emails sent to you 'in case you want to know', but you don't? Email is an abused communication form, and that's partly because it's so easy. Your name can be put on a distribution list in moments, and you have to live with the consequences for months. Communications used to be largely by phone, but then came email so people emailed instead. Now, because they know that you get a huge amount of email, after they have sent you something, they phone you up to tell you to look out for it. And while they're on the phone, they can't help telling you what's in the email.

So much for other people bombarding you with information that you don't want, but are you an offender too? Do you send other people masses of information about what's happening on your project 'in case they want to know'?

If a significant number of people (including staff in other projects) need to know what's happening on your project, consider setting up a website. You can put key information there, and then send everyone a single email to say that if they want to know what's going on in the project, to look at the website. If they need more information than that, they should simply ask.

Websites are great for making information available, but remember they're not usually very secure. You may need to sanitise the information put up on the site – which is fine for most people who need to look at it – but have a secondary line of communication such as an email to the sponsor for more sensitive information. You can put both of those communications into your plan – see the section 'Preparing a Project Communications Management Plan', towards the end of this chapter.

# *Making a business presentation*

An increasingly popular medium for getting information across is a business presentation. This may be suitable, for example, for regular project progress meetings. Instead of having a written report, the Project Manager gives a short presentation with a few PowerPoint or Keynote slides. The Project Manager then hands out the essential figures such as the spend against plan and products completed, on a very short note.

Preparing a presentation needs some thought and, strangely, the shorter the presentation then usually the more preparation is needed. It takes some practice to get the information across in a short time.

### *Planning the presentation*

Start out by planning carefully. Think who'll be attending, what their interests are and so what information you need to include and what you don't need. Beware of putting in superfluous detail that you find interesting but your audience won't.

In terms of the overall content, packing a presentation with a mass of facts and figures and delivering it all in a high-speed gabble isn't going to be effective, because the people listening to you simply aren't going to take it in. It's much better to have a much more limited amount of information delivered in a measured way.

When planning the content of a presentation, don't ever fill the time available. Always aim to underfill the time for two reasons: first, you will speak more slowly in front of a group of people than you will on your own when rehearsing; and second, people will ask questions and you need to allow time to answer them. It's no good saying 'please leave your questions to the end' either. It's not fair to move on to new material in the presentation when someone's not clear about some vital information you've just covered. But in any case, if you're talking to senior managers, they'll ask questions as points arise, irrespective of whether you have asked them to leave questions until the end.

### *Using visuals*

The proverb 'A picture is worth a thousand words' is true. Make use of visuals, but use images and not too many words. Repeated lists of bullet points are deadly boring. Rather, use illustrations, graphs and diagrams. Most of the words in your presentation should be what you say not what you display.

On visuals, then, keep the number of words down. As the actor John Cleese said, don't put more words on a slide than you would on a t-shirt. You may not be able to follow John Cleese's advice completely if you need to show key project performance data, but it's a good saying to keep in mind and keep as close to as you can. And it's surprising how much you can avoid words if you use charts and diagrams.

When you're planning your use of visuals, avoid the temptation to have a lot. In a 15–20-minute presentation, plan to use no more than about five or six slides, including a title slide. A lot of slides flashing before the eyes is distracting.

Nick Graham has a rule in his project training company, Inspirandum, that in a course session of 40–60 minutes, there are never more than 16 slides, including the title slide, and the slides are highly visual with lots of images. He was amazed to see some materials from another training company that comprised 45 slides for a 40-minute session, and most of those were long lists of bullet points. Given that those attending the course also need to listen to the presenter, there wouldn't be time for people attending the course to even read all the information on the slides, let alone remember any of it.

### Rehearsing

Rehearsing your presentation is essential to make sure that you can fit it into the time and also to make sure that the slides make sense. US president Abraham Lincoln put it well when he said: 'Give me six hours to chop down a tree, and I will spend the first four sharpening the axe.'

If your presentation is very high profile, such as to key stakeholders, go through it several times and perhaps get some of your project team to stand in as members of the audience. Get them to ask questions too, and the tougher the better, so that by the time you get to the presentation, you've covered every angle that you might get asked about.

### Dealing with questions

In the presentation itself, answer any questions honestly and, whatever you do, don't invent things. If you make up information, that's not only dishonest but it's likely to get you into trouble if someone in the audience knows it to be untrue or finds that out later when checking up on it. Your attempt at cover-up will merely result in a complete loss of credibility.

If you don't know the answer to a question, say so and tell the person that you'll find out and get the information to him. And then make absolutely sure that you do get back to the person with that detail, and quickly.

If you have a troublemaker in the audience – and you'll get them occasionally – who asks questions that will take you off track, you must take control the situation. You exercise that control in order to keep your presentation to time and on the subject that is of interest to the bulk of the audience. One way of dealing with the problem is to say to the questioner that the subject isn't the main focus of the presentation but that you'll be happy to take the discussion 'off-line' and talk to him at the end or at some other time.

### Sticking to time, and going for the kill

Time management is very important in a business presentation, not least to convey to your audience that you understand that their time is valuable. That emphasises the need to rehearse the presentation and trim the content to fit the time available, with some spare. You must leave time to 'go for the kill' if you're asking the meeting for approval or permission, such as to start work on the next project stage. Don't end up in a fluster trying to cram your last points in and then realise, when everyone has left the room, that you didn't actually ask for the approval or permission you needed.

# Preparing a Project Communications Management Plan

With the diversity of people who will be looking for information about your project and the array of data that you will be collecting, it's helpful and sometimes essential that you prepare a project Communications Management Plan (Comms Plan for short) to record what communications are to be made and how. As with most of project management, the Comms Plan isn't difficult.

You'll normally think through the communications needs in detail when you are doing the project planning in the Organising and Preparing stage – see Chapter 2 for details of the four stages of a project. However, you may uncover communication needs before that in the Starting the Project stage when you're sketching out the preliminary ideas for the project. Don't run the risk of forgetting those communications needs, so make a note of them ready for the Comms Plan.

As you come to think about project communications, it can be helpful to break them down into three areas to give more focus and structure to your thinking. Figure 15-2 shows the three areas.

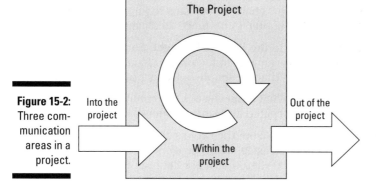

**Figure 15-2:** Three communication areas in a project.

The Project

Into the project

Out of the project

Within the project

# Identifying the communications

Within each of the three areas of communication in Figure 15-2, think through what communications are likely to take place, or which you need to set up or ask for. Then for each one, make an entry in the Comms Plan – see the 'Writing a Communications Management Plan' sidebar, later in the chapter.

## Identifying inbound communications

Inbound communications can be from outside the organisation, or from within the organisation but outside your project, such as from other projects. Some of this information may be sent automatically, but you need to think about who'll receive it, and in other cases it won't arrive unless you specifically ask for it. You may need to include:

- **Business information:** New policies and strategies, changes in the business or interfacing business procedures.

- **Financial information:** Statements of project funds committed, information on project finance available (perhaps dependent on company profits at the end of the financial year).

- **Interdependency information:** Such as progress on other projects interfacing with yours, or changes in those projects that will affect deliverables in your project.

- **Staff resource information:** Details of when staff will be available to work on your project, or which staff can be made available. This may run counter to the recorded assumptions in your plan and so need change-control action to re-plan it.

## Circulating information within the project

You can think of internal communications within the project as being at two levels. The first is communications between the sponsor or steering committee and the Project Manager, and the second is between the Project Manger and the team leaders or team members. You can include:

- **Change control:** Asking for changes, perhaps to improve the project or to correct errors. (See Chapter 14 for more on change control.)

- **Direct communications to the Project Manager:** Sometimes known as *Project Issues*. This allows anyone in the project to communicate directly to the Project Manager – that's a simple but very powerful mechanism.

- **Financial information:** What money is being committed by team leaders, where they have delegated authority to spend.

- **Product control:** Authority from the Project Manager to a team manager to start working on a work assignment, or *Work Package*, and then notification by the team leader when that Work Package is complete.

✔ **Progress information:** Regular progress reports from team leaders to the Project Manager, then regular progress reports from the Project Manager to the sponsor or steering committee.

### Sending information out of the project

Think about the following areas:

✔ **Business Case information and updates:** Including benefits projections, project costs and estimated delivery times in the project. (Please turn to Chapter 3 for more on the Business Case.)

✔ **Financial information:** Funds spent or committed in specified reporting periods, typically monthly.

✔ **Operational units:** So that they can be aware of what changes they need to make when the project is delivered, and the timescales for those changes.

✔ **Progress information:** From the sponsor or steering committee to corporate management.

✔ **Stakeholder information:** Information targeted at specific stakeholder interest areas to keep key people on board, supportive and enthusiastic.

# Writing a Communications Management Plan

The Comms Plan is simply a list of the communications that will take place in the project and how they will be conducted. You can see most communications coming, but others come to light as the project progresses, so the Comms Plan must be kept up to date.

The Comms Plan lists each communication with some or all of the information in the bullet points below. For some communications, you may also need to include details of an agreed format, such as with the layout of a dashboard for a project progress report (see the section 'Using a dashboard for progress reporting', earlier in this chapter).

✔ **Communication name:** An easily recognisable name such as 'Team Progress Report'.

✔ **Security:** You may not need this heading for your project, but a surprisingly high proportion of projects do include data that must be looked after. It's not just classified data within government, but commercially sensitive information involving clients or company plans, or privacy in the context of financial or medical records.

✔ **Recipient(s):** Who'll receive the communication.

✔ **Producer:** Who'll be responsible for the communication.

✔ **Content:** The information content decided or agreed for the communication.

✔ **Frequency:** How often the communication will be made. This may be regular such as weekly or monthly, on demand as the need arises such as with problem reporting, or fixed to a particular event such as an End of Project Report being at the end of the project.

✔ **Media:** How the communication will be made, such as phone call, email, website entry or business presentation.

✔ **Data collection:** How and when the data for the report are collected. This collection may have to be done some time in advance of the communication and involve resources beyond the person responsible for the communication, the Producer (see the earlier bullet).

# Chapter 16

# Bringing Your Project to Closure

. . . . . . . . . . . . . . . . . . . . . . . . . . . . . . . . . . . . . . . . . . . . . . . . . . . . . .

## In This Chapter

▶ Planning for a successful project termination

▶ Dealing with early closure of the project – a 'crash stop'

▶ Helping your team members move on to new work

▶ Evaluating your project's successes and failures

. . . . . . . . . . . . . . . . . . . . . . . . . . . . . . . . . . . . . . . . . . . . . . . . . . . . . .

*O*ne characteristic that distinguishes a project from 'business as usual' work is its distinct end – the point at which all work is complete, the results are achieved (of course) and reviewed, and the project team disbanded. However, with intense demands pulling you to your next assignment, you may need to show some determination in order to finish the project properly and thank all the people who made it possible.

Unfortunately, not bringing your projects to full closure hurts both the organisation and the people who performed the work. When you don't assess the extent to which your project achieved the desired outcomes, you can't determine whether you conceived, planned and performed the project well. Furthermore, team members don't have the chance to experience closure, achievement and a job well done.

This chapter shows you how to close your project successfully by finishing all substantive work, performing the final administrative tasks and helping team members complete their association with your project and move on. In addition, this chapter helps you carry out a project evaluation, which is important to pick up on good and bad things that happened in this project, from which you and the organisation can take lessons to help future projects.

Most projects run their full course, but occasionally you may need to stop a project early. The early closure is a sort of 'crash stop' if something goes significantly off target. You may need a crash stop if company profit or government funding is less than expected and the project can no longer be afforded. Or perhaps business circumstances have changed and the project is simply not needed any more. Whatever the reason for the closure, whether it be the planned closure or a crash stop, you still need an orderly shut down.

In a crash-stop situation, still look to see what can be used from the project. It's often the case that something can be saved and used, so that not all the effort is wasted. It may even be worth finishing some of the products if they're almost complete and could then be used. Both of these are reasons to have a closure stage, even if the project is shutting down early.

# Staying the Course to Completion

Sometimes a project just sort of fizzles out and nobody is really clear whether it's still running or not.

*'I thought that project was finished.'*
*'No, Jane and Bob are still working on it, aren't they?'*
*'Well, Jane isn't because she moved to headquarters and a new job last week, and I thought I heard Bob saying he'd finished his project work now.'*
*'Oh well, in that case perhaps it has finished.'*

Projects should have a clear start and a clear finish. If you follow the product-based planning approach set out in Chapter 5, you automatically know when the main work of the project is over, because all of the deliverables are complete. You're now left with some close-down work to do, which also needs planning.

## Thinking ahead about project closure

The time to start thinking about project closure is when you're setting up the project in the first place. However, be aware that you may not be able to plan the detail until you get close to closure and can see exactly what's needed. In that sense, planning for closure is no different from the normal stage planning (more on stages in Chapter 9). If you wait until the end of your project to start thinking about its closure, it may be too late to gather all the necessary information and resources. Instead, start planning for your project's completion at the same time as when you prepare your initial project plan.

### Looking at the options for closure

You have two basic options open to you for how you fit closure to project stages:

- ✔ Have a closure stage that runs after the final products have been delivered.
- ✔ Make the shutdown work part of the final delivery stage.

Arguments exist for both, but a strong argument for having a closure stage is that frequently the recipients of the project's products need some 'hand holding' in the early days, and also final adjustments may be needed before those products are completely ready for their operational life. You may be slightly constrained if you're using a standard project method (Chapter 2 explains other project methods). The PRINCE2 project method, for example, has always included closure work as things to do towards the end of the last delivery stage, although in its latest edition it is now leaving the door ajar for having a closure stage. The PRIME project method strongly commends a closure stage because of the fine tuning and handholding work that's typical of the end of the project.

### Thinking about closure from the start

Even in the outline planning, closure should be in everyone's mind, and especially yours. It's logical to think through the implications of project delivery, and that includes being clear on, and agreeing, what that delivery is. If you're delivering a project to someone else, you need to be absolutely clear on how the project will be handed over at the end. There may be particular conditions for that handover, such as that project deliverables are functioning correctly, but also regarding flexibility. For example, will the customer of the project really refuse to take delivery if the 24-month project comes in 10 days overdue? It's possible that the delivery date is fixed and paramount, but in most cases you will find there is some flexibility.

An argument developed towards the end of a high-profile construction project. The construction company said that the customer should check the building, and then it could be handed over. The customer said that the building should be handed over then they would check it. The argument was finally resolved and narrowly avoided a £2 million court case that was looming to resolve the matter. Such a dispute is inexcusable in a small project, let alone a major one. The handover should be absolutely clear and agreed at the outset, and built into the plans. This is extremely easy if you use the product-planning approach covered in Chapter 5, in which the Work Flow Diagram not only shows the deliverables but also the order in which they occur. So, going back to the construction project, was 'Signed Handover Document' before 'Customer Building Check Report' or vice versa?

## Dealing with a crash stop

If your project is shutting down early, perhaps because it's no longer needed because of a change in corporate policy, then you still have some planning to do for closure. The emphasis is slightly different from a planned closure, so consider the following questions for your closure plan:

✔ Can any of the project products (deliverables) be salvaged so that there is some benefit from all the project effort – not everything gets thrown in the bin?

✔ Even though the project is closing, is it worth finishing any products? It may be, for example, that some are almost complete and would be usable. It doesn't make sense to stop work on a £100,000 product if it's within £1,000 worth of effort to complete and you can still use the product to save the organisation £50,000 a year.

✔ Is a more thorough review needed to examine the causes of the fast shutdown and see whether it could have been spotted earlier that the project was no longer viable or needed? That knowledge could save money in the future.

✔ Do you need to warn the organisation or individual managers that project staff and other resource – such as accommodation and equipment – will be released early?

✔ Do you need to warn finance managers that the project budget now won't be fully used, and inform them how much will be released and what amounts are involved in what financial years, if the project was planned to run across a financial year end?

✔ Do you need to stop supplier work prematurely and pay off remaining amounts on the contract? Of course, you'll be using that 'early shutdown' clause you had put into the contracts so you don't have to pay the full amounts!

✔ Do you need to tell the stakeholders who wanted the project that it now won't be completed? That may need particular thought and care if some stakeholders needed the project badly and the early closure has significant implications for them.

# *Planning Closure*

As you approach the end of the project, you need to adjust your closure plans in the light of what's happening in the project, and then work them into detail so you know exactly what's involved and what time and resource will be required. As we point out earlier in this chapter, this work is very much like the standard delivery stage planning that you do at the end of the preceding stage. The difference with closure work is that it tends to be a bit more unpredictable. For example, if those receiving the deliverables find that they are exactly as they wanted and everything works really well for them, it may be that only a few minor adjustments are needed. However, if users find that there were a lot of things that neither they nor the team had thought of, then rather more adjustment may be needed.

# Outlining closure activities

Here are some examples of closure work to include in your plan:

✔ Establish what adjustments, if any, are needed to fine-tune the project deliverables, and what priority they have. Some changes may be essential and the deliverables won't be properly usable without them. Other things may be cosmetic and nice to have if they can be accommodated.

✔ Establish the amount of funding needed for adjustment, and its source. If something is a change from the original requirement (which most changes at this point will be, or the products would have failed when tested), then the customer may have to find extra budget unless the remaining change funds are sufficient.

✔ Schedule remaining work to adjust products and support user staff in their early use of them.

✔ Fix or confirm the date for the final handover and the close of the project.

✔ Check any business benefits that are immediately visible at the end of the project.

✔ Check the plans for measuring and reporting benefits that won't be clearly visible until some time after the project has shut down.

✔ Identify any elements of project control that will need to be passed forward into the working life of products. This includes version control systems, risk management and maintenance requirements.

✔ Terminate contracts for project work and pass on to the business area any contracts for ongoing supplies and support. This includes authorising any final payments under the contracts.

✔ Ensure that all support documentation is in place for ongoing maintenance and operations. You should have included such documentation in the products earlier in the project, so this item should be a fast confirmation to be quite sure that everything is in place.

✔ Ensure that any necessary licences, permits or other authorities are in place, ready for handover.

✔ Plan the release of project staff, because support requirements will wind down during closure, liaising as needed with their line managers, and then release staff in line with the plan.

✔ List any organisational actions that will be needed or which are recommended after the project. This might include picking up on good ideas that the project didn't have time to implement, or adjustment of project management standards following experience in this project.

Although not necessarily appearing on the official list of project closure work, some sort of project celebration is appropriate for a successful project. It's not only right to thank staff for their part in the success of the project, but it's a great boost to see and celebrate the result of all the effort.

Some organisational managers have a very strange approach to such celebration and may object to any funding of it. It's unlikely, though, that they carry that way of thinking through when they support their football teams. When the manager's friend shouts excitedly as the final whistle blows, 'We won! Our team scored two goals and we won two-nil – hurray!' does the manager reply, 'Well, it's what they get paid for, isn't it?' Seeing a result and then that result being recognised are both extremely powerful in motivation, as Chapter 13 explains.

## Motivating teams to the finish line

As team members work hard to fulfil final project obligations, their focus often shifts from accomplishing the project's overall objectives to completing their individual assignments. In addition, other stakeholders who were initially very interested in the project's results may become involved with other priorities and activities as the project continues (which means they likely lose interest and enthusiasm for your project). Yet, successful project completion requires a coordinated effort by all key participants.

To reinforce your teams' focus and interest, do the following:

- ✔ Remind everyone on the project of the value and importance of the final results.

- ✔ Visit your teams, and reaffirm your mutual commitment to bring the project to successful completion.

- ✔ Monitor final activities closely, and give frequent feedback on performance.

- ✔ Encourage teams and individuals. You should be doing this throughout the project, but it is specially important towards the end.

# Providing a Good Transition for Team Members

Team members can get very concerned when it's first suggested that they move over to work on your project. *Transition planning* – how team members get back into the mainstream after the project, or onto a new project – is extremely important. In some organisations, being assigned to a project is seen as a career death sentence. You not only need to make sure that arrangements are in hand for the return of staff, but that these arrangements are carried through.

Even if bad things don't happen to team members after a project, they're likely to worry that those things will. The worries include:

✔ Someone else has been put in my job while I'm on the project, so I won't be able to go back afterwards and will be given a rubbish job somewhere else that I will hate.

✔ My department will reorganise while I'm away and there won't be a place for me any more.

✔ The organisation is hitting problems and is downsizing, and as the department has managed without me during my time on the project, it will see me as disposable and the first in line for redundancy.

✔ The project is quite long and I will get out of touch with what's going on and with the technical aspects of my normal job.

If team members have been assigned to you for the project, rather than the team being people in your own organisational area, it's important that they know what's going to happen to them at the end of the project, and then that what is promised actually happens. If they spend time worrying about their future, they're not going to concentrate too well on the work, and are likely to spin it out and miss deadlines in order to put off the time when they leave the project. In the worst case, team members may jump ship before the end of the project and find another more stable job in another organisation (and perhaps take all their valuable knowledge and experience to your arch competitor).

If promises are made about transition but are then never carried through, there will be organisational implications for future projects. Word will get around that the assurances made by organisational managers are worthless, and people will fight tooth and nail not to get drawn into project work.

As far as you can, make the environment one where project work is seen as a career opportunity and something that's valued in the organisation. If it's not in your power to create that environment, do your best to influence others to see the logic of it.

As part of the transition work, consider the following:

✔ **Acknowledge and document team members' contributions.** Express your appreciation to people for their assistance on your project, and share with them your assessment of their performance. Take a moment to thank their supervisors for making them available to your project, and provide the supervisors with an assessment of their performance.

   As a general rule, share positive feedback in public; share constructive criticisms and suggestions for improvement in private. In both cases, be sure to share your comments with team members personally.

✔ **Help people with their personal plans for transition to new assignments.** If appropriate, help people find their next project assignments. Help them develop a schedule for winding down their involvement with your project while making sure they fulfil all their remaining obligations.

✔ **Announce to the organisation that your project is complete.** You need to advise closure for the following three reasons:

- To alert people in your organisation that the planned outcomes of your project are now available

- To confirm to people who supported your project that their efforts led to a successful result

- To let people know they can no longer charge time or resources to your project

---

# Using a novel approach to announce your project's closure

If your project was small, chances are all the participants already know it's over and are aware of its results. But if the project took a long time (six months or more) and involved many groups in your organisation, people who participated early may never see the actual results of their efforts.

A while back, one of Stan Portny's clients had just completed a one-year project that entailed the design, development, production and introduction of a small piece of equipment for an aircraft cockpit. At the official end of his project, the client reflected on the many different people from all areas of his organisation who'd played some role in the project. In addition to the engineers who completed the final installation and testing of the equipment, contract officers, procurement specialists, financial managers, human resources specialists, test lab personnel, logisticians and others had all helped make the project a success.

The client realised that, if past experience was any indicator, the vast majority of these support people would never see the final result of their efforts. So he decided to do something that his organisation had never done before: he put together a small display in his workplace that

illustrated the birth, evolution and fruition of his project. He included everything from the signed contract document and purchase orders, to the initial design model and engineering drawings, to pictures of the device in an airplane and a pilot who would use it, as well as the maintenance people who would support it. He then sent messages to all the people who'd worked on the project, announcing the display and inviting them to come by his workplace to visit.

The response was overwhelming. He estimated that more than 100 people came by to look at the display. He overheard comments by people throughout the organisation about how they'd performed individual tasks large and small that contributed to the success of this equipment – equipment that they now could see would affect people's lives. The most poignant comment Stan's client received was from a technician who worked in the test laboratory. The technician told him this was the first time in his 11 years with the organisation that he'd ever seen the final results of an item he'd tested.

Stan's client had spent several hours assembling the display but the positive results he and his organisation received were immeasurable.

# Reviewing the Project

Lay the groundwork for repeating on future projects what worked well on this one (and avoiding what didn't) by conducting a project evaluation or review.

A *project evaluation* is an assessment of project results, activities and processes. It contributes to noting lessons learned (both good things and bad things) that will help improve project management on future projects.

Avoid the term *project post-mortem* because it conjures up the image of an autopsy to determine the cause of death! The term alone gives people a very negative outlook and suggests that the evaluation is looking only for problems and culprits. The project review is as much, or even more, about what went well as what went badly.

## Beginning with the end in mind

As mentioned in Chapter 2, the second habit in Stephen Covey's book *The 7 Habits of Highly Effective People* is 'Begin with the end in mind'. That's great advice when it comes to project review. You can't review properly unless you have something to review against. Right at the beginning of the project, you need to think what you'll review against. It makes good sense anyway to be clear about what the project is to achieve before you decide to do it. As always, don't get worried about this, because it doesn't have to be difficult. Just think about what you want to check at the end of the project and then put in place the things that will enable you to carry out that check, such as:

- ✔ Benefits
- ✔ Finance targets
- ✔ Meeting deadlines – perhaps key deliveries that need to be made during the project as well as at the end of it
- ✔ Objectives – what the project is to achieve
- ✔ Productivity levels
- ✔ Quality
- ✔ Risk mitigation

You can conduct a review by going around and talking to people or by a meeting that you can hold in person, or by video or in a telephone conference. As always, face to face is better, so only resort to other means when you really must. A good review, whether by interview or meeting, requires that you address the right topics and that people share their project thoughts and experiences openly and honestly.

As you plan your consultation with others, consider asking about the following issues:

- ✔ Could anything have been done better, faster or more cheaply?

- ✔ If you did the project again, what would you like to be done differently in the light of this project experience?

- ✔ If you did the project again, what would you like to see done the same way next time because it worked so well?

- ✔ Was anything unnecessary and, if so, was that just because of the way things turned out or because, on reflection, the activity was over the top from the outset?

- ✔ With any mistakes or misunderstandings, could someone have seen them coming and prevented them, or were they just the sort of things that you can never completely eliminate?

- ✔ Could anything have made your work easier, such as more support or better equipment?

- ✔ With regard to problems during the project:

  - Could you have anticipated and planned for them? If so, how?

  - Did you handle them effectively and efficiently when they arose?

- ✔ Did you use the organisation's project management systems and procedures effectively?

- ✔ Were any of the organisation's project management systems and procedures ineffective or inappropriate? If so, should this type of project be exempted from such procedures, or should the procedures be changed for all projects?

## *Recording project information*

For many of the review areas, having established at the outset that you'll review them, you then need to set up mechanisms to record the data so that you can review it at the end. Finance is an obvious one, and you'll undoubtedly be recording spending information anyway, but what about quality and what about team performance? Just how many products did fail test and need rework? Did the teams deliver products within the expected number of staff hours, or was the number of hours significantly less or more?

As we explain in the introduction to this chapter, project review brings to light important information, and missing it out damages the organisation. Project review shouldn't normally be a huge amount of work, but the information that flows out of it can be hugely valuable for future projects.

## Lessons – storage and retrieval

Writing down details of experiences in a project is pointless if nobody knows that the record exists, or if they do, what's in it and whether it's of any use. Unless you're a Project Manager with an interest in history and with far too much spare time on your hands, you're not going to have time at the start of a project to start wading through loads of project records in the hope of finding some lessons reports, and within the dozens of reports that you do find, one or two tips that will help you now. Instead, ideally you will want some fast reference system that will take you quickly to what you want to know.

A key factor in storing information is understanding how it will be retrieved. Strangely perhaps, lessons reports, as commended by some of the older project methods, aren't the best way of recording information. It may be convenient for the project to store data in this way, but it isn't convenient for those wanting to retrieve it, and if it can't be retrieved, what's the point of storing it?

Dealing with lessons information needs a corporate response not a project response. If you have a Project Office in your organisation, that's the ideal place to store information on project lessons. But even then, it's bad practice to rely on the memory of staff in the Project Office. 'Oh,

you're starting up the global distribution project? Ah well, you need to look at these two lessons reports from earlier projects and, oh yes, I think you'll find some useful stuff in this one as well.' Good though that may be, what if that staff member leaves?

What you need is for lessons to be treated singly with a predetermined set of key words. They can then be put in a database and you can search for particular areas such as 'product planning' or 'risk involving suppliers'. Text searching on computers is getting increasingly sophisticated, and if you have the right kit, text searching can effectively act as a database because the words are all keyed. If the lessons reports are in one place, searching that directory under key words may be sufficient.

Either way, lessons information is extremely valuable. It's sad if a good project fails. It's even sadder if a second one fails because nobody took on board the lessons from the first one. It's been said that history repeats itself because no-one listens the first time. Don't let that happen in your organisation's projects. Instead, have some central repository of lessons where you can find specifics on topics like risk and advice by type of project, so you can pull up lessons from similar projects from the past.

## *Learning lessons – and passing them on*

There's a clear and obvious link between project review and learning lessons to be passed on to future projects, but the two aren't the same thing. Some aspects of review, such as whether the project met its objectives, are usually for this project alone. Similarly, lessons learned may be identified and passed on throughout the life of the project, particularly if it is a long one, not just left to the end.

One public sector health organisation in the UK asked Nick Graham to take part in a couple of its Project Managers' days to give advice to Project Managers. These sessions are held about three times a year and all the Project Managers in the organisation take the day out to meet together, talk about their projects, swap ideas and maybe ask for help on particular aspects. All

Project Managers reported that they save considerably more than three days a year from the valuable insight and help they get from their colleagues and invited consultants in these meetings.

Identifying the cause of problems in order to avoid them wherever possible on future projects is very important, but the main thrust of lessons learned is to see what worked really well and pass on that experience so other projects can benefit from it in the future.

Having learned lessons, it's vital that they are passed on and not just left to get dusty along with the other project records in some forgotten corner of a corporate network drive. A central repository should exist somewhere so that future Project Managers can get at the lessons easily: have a look at the nearby sidebar 'Lessons – storage and retrieval' for more.

# Measuring benefits

If benefits are visible at the end of the project, which some may be, no sponsor is going to wait six months for some post-project benefits review if there's already some indication as to whether the project has been a success.

Many benefits won't be clear for some time. For example, if the project has put some new business process in place and at the end of the project the business staff start to use it, it's no good looking at time savings immediately. Staff will still be going slowly as they learn the new approach. The best time to measure the time saving of the new procedure will probably be in four or six weeks' time when things have settled down and staff are up to a normal speed of working.

### Measuring benefits now

While the project is still running, there are either one or two end points where you may want to measure and report benefits. Whether there are one or two points depends on whether you have a closure stage or if closure is just at the end of the final delivery stage.

When final products are delivered, some benefits may be seen immediately, such as that maintenance time drops as soon as the new machines are commissioned and the old ones are taken out of service, or that customer complaints are dramatically reduced the moment the new delivery procedures start up. You can measure and report such benefits at the end of the final delivery stage, which in some approaches may mark the end of the project.

If you have a closure stage, though, it may well be that the six-week measures can be taken within the life of the project, before final closure, and reported.

### *Measuring benefits later*

If benefits will come on stream after the end of the project, either because you don't have a closure stage or because the benefits will take a longer time to become clear, then it's not within the remit of the project to measure and report on them. However, you should make arrangements for such measures and reporting back to corporate management on the eventual level of benefit from the project.

It's vital that the organisation does review project benefits systematically or else poor management decisions may be made in the future. If the bulk of a project's benefits only came on stream six months after the end of the project but were never measured or reported, the organisation may be reluctant to run a similar project, because the only information available massively understates the benefits. Or, vice versa, expected benefits never actually materialised and now the organisation runs a second project on the assumption that they were all delivered as the original Business Case claimed they would be. This area is tricky, though, because as a Project Manager you don't have authority over corporate management. But sometimes you have the opportunity to influence things, such as by having a word with the sponsor or members of your steering committee who are corporate managers.

Nick Graham was talking to staff from a local authority in Scotland about their current project, its justification and its projected benefits. The staff told him that the project was justified because it would make a 5 per cent saving. When he asked how that had been calculated, the staff told him that it hadn't been, but it would surely save at least 5 per cent. When he asked if they would measure at the end of the project to check the saving, he was told that they never did, because the pressure to do other projects was so great they just moved straight on to the next one. Nick said, 'Don't tell me, you justify the next project on a 5 per cent saving as well!' He intended it as a light-hearted remark, but to his astonishment the staff replied seriously, 'Yes, that's right.'

# *Planning for Things After the Project*

The final part of the closure work is to consider what work needs to be passed on to organisational managers such as operations staff. The nature of this post-project work varies depending on the nature of the organisation and the project, but here are a few areas to think about:

- ✔ Considering changes to organisational standards and procedures such as project procedures and risk handling

- ✔ Making sure that if suppliers delivered sub-standard items that were temporarily usable, but not correct, that the supplier replaces those items

- ✔ Incorporating maintenance work

✔ Measuring and reporting benefits that will come on stream after the end of the project

✔ Picking up on good ideas developed during the project but which the project didn't have time or money to do

✔ Monitoring risk-related work that's ongoing, such as use of dangerous machinery

✔ Enforcing version control

In each case, discuss the work with the person who'll be taking it on to be sure that she's the right person and that she has the capacity to do the job. If there's a problem, discuss it with your sponsor or steering committee, but make sure that it's resolved so that the item isn't left unmanaged.

# Part V
# Taking Your Project Management to the Next Level

'He's never given up awaiting a decision on the project he managed 60 years ago.'

# In this part . . .

You become a truly skilled project manager by continuing to increase your knowledge and refine your practices and by effectively using tools and resources from start to finish. This part is here to help you do just that.

In this part you can get some ideas about the sort of computer software that can help you, and how you can get a lot for free. There's also information on the powerful Earned Value Management (EVM) technique. Also, if you're working in a multiple project environment, you'll find some guidance on programmes and portfolios. Not sure what they are? Read on!

# Chapter 17

# Managing Multiple Projects

· · · · · · · · · · · · · · · · · · · · · · · · · · · · · · · · · · · · · · · · · · · · · · ·

## In This Chapter

▶ Understanding programmes and portfolios

▶ Looking at the implications for your project of being in a multi-project environment

▶ Seeing how being in a programme can affect your plans

▶ Looking at project interfaces in a multi-project environment

· · · · · · · · · · · · · · · · · · · · · · · · · · · · · · · · · · · · · · · · · · · · · · ·

T his chapter is a little different to the others in the book because it gives you some information and advice on working with multiple projects. You may find this guidance helpful for two reasons. The first is that if your project is part of a group of projects, then it will affect how you set it up and then run it. The second is to give you some outline guidance if you end up being responsible for a group of projects yourself, rather than just a single one.

Business-based organisations are now more aware of the need for projects and project management. Unfortunately, in the UK at least, this has led to over-excitement in the marketplace over what people can sell to make money out of this increasing interest. After intense interest in some project management qualifications, attention turned to finding the next big catchphrase and money-spinner, and that catchphrase was *programmes*; and now that many people have become qualified in programme management, attention is increasingly turned to *portfolios*. Now programme and portfolio management are both important (don't worry, the terms are explained in this chapter), but you need to be careful to apply the disciplines correctly and intelligently so that you don't incur unnecessary overheads, bureaucracy and delays on your projects. Sometimes, even though everyone is banging on about programmes and their latest shiny qualifications, you might even raise eyebrows by arguing that your project simply shouldn't be part of the programme.

This chapter helps you understand the nature and dynamics of programmes, including different types of programme and how a portfolio works. It gives you advice on when a group of projects need to be in a programme and, importantly, when they don't.

# Talking the Talk

As a first step then, what exactly is a programme and what is a portfolio? The terms are increasingly used but widely misunderstood.

## Defining a programme

A *programme* is a group of projects that:

- ✔ Are connected in some way, such as each project needing deliverables from the others in order to proceed
- ✔ Need to be coordinated and managed together as a group, not merely as separate projects
- ✔ Need specific people to coordinate the projects as a whole as well as people to deal with the management of each of the member projects

A great definition of a programme is from something that has absolutely nothing to do with programmes! It's a quotation from the leader of the Red Arrows – the Royal Air Force aerobatic display team. The leader said this about his role: 'My job is to fly nine aeroplanes as though they were one.' That's a brilliant description of the tight formation flying that the Red Arrows and similar aerobatic teams do, but it's also a great picture of a programme. Running a programme is like flying a formation of projects. Each project is distinct and has its own 'pilot', but the projects within the group need to be closely coordinated.

## Following the crowd

Nick Graham was talking to a Programme Manager on one of his project training courses. The manager was confused about his role, and Nick asked about the projects he was involved in and which were included the programme. As the discussion continued and Nick probed deeper, the person came to see that not only was he not a Programme Manager (despite his job title) and he didn't have a programme, the projects weren't even true projects. He had been swept along in the organisation's rush to have programmes because 'that's what everyone is doing these days'. Instead of having work allocated to him and then deciding the best way of managing it, the manager had been told it was a programme and he was now trying to retro-fit that structure onto the work.

In the rush to establish qualifications with associated training courses in the UK, the term *programme* got hijacked by the UK government organisation responsible for a particular programme approach and qualification. It was taken to mean strategic programmes, as if no other sort existed. In fact, other sorts of programmes exist, and you need to be aware of them. Having said that, some people are setting up programmes when they're not needed (see the nearby sidebar 'Following the crowd' for one example), and other people are making the opposite error of not setting up programmes that are needed, all because of that restricted understanding of the word *programme*. Make sense? Have a look at some different types of programme and all will become clear:

- ✔ **Coordinated delivery:** This is where a group of projects must finish at the same time and need to be carefully controlled in order to do that. Often there is technical coordination and some interdependency between the projects as well. An example is with developing a new version of office software. Different projects will update the word processor, spreadsheet, database and presentation graphics components, but they must have the same look and feel and all be brought to market together as a set.

- ✔ **Linear:** A common mistake people make with projects is trying to do something too substantial and launch it with one big bang. That's a very high-risk strategy and it often makes more sense to break the job down into a consecutive series of smaller projects. It's then possible that two or more of those projects can run consecutively, but that's unusual and it's more often a linear string of projects.

- ✔ **Strategic:** This is a rolling group of projects that will completely change the way an organisation operates. It's common that this sort of programme will last around five years. Although some projects are known at the outset and can be started when the programme starts, others emerge as the programme continues.

- ✔ **Heavy product interdependency:** Where significant product interdependencies exist between projects, the complexity is such that it makes sense to have an overall plan and exercise overall control to manage those interdependencies. Have a look at Chapter 5 for more on products and product planning.

- ✔ **Heavy resource interdependency:** Where a group of projects are calling on the same resource pool, some coordination is necessary or the projects will all go rapidly off plan when the projects find that the people they need at a particular time are already fully committed on one of the other projects. Resource levelling is needed in each project anyway, and this will deal with project dependencies – Chapter 6 on activity planning explains this resource levelling. But where that resource planning between projects gets really complicated, it can make more sense to establish a higher management level above the projects with an overarching plan and resource schedule. This higher-level resource plan will help avoid conflicts where two projects want the same staff at the same time, and helps managers look quickly at the implications across projects if a project experiences a delay and doesn't release staff at the expected time.

## Defining a portfolio

A *portfolio* is simply a list. It would be nice to be really complicated about portfolios so we can sound clever, but basically a portfolio is a list of projects that your organisation would like to run as and when resources become available. There may be a single list across the whole organisation, or separate portfolios may be maintained by different specialisms or departments.

The management of a portfolio concerns the control of how a project gets onto that list in the first place, how the list is organised, and then how the project gets off the list. A project may be taken off the list because it's now underway or because it no longer warrants a place there, perhaps because changed business circumstances mean that the project is no longer needed.

As with so many buzzwords, a lot of confusion has arisen around the terms *programme* and *portfolio*. Some organisations talk about their 'IT programme' and their 'accommodation programme'. Actually, the IT programme is just a list of pending IT projects. There's no coordination of projects involved, so actually it isn't a programme at all – it's a portfolio but made up of a single type of project. Keep quiet if it's you that controls the list and your organisation now calls you a 'Programme Manager' – with the appropriate pay rise – because of it.

# Deciding on a Programme

So when is a group of projects just a group of independent projects, and when is it a programme? All sorts of complicated arguments can be brought into play to answer the question, but a simple way of cutting through this is to look at whether the additional level of management is justified. If you appoint a programme structure with programme staff, is it really necessary; will it earn its keep?

In many cases, the line between having a group of separate but related projects and having a programme is a blurred one. In fact, that's what causes many people to become confused and set up programmes where they're just not needed. Just because a project has a product interdependency with another project doesn't mean that the two projects are part of a programme. It just means that two projects have a product interdependency! The respective Project Managers may be able to control the product transfers quite happily between them with the interdependencies shown clearly on their plans. The same applies to shared resources.

The balance tips where it's more effective, including cost effective, to have a higher level of management doing the coordination. After the programme level of management has been established, its cost effectiveness may then be enhanced by providing services that give economy of scale, such as having centralised project administration for all the projects in the programme and doing some management functions such as risk management. If the same business risk could affect five out of the eight projects in the programme, it often makes sense to monitor it once at programme level rather than five affected projects each having to monitor that same risk.

A programme has its own level of planning, management and control that's positioned above the projects. It follows that you have a number of things to bear in mind if your project is part of a programme.

## Understanding programme roles

The roles used at the programme level may vary a bit depending on whether you're using a particular approach to programmes, but typically there will be the following roles:

- ✔ **Project Director:** Someone who has overall responsibility for the programme and all the projects that make it up. This is similar to the sponsor of a project, but at a higher level.

- ✔ **Programme Manager:** A person with project management skills who can draw up and maintain the overall Programme Plan. This person will liaise with the Project Managers of the projects in the programme.

- ✔ **Programme Administration:** An administrative function that can offer support to projects as well as to the programme level. It may be in the form of an office called the Programme and Project Office (PPO) with a manager and other staff.

There may be additional, optional, roles with which your project will need to work, depending on the nature of the programme:

- ✔ **Programme Risk Manager:** As the name suggests, a risk specialist keeping track of risks across the whole group of projects.

- ✔ **Business Change Manager:** If the programme is causing substantial change across the organisation, this person will liaise with departments to ensure that the change is coordinated so it happens smoothly and the interfaces are properly thought through.

- ✔ **Audit:** This is a centralised project audit function to check that projects are running properly and that the information coming out of them is correct. It's the project equivalent of financial audit.

It's possible and sometimes advantageous to have staff from the programme level, often the programme director, also taking a role on project steering committees; it forms a natural link between each project and the programme. However, if some projects have programme staff directly involved while others don't, it can sometimes lead to favouritism when it comes to resource, so such role sharing needs to be done carefully and thoughtfully.

## *Fitting in with Programme Plans*

A programme has an overall plan at a higher level of detail than the Project Plans. This shows dependencies between projects, both product dependencies and resource dependencies.

You often sketch out the plan for the programme first and then break it down into the parts that will become the member projects. In other cases, though, the component projects will already be clear, and after a decision has been made to group them into a programme, the Programme Plan will be drawn up from the Project Plans, with particular attention now being given to the interfaces.

## *Mapping interdependencies by product*

An excellent tool for mapping product interdependencies is the Work Flow Diagram. Chapter 5 covers product planning in the context of planning for a single project, but you can adapt the Work Flow Diagram to show dependencies across projects in a programme. Figure 17-1 illustrates the Work Flow Diagram, but if you haven't yet read Chapter 5 it's probably best to do so before coming back to look at Figure 17-1.

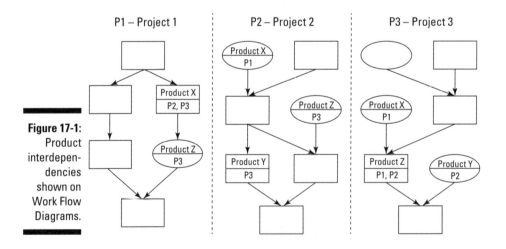

**Figure 17-1:**
Product interdependencies shown on Work Flow Diagrams.

Figure 17-1 uses notation from Inspirandum's publication *The Project Techniques Toolbox* to show the product interdependencies. Team products are shown in rectangles, and where the product is being passed to another project as well as being used in its own project, a bar across the bottom of the rectangle shows what other projects it is being sent to. Where an external product has a bar across the bottom of the symbol, it shows that the product is coming from another project in the programme, and the notation shows which project it's coming from. Figure 17-1 shows the three Work Flow Diagrams from the three Project Plans, but the Programme Plan can show these product dependencies in one view and without all the detail of the Project Plans.

Colour-coding is particularly effective on cross-project diagrams, but it's best to keep the bar and the identifier on as well for complete clarity.

## Controlling a programme

Programme-level controls focus primarily on coordination, not on running the projects. Having made that point, some central control can also be exercised in other areas, for example:

- **Business Case and benefits projections:** The project's Business Case may be part of the Business Case for the whole programme (Chapter 3 explains the Business Case). Therefore, any changes, such as in the levels of benefit anticipated, may have programme implications.

- **Change control:** Each project may have a change budget, but the programme may hold a bigger change budget. If a project comes up with a really good idea, it can bid for programme change funds.

- **Problem reporting:** Some problem reporting may have to be copied to programme level if there are implications for other projects. You need to be specially careful to consider impacts on other projects when looking at things happening in your own project.

- **Progress reporting:** In order to monitor and control the interfaces between projects and keep them coordinated, the programme staff will need accurate progress reporting from projects. This can often be simple, with the progress report that is prepared by the Project Manager and passed to the sponsor or steering committee simply being copied to the programme level. In addition, milestone reporting with Work Checklists is particularly effective – see Chapter 14 for more on Work Checklists.

- **Reporting line:** The programme management level will change the reporting line from the Sponsor or steering committee. In a standalone project, the Sponsor would report on the project directly to corporate management. In a programme, the Sponsor normally reports to the Programme Director and the Programme Director then reports to corporate management.

- **Risk management:** Some risk monitoring and management may be carried out at programme level. In addition, projects may need to notify new risks so that a check can be made at programme level to see whether they affect other projects in the programme.

For coordination within the programme, two-way communications are essential so that each project keeps the programme management well informed on progress and resource utilisation, and to make adjustments in the project in response to information and instructions from programme management because of what's happening in the programme. Using the resourcing example, if another project experiences a delay, it may result in a delay to the release of specialist staff due to work on your project, so you will need to re-plan accordingly.

# Managing a Portfolio

Managing a portfolio involves three key areas:

- ✔ Controlling the entry of projects onto the list
- ✔ Determining priorities and dependencies between the projects
- ✔ Regular review of the list to reassess priorities, confirming that projects should remain on the list and removing them if they shouldn't

## Understanding the project implications

To get a project onto the portfolio, you normally need to produce a paper to outline:

- ✔ What the project is about
- ✔ How much the project will cost and how long it is expected to take
- ✔ How the project fits with other projects, such as by showing dependencies
- ✔ How the project fits with organisational strategy
- ✔ What call the project will make on staff resource, particularly specialist or scarce resource

If you've already read Chapter 2, you may think that the content of the bullet points sounds familiar and rather like the outlining work you do in the stage Starting the Project. You'd be right to think that, and in fact there is sometimes a break between the Starting the Project stage and the full planning while the project waits for authorisation and resource. In turn, that can mean that someone other than you does the outline planning, and when you get the go-ahead to start the project, you need to review that outline before going on to full planning. It could be that some things have changed in the time since the outlining was done and you get the go-ahead to start the project with the Organising and Preparing stage.

# *Maintaining the portfolio*

For a project to get onto the portfolio in the first place, the outline should demonstrate that the project is justified. That means that the outline should include some business view, and depending on your organisation there may be a need for a costing or other justification (such as that it is a mandatory project) or even a simple Business Case. Chapter 3 provides a lot more information on project justification and Business Case preparation.

A danger is prioritising projects according to the amount of benefit that they will deliver. That's a wrong approach because benefits are only part of the story. Those responsible for the portfolio should consider:

- ✔ **Benefits:** Yes, they're important.

- ✔ **Organisational imperatives:** Imperatives include organisational strategy, but also tactical considerations such as the need for a 'quick win' project to boost confidence.

- ✔ **Project dependencies:** A low-return project may need to be run before a high-return one because it delivers things that the second project will need.

- ✔ **Return on investment:** A project with a modest return of benefits may be very attractive because it will be fast and cheap to run. A project with much more benefit may be much more costly and take a longer time before giving a return.

You should then regularly review the portfolio to check that each project still deserves a place on the list, and for changing priorities resulting from changes in the organisation and new projects added to the portfolio.

# Chapter 18

# Using Technology to Up Your Game

. . . . . . . . . . . . . . . . . . . . . . . . . . . . . . . . . . . . . . . . . . . . . . . .

*In This Chapter*

▶ Recognising software's role in project planning, control and communication

▶ Sizing up the benefits and limitations of technology in project management

▶ Making data available and supporting virtual teams

▶ Getting computer software and services for free

. . . . . . . . . . . . . . . . . . . . . . . . . . . . . . . . . . . . . . . . . . . . . . . .

*A* major part of project management is information – getting it, creating it, storing it, analysing it and sharing it. But the key to successful project management is using this information to see what's going on in the project and exercise control, and to guide and encourage people's performance.

Technology is providing ever easier and more affordable ways to handle information and also to help with the work involved in areas such as project planning. For example, computer software allows you to enter, store and analyse information and then present the results in professional formats. Email allows written communication with people in remote locations at all hours of the day (and night!), and video conferencing allows you to talk to them too. Computer scheduling tools allow you to draw up activity networks and Gantt Charts (see Chapter 6) much more quickly and easily, but then also help you to make changes easily and rapidly and so keep the plans up to date.

Even with all these advances, however, technology has its limitations and, for example, can't ensure focused and committed team performance. In fact, excessive reliance on technology can actually result in poor morale, confused and disorganised team members and lower overall performance. Used inappropriately, technology can become a distraction and even a problem, as you surely know if you have to plough through a massive email inbox each morning.

This chapter shows how you can use technology in jobs that benefit from it. For the jobs that aren't so well-suited for technology, the chapter covers other, more appropriate, means for handling information needs.

# *Using Computer Software Effectively*

Software for special analyses, project planning and reporting now looks so good that you may be tempted to believe it's all you need to ensure your project's success. However, even though the software works effectively and efficiently, it *can't* perform the following essential tasks:

✔ **Ensure that information is appropriately defined, timely and accurate.** In most instances, people record information to support project planning and control, and then they enter the information into a computer. You can set up the software to check for correctness of format or internal consistency, but the software can't ensure the quality and integrity of the data.

Suppose you use a computer program to maintain records of work hours that team members charge to your project. You can get time-recording software to reject hours that are inadvertently charged with an invalid project code. However, you can't set the package to recognise hours charged to the wrong project with a valid code.

✔ **Analyse all information or make project decisions.** Software can help you objectively determine the results of several possible courses of action. However, software can't effectively take into account all the objective and subjective considerations that you must weigh up before making a final decision.

✔ **Create and sustain dynamic interpersonal relationships.** Despite people's fascination with Facebook, email, texts and other types of social networking, computers can't ensure trusting relationships between people working together on a team. Technology can even make relationships more difficult to develop. Developments such as video communications through Skype and similar services help because they give some ability to see facial expressions and body language, but it's still nowhere near as good as face-to-face communication, and the limited duration of each communication isn't the same as working alongside a colleague in a team room.

So how *can* computer facilities help you during the life of a project? This section looks at what functionality is available and how technology can help you manage your project.

## *Seeing what software you need*

You'll find computer software helpful in three core areas:

✔ **Office software:** This is the standard package of a word processor, spreadsheet, presentation software and, possibly, database and contacts (address book) functionality. The presentation software gives some graphics capability, and perhaps enough for your needs, but you may choose a different package for graphics.

✔ **Project management software:** Well, so-called project management software anyway. The *so called* is because the packages are mostly scheduling software to do activity networks, Gantt Charts and resource scheduling. There is much more to project management than that, as you can discover by flicking through this book.

✔ **Communication software:** This includes email, but also things like RSS feeds (to notify changed information on a website), tweeting and, perhaps more importantly, Skype and its equivalents for video calls.

An area where software may be necessary, not merely a benefit, is if you're maintaining a website for your project and need web management facilities. Then again you may need software support for things like version control, MindMap diagrams and time management. This chapter focuses primarily on the core areas that cover the bulk of the project management work you'll encounter.

## Understanding where to use software

It's pretty obvious where you use some of the software. If you want to do an activity network, you'll naturally be drawn to a project management package. However, some uses aren't so obvious, so this section points out where you might use software applications and where you might use them in more unusual circumstances if you need to or even have to.

### Using the best software for the job

Try to resist, and then try to reverse, illogical software standards imposed by project offices that have a primary objective of making centralised reporting easy rather than making project management effective. In one multinational company, a project office insisted that the overview of the Risk Register (see Chapter 10) was held in a word processor table rather than on a spreadsheet, because that was its standard. The Project Manager had wanted to use a spreadsheet so he could sort the data in different ways using the powerful inbuilt sorting functions of a spreadsheet, such as for presenting rows in order of risk severity, or by who reported risks or by type of response; you just don't get that power and flexibility in a word processor table. The restriction was both unthinking and counter-productive, because the table and spreadsheet both look the same when included in the project office's report, and the project office could even have converted the spreadsheet to a table when reporting. We won't get into who gave the project office such authority over the Project Managers!

### *Office software*

Office software is important for things like reporting, but remember that a report may be in the form of a presentation to a steering committee or project board, where the presentation element of the software will be more than useful. The most common package is Microsoft Office, but there are others.

Here's some core software you'll need:

- ✔ **Database:** Useful for things like a Risk Register and an Issue Register, if you want something with more power than a spreadsheet.

- ✔ **Presentation graphics:** Useful for reporting and passing on information in the form of a presentation, but the facilities in these packages are powerful for general graphics work too and are great for things like the product-planning diagrams.

- ✔ **Spreadsheet:** Budget information, 'what if' calculations and also reporting if you use a 'dashboard' format for progress reports (see Chapter 15). Interestingly, spreadsheets are widely used for resource planning in larger projects, where many Project Managers find that the project management software just doesn't give them the flexibility and detail they need. You might also hold register overviews on a spreadsheet, such as a summary of information from the Risk Register. You can even produce an activity network on a spreadsheet, but it's hard work both in creating the network and then keeping it up to date, and project management (scheduling) software is considerably better. If you're thinking that you can't afford project management software, have a look at the section 'Getting Really Good Stuff for Free', later in this chapter.

- ✔ **Word processor:** For written communications, including reporting, and document preparation such as the Project Charter. You might also produce a project news sheet if you need to keep stakeholders informed of developments and you don't need the sophistication of desktop publishing software.

### *Project management software*

This title is a misnomer because the package doesn't help with all of project management or anything approaching it. Really, the tools are scheduling tools and cover activity networks, Gantt Charts and resource planning including resource levelling. The best known is Microsoft Project, but there are many others.

Project-scheduling software is generally excellent in what it does, but it can prove very frustrating as well because of the limitations it can impose. As you get used to the software, you quickly learn the tricks to make it display what you want, even if that means telling 'lies' to the software to get the effect you need. On the other hand, though, who'd want to recalculate a hand-drawn, 100-task, two-year duration activity network because a duration changed in Week 1?

Some packages are available that fit with project methods, but be careful to check what they do, what they don't do and the nature of their support. These tools, for example, generally don't include scheduling functionality but require you to use something like Microsoft Project alongside them. Some also start at the wrong end. They provide a huge amount of documentation and the boast that the software will help you control it all. A better start is to minimise the documentation and limit it to what you really need, not get help controlling some vast and unnecessary project bureaucracy.

A typical project management package allows you to:

- ✔ Create a hierarchical list of activities and their components.
- ✔ Define and store key information about your project, activities and resources.
- ✔ Define activity interdependencies (see Chapter 6 for more information on activity interdependencies).
- ✔ Develop schedules by considering activity durations, activity interdependencies, and resource requirements and availability.
- ✔ Display your plan for performing project activities in a network diagram (see Chapter 6).
- ✔ Display a schedule in Gantt Chart and table formats (see Chapter 6).
- ✔ Assign people to work on project activities for specific levels of effort at certain times.
- ✔ Schedule other resources for project activities at specified times.
- ✔ Determine your overall project budget (see Chapter 8 for how to prepare project budgets).
- ✔ Determine the effect of changes on the project's schedule and resources.
- ✔ Monitor activity start and end dates and milestone dates.
- ✔ Monitor person-hours and resource costs.
- ✔ Present planning and tracking information in a wide array of graphs and tables.

Project management packages offer benefits as well as drawbacks. The benefits include the following:

- ✔ **The package's functions are linked.** For example, if you enter staff availability in the form of personal calendars, the program uses them when developing the schedule and won't allow an activity for a team member to run in a week when she'll be on holiday.
- ✔ **Packages typically have a variety of predesigned report templates.** Having predesigned report templates allows you to use formats that are proven to be effective. It also saves you time and money when preparing and distributing your reports.

Integrated project management packages also have their drawbacks:

✓ **The package may not be immediately available.** If it isn't currently available, you have to devote time and money to buy and install the software before you can use it to support project planning and control.

✓ **Most people require training to become comfortable with the package.** Training takes additional time and sometimes money, particularly for the more sophisticated packages.

✓ **Having a wide range of capabilities in a software package doesn't guarantee that you'll use them correctly.** Remember the old adage: garbage in, garbage out. Even the most advanced software package can't help your project if people don't submit accurate and timely data.

If you decide to use a project management package, consider the following factors when choosing your program:

✓ **Types and formats of reports:** Choose a package that supports your reports and means of reporting with minimum customisation.

✓ **Your organisation's present software:** If several software packages are equal in most aspects, choose a package that's already available so you can share both expertise and files.

✓ **Your organisation's existing systems to record staff hours and expenses:** If your organisation has such systems, consider a package that can easily interface with them. If the organisation doesn't have these systems, consider a package that can store the information you need.

✓ **The project environment in your organisation:** What's the size of the human resource pool for projects, the number and typical size of projects and so on? Choose a package that has the necessary capacity and speed.

✓ **Software used by clients and companies you work with:** Choosing a package that allows you to communicate and coordinate easily with your customers' and collaborators' software saves you time and money.

Check out *Project 2010 For Dummies* by Nancy C. Muir (Wiley) for more information on effectively using this software's capability.

Before you rush out and buy any project management software, plan how to maximise its capabilities and avoid associated pitfalls. Do the following to help you select and install your software:

✓ Be sure you have a firm grasp of project planning and control approaches and techniques before you consider any software.

✔ See what software other groups in your organisation are using or have used; find out what they like, what they don't like and why.

✔ If possible, ask someone who already has a copy of the software whether you can spend a few minutes exploring its operation.

✔ After the package is on your computer, load a simple project or a small part of a larger project to practise with (that is, enter the activities, durations, interdependencies, resources and so on).

✔ Use only a few of the program's capabilities at first (determine the effect of small changes on your schedule, print out some simple reports, and so on); use more capabilities as you get more comfortable with the software and feel the need for the facilities.

✔ Consider attending a formal training course after you've become comfortable accessing the software's different capabilities.

After you've undertaken these steps, you can effectively use software to support your project planning and control activities. On an ongoing basis, ensure that you obtain all updates and changes to the software, and consider purchasing software upgrades that introduce significant new capabilities.

PROJECT SPEAK

# Programme management software: Raising the bar on project management

Most integrated project management software packages support the planning, tracking and reporting of an individual project. Programme management software, however, is special because it also:

✔ Supports the assigning and tracking of people to activities on more than one project

✔ Takes into account inter-project activity dependencies when determining different schedule possibilities

✔ Tracks and reports the progress and accomplishments of numerous projects simultaneously

✔ Supports communication throughout the organisation regarding the planning and performance of different projects

Consider using programme management software to support project planning and control when your organisation meets these criteria:

✔ It has several large, cross-departmental projects underway.

✔ Inter-project dependencies are common and significant.

✔ It staffs these projects from a common resource pool.

✔ It has well-established project management and data-collection practices and procedures.

### *Communications management software*

Communications problems are a primary cause of project failure, so the whole area of communications in your project justifies some very careful thought; Chapter 15 goes into the detail. Technology can help with communication but it can also hinder it, so you need to keep your brain in gear when considering communication.

Communications technology is particularly good when it adds something that can't easily be done otherwise, and this section covers five examples.

#### *Tweeting*

A relatively new technology is tweeting using the Twitter social networking service. Having first been associated with teenagers filling their many spare hours with idle chatter, its potential was quickly spotted by other and perhaps more serious users. Organisations such as political parties in the UK have been quick to see the value of keeping people in touch, but so have businesses to keep customers informed of the latest services and offers and to keep their names regularly in front of the customers.

In the context of a project, tweeting may be worth considering to keep information flowing to large teams who are spread out geographically, but also as a mechanism for keeping key stakeholders in touch with developments in a fast-moving project environment.

#### *Emailing*

Email is powerful, and would be more powerful still if it wasn't so widely misused. This book isn't about email, but it's worth setting down a few pointers in the context of projects.

- ✓ Email is fast. Sometimes people fire off an email without thinking too much. Be aware of the communication limitations of emails. Emotions are hard to convey and a poorly worded comment that is intended to be light hearted may be taken as a criticism or even insult. People do use 'emoticons' such as :-) to convey when they're attempting to be funny, but scope for misunderstanding and miscommunication still exists.

- ✓ In larger organisations, people tend to get a lot of email. Consequently, the fact that you've sent an email doesn't necessarily mean that all the recipients have read it, or at least not immediately.

- ✓ Following on from the last bullet point, keep email traffic down. Beware of putting people on distribution lists 'for information' when they really don't need to be included. Equally, ask for your name to be removed from distribution lists where you don't have an interest. This is all relevant to the communications planning for the project that we cover in Chapter 15. Overcommunication is often much more of a problem than under-communication.

✔ Email can be time consuming. It's not uncommon for someone to spend time composing an email on a minor matter and then send it . . . to the person sitting right next to her! She could have just turned to her colleague and used the older but often more reliable technology of speaking. Also, less disciplined team members can waste significant time by chit-chatting with emails in the same way that they do with friends when texting, rather than focusing on project work.

✔ Email can be seen as an informal communication. Be sure that if you receive or send an email that's important, you take care of it in the same way you would take care of an important letter. Set up some systematic way of storing project emails so that you know what's been said on a given subject and can find the emails again.

Take note that email *can't* be the exclusive means of communication to do any of the following tasks:

✔ **Brainstorm to analyse problems and develop new ideas:** Use email to announce the brainstorming session, invite people to attend, identify the topic(s) you'll explore and provide relevant background material for people to review before the session. Use email to share a summary of the results and future actions. But conduct the actual interchange of ideas in a face-to-face session.

✔ **Build and sustain team members' trust and commitment:** Even though you use email to inform team members of each other's background and experience, commitments and accomplishments, be sure you provide sufficient opportunities for face-to-face meetings so team members become familiar and comfortable with each other.

✔ **Share an important message:** Perhaps you can share the message initially through email, but follow up with phone calls and in-person meetings to emphasise its importance and ensure that your recipients have correctly understood its content.

### *Video conferencing*

Video conferencing has been around for a while of course, but changing technology has made it readily available and, importantly, cheap to the point of being free when you have a camera that is built in on many computers anyway. A major service provider is Skype, but there are others on offer including services from Apple and Microsoft.

Where you need a meeting, nothing beats face-to-face, but where that's difficult or expensive, then video calls are a great advantage over the phone, because it does make for better communication when you can see people and gauge their reactions in a discussion. With international projects in particular, the video conference is a powerful and economic addition to your communication options.

### *Working collaboratively with software*

Major players such as Microsoft increasingly allow for online collaborative working with their software. An example is with a shared 'whiteboard' where people can join in remotely to add to diagrams and comment, but collaborative environments often offer shared file storage as well.

Collaborative working like this comes second place to working around a whiteboard face to face. However, if getting everyone together isn't possible or is prohibitively expensive, then such electronic collaboration is much better than phone calls during which participants can't see diagrams and certainly can't directly draw onto the diagrams. Email is worse, with the inbuilt time delay. Using online collaborative environments also retains the 'shared experience' dynamic where ideas spark backwards and forwards more easily and where participants get more engaged than they would with some form of written response.

### *Setting up a website*

A useful technology in bigger organisations and projects is . . . the web. A website dedicated to the project can be extraordinarily effective both in making information available and keeping people in touch with the project.

Part of the advantage of setting up a website relates to the problem of email distribution lists. If you have a website for your project, then you can email your fellow Project Managers, once, to say that you have a site and if they want to know anything about your project then to go and look on the site. They'll be extremely grateful that you haven't merely added them to yet another email group to pump megabytes of text into their inboxes 'in case they want to know'. Hopefully, they'll be so impressed and appreciative that they'll follow suit and set up websites for their projects and stop sending you trayfuls of email 'in case you want to know'. You'll find more in Chapter 15 about the implications of using this technology to circulate project information.

A second way that a website can be really useful is to keep people in touch with, and interested in, your project. If you have a public interface or customers who are very interested in how things are going, then a website could be the answer. The Royal Shakespeare Company had such a site when rebuilding its theatres at Stratford upon Avon recently. The site not only explained why the rebuild was needed, but added interest with photo galleries showing the theatres at the various points in the project, and also invited contributions to help with the work. That's imaginative and effective communication.

In terms of project information held on the site, adding an RSS feed makes it even more useful. With RSS, as you're probably aware from your own use of the web, people who are subscribed get notified automatically when something has changed, and don't need to keep checking the site themselves.

# *Having Your Head in the Clouds*

Cloud computing is now with us, and its use is expanding very rapidly. A *cloud* is where you have data and even software stored centrally by an Internet service and you access that data over the Internet. Cloud computing is exciting for projects because it makes access to data so much easier (working at home as well as in the office) and because it brings with it functionality such as computer synchronisation.

If you store your project data in a cloud, then everyone to whom you give the necessary authority can access it over the Internet, wherever they are in the world and at any time of the day or night. If you update a file and upload it, then immediately everyone has access to that new version.

Many cloud services incorporate synchronisation of data. Each computer has a copy of the cloud on its local disk and from time to time will check that the local copy is an exact copy of the folders and files on the cloud. If the local computer has a more recent file (because the user has updated or created something) it will be sent up to the cloud, and if the cloud has a more recent copy or something new, it will be downloaded to that local computer.

The speed at which computers are synchronised varies with the service you are using. Some only synchronise at intervals, so there can be a gap before the new file goes up to the cloud and another gap before other computers check the cloud and download any changes. That delay is currently true of Apple's MobileMe. Other services are almost instantaneous, such as Dropbox.

This section of Project Management For Dummies is hard to write because even before this UK edition gets onto the shelves, things will inevitably have changed. However, in an attempt to be helpful, here are three simple guidelines on cloud computing:

- ✔ **Back up:** Commercial cloud storage is reliable, but don't rely on it. Don't keep a backup copy of your files either; keep several (!) and in different places too. Just two sorts of computer hard disk exist: those that are going to fail and those that have already failed.

- ✔ **Be careful with synchronisation:** Synchronisation is great, but it has a drawback. If some junior team member deletes a file on her local copy of the cloud, that deletion instruction will get transmitted up to the cloud and then onto everyone else's computers, and the file will be wiped out everywhere. The more sophisticated suppliers of cloud services have an archive from which you can retrieve deleted stuff as much as six months afterwards. That archive service is valuable, provided you realise within six months that something has been accidentally deleted.

✔ **Watch security:** Cloud storage is not 100 per cent secure, even if you have got good access controls. That lack of security can simply be because a rookie team member has written her complicated 'secure' password on a sticky note and stuck it on the wall above her desk. But even if the access and the cloud storage itself is safe, the transmission of data to and from that storage generally isn't. Storing information such as project plans is probably going to be fine. But you probably shouldn't put important commercial information on your company's finances that's embedded in the project Business Case on cloud storage.

# Getting Really Good Stuff for Free

No, it's true, you can. The days are long gone when the free software on the front of a computer magazine turned out to be some barely functional amateur offering that took more time to use than it saved and then crashed anyway. Powerful, reliable and highly functional services and software are available for free on both PC and Mac platforms. On the software side, you have *freeware*, but more significantly you can download *open source* software, which is the fruit of collaboration on a huge scale worldwide.

A search on the Internet can help you find such software and services. New stuff is emerging all the time, but this section gives you a starting place and also provides a few hints on what to look out for:

✔ **Activity planning:** Lots of free tools are highly functional for activity networks, Gantt Charts and resource planning (see Chapter 6). They're the equivalent of Microsoft Project. You find them for both PC and Mac platforms, and a sophisticated example for the PC is Open Workbench.

✔ **Cloud storage:** Internet service providers often give some online cloud storage (see the previous section) for free. Other commercial services are paid for but can be free in two respects. First, you can sometimes get a fairly generous trial period for free, and that period may actually be enough for your project. Apple's MobileMe service currently offers six months use for free. Second, some services like Dropbox give a basic amount of storage for free, but you then pay if you want more. That last option might not sound so good until you see just how generous the free allowance is; it's quite substantial when you are storing things like documents rather than large libraries of music and photographs. Having said that, even if you do want more space, the extra storage is usually reasonably priced and available in increments.

✔ **Mind Mapping:** Many free packages are impressively functional. These are great if you like Mind Maps and want to use them for things like product planning and risk analysis.

✔ **Office packages:** Many cheap office packages offer word processor, spreadsheet and graphics programs, but you also have the choice of some free ones. The most widely recognised is Open Office, which is available on both PC and Mac platforms. Open Office has the advantage that it is very powerful and it reads in and out of Microsoft Office formats.

### Watching out for file formats

When looking at the free software, check out the file formats and the import and export features. You need to ensure that you can communicate with other people. It's no good working late into the night at home on an update to your project plan if you can't then load the file into the software back at the office.

### Obeying security restrictions

In all cases when you're shifting data about, do make sure you take on board any security restrictions in your organisation. It takes the shine off delivering a really successful project if you then get fired for security violations. In this context, security includes virus-checking procedures. Don't think either that viruses don't matter if you're in the happy world of Macs because, of course, nasty things can find their way into macro-enabled documents as well as programs and operating systems.

# Supporting Virtual Teams with Communication Technology

The globalisation of today's businesses creates a greater need for people around the world to work together on projects. This lack of proximity creates unique challenges when encouraging successful team performance. Imaginative use of technology can support the communication needs of these virtual teams. But we're not just talking about globalisation. On the smaller end of the project scale, you may face similar issues if your organisational policy is for people to work mostly at home with only a small central office and those dreaded 'hot desks' – see Chapter 7.

A *virtual project team* is a group of people who work together across geographic, time and organisational boundaries to accomplish a common set of goals and objectives. Although the needs of a virtual project team are the same as those of more conventional teams, many processes and resources used by conventional teams aren't available to the virtual team. Only through creative use of the communication technology available can virtual teams perform at peak capacity.

High-performance team members on both virtual and conventional teams must successfully accomplish the following tasks:

- ✔ Share project and team-related information in a timely and accurate manner.
- ✔ Create and sustain trusting and productive interpersonal relationships.
- ✔ Effectively collaborate to perform project work.

Each of these tasks requires effective and timely communication. But, as virtual teams approach these activities, they face these unique challenges:

- ✔ **Members may never meet each other in person.** Becoming familiar with and trusting each other is more difficult; the use of nonverbal signals and body language when communicating is severely limited.
- ✔ **Members may have different primary languages.** This challenge increases the chances that people may incorrectly interpret a message.
- ✔ **Members may come from different organisational and cultural environments.** People's work styles and communication practices may differ.
- ✔ **Members may be in different time zones.** People may not be available to interact with each other during certain periods.

Today's communication technology can help you and your virtual team address these challenges (see Table 18-1 for specific ways that today's technology can support communications on a virtual team).

| Table 18-1 | Using Communication Technology to Support Virtual Teams | |
|---|---|---|
| *Communication Need* | *Approach* | *Application* |
| Share project-related information | Email, Twitter | Sharing factual information; confirming and recording discussions and agreements |
| | Cloud, collaboration services, website, RSS feed on web | Storing plans; entering, storing and reporting on progress data; storing project management forms and procedures |
| | Video conferencing | Discussing and clarifying issues |

| Communication Need | Approach | Application |
|---|---|---|
| Support interpersonal relationships | Video conferencing, website | Introducing new team members; acknowledging team and individual accomplishments |
| Collaborate on project activities | Video conferencing | Discussing technical topics; brainstorming |
| | Software collaboration | Dynamically sharing a 'whiteboard' or drafting a document |
| | Email | Sharing data and reports |
| Inform and heighten interest | Web, RSS feed | Sharing information but also creating interest with imaginative content |
| | Twitter | Instant updates on progress, decisions and points of interest, maintaining the immediacy of the project |

Available communication technology can address a wide range of the virtual team's routine communication needs. When possible, however, people should meet in person to periodically reinforce their relationships and the team's focus and identity.

# Saving Time With Software

Using computers can make life much easier for the Project Manager, such as by enabling her to quickly find previous versions of plans by nipping into an archive directory on a computer rather than going through a mass of papers thrown in the bottom drawer of the filing cabinet. It can also make for great time savings:

- ✔ **Easy retrieval:** For other project staff, not just the Project Manager, to get at documents quickly, but also to be able to retrieve an older version if you're updating something and now realise you've done it wrongly and want to start over. Which, in passing, means that you should routinely save the different versions of project documents; it takes seconds and could save hours.

- ✔ **Fast transmission:** A report sent as an email attachment rather than through the mail – internal mail, national or international.

✔ **Fast update:** Such as putting new estimates based on recent information into an activity network then recalculating the critical path (see Chapter 6) before printing off a new version of the plan.

✔ **Re-use:** Storing project documentation such as plans that might be adapted for future similar projects, so saving time and helping ensure completeness.

✔ **Template documents**: A stock of basic templates for things like budgets and reports that save having to start from scratch for each project.

# Chapter 19

# Monitoring Project Performance with Earned Value Management

Suppose you are a senior manager responsible for a particular Project Manager. On the current project, the plan shows that your Project Manager should have spent £110,000 by the end of Week 6. Today it's the end of Week 6 and you receive the regular report on the state of the project. You look at the section on project financials and see that the Project Manager has spent *exactly* £110,000. You're a bit surprised that the figure is correct to the penny, so you crosscheck the project code on the report screen of the organisational finance system. The finance system confirms that the project spending to date is on the button at £110,000.00. Are you pleased with the Project Manager? Will you recommend him for promotion to extremely senior Project Manager? Everyone knows, after all, that money and budget control is everything in organisations.

Well, you might not be so pleased if you then look further down the status report and see that of the work due to be completed by the end of Week 6, less than half has been done. Your Project Manager has spent the money for you okay; he's good at spending money. What he hasn't done is the scheduled work, and what has been achieved actually cost more than twice as much as projected.

What's important in projects isn't just money but delivery. If you've already read Chapter 5, you'll know that a very powerful planning technique is based on products; in other words, what's being produced or delivered. Building on that, this chapter covers a technique that works well with product planning and it's called *Earned Value Management* (EVM), formerly called *Earned Value Analysis* (EVA). EVM is a technique that helps determine your project's schedule status and cost status. It identifies what you have spent, but it also identifies the value you have *earned* in the project in terms of completed work. *EVM* is particularly useful for identifying potential problems on larger projects, but you can use it on smaller ones too as an effective project monitoring tool.

Monitoring your project's performance involves determining whether you're on, ahead of, or behind schedule and on, under, or over budget. But just comparing your actual expenditures with your budget can't tell you whether you're on, under or over budget – and that's where EVM comes in.

# Understanding EVM Terms and Formulas

EVM has some complicated-looking formulas, but they're quite simple when you look at the principle underneath them. In fact, before we set out the detail of the formulas, you can already work out what's going on. Have a look at the following figures and then the project example and see whether you can determine what's happening in the project.

Here are the figures you need to work out:

- Planned cost of the work to be done (PV – planned value)
- The value of the work done to date at the original price estimates (EV – earned value)
- The actual cost of doing the work, which may be the same as the planned cost, or the work may have cost more or it may have cost less than expected (AC – actual cost)

## Looking at a project example (1)

For a project, you get a report that gives you the three figures. Can you see what's going on?

Planned cost of the work to this point in time = £5,000

Earned value of the work done to this point = £6,000

Actual cost of the work done to this point = £6,000

So, the plan showed that £5,000 worth of work would be done by now, but actually, at the original planned prices, £6,000 worth of work has been done. To do that work actually cost £6,000 too. So, the project is ahead of schedule but bang on budget because things are costing exactly what you thought they would.

## Looking at a project example (2)

Try another. This example tells a different story so see whether you can work out what's happening:

Planned cost of the work to this point in time = $5,000

Earned value of the work done to this point = $5,000

Actual cost of the work done to this point = $6,000

In this second example, the plan showed $5,000 worth of work being done by now. The earned value, based on original prices, shows that $5,000 has been done. So the project is on schedule. What should have been delivered by now has been delivered. However, the actual cost of doing that work was $6,000, so the work has cost $1,000 more than expected. Things may be okay in terms of the schedule, but the project is overspending.

## Looking at a project example (3)

Are you following the formulas? Okay, go for a third then:

Planned cost of the work to this point in time = $5,000

Earned value of the work done to this point = $7,000

Actual cost of the work done to this point = $6,000

By this point, the project was scheduled to do work that would cost $5,000. In fact, the project has delivered $7,000 worth of work at the original prices, so it's significantly ahead on time and more has been delivered than planned for this point. However, although $7,000 worth of work has been done, it's only cost $6,000 to do it. So the project is ahead of schedule at the moment, and is coming in under budget. Looking good then – the figures must have come from one of your projects.

EVM then associates delivery with cost. It isn't simply a matter of what has been spent, but rather whether the scheduled work has been done and how much it has actually cost to do it. When you're used to EVM, it's quick to see what is happening on the project, which makes this an excellent technique to use in progress reporting.

## Getting the three key figures

Here are the names for the three key figures that the preceding sections help you calculate. You may come across some slightly different terms for the three figures, including those mentioned in the following bullets, but if you do, don't get thrown by it, because it's just different terminology.

✓ **Planned value (PV):** The approved budget for the work scheduled to be completed by a specified date, also referred to as the *budgeted cost of work scheduled* (BCWS). The total PV of a task is equal to the task's *budget at completion* (BAC) – the total amount budgeted for the task.

✓ **Earned value (EV):** The approved budget for the work actually completed by the specified date, also referred to as the *budgeted cost of work performed* (BCWP).

✓ **Actual cost (AC):** The costs actually incurred for the work completed by the specified date, also referred to as the *actual cost of work performed* (ACWP).

Figure 19-1 illustrates the three figures on a graph.

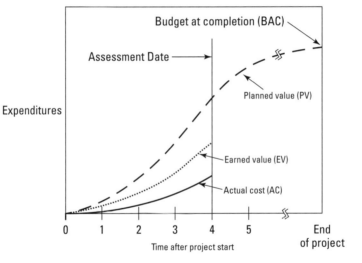

**Figure 19-1:**
Monitoring
planned
value,
earned
value and
actual cost.

To describe your project's schedule and cost performance with EVM, you can move on to use the following indicators that come from comparing the three main figures:

✓ **Cost variance (CV):** The difference between the amount budgeted and the amount actually spent for the work performed. The CV shows whether and by how much you're under or over your approved budget.

✓ **Schedule variance (SV):** The difference between the amounts budgeted for the work you actually did and for the work you planned to do. The SV shows whether and by how much your work is ahead of or behind your approved schedule.

✓ **Spend variance (SV):** The difference between the amount budgeted to have been spent by this point in the project and the amount actually spent at this point in the project.

Given that there are three key figures and then three comparisons between them, you could be forgiven for thinking that this suggests a triangular model. Sure enough, you can show the figures that way, and having described such a picture it's only fair to provide it, so have a look at Figure 19-2.

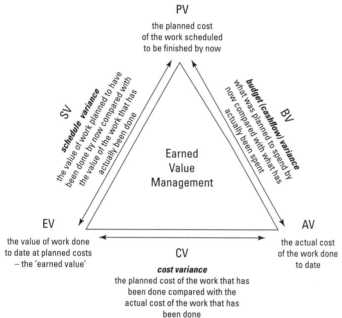

**PV**
the planned cost
of the work scheduled
to be finished by now

**SV**
*schedule variance*
the value of work planned to have
been done by now compared with
the value of the work that has
actually been done

**BV**
*budget (cashflow) variance*
what was planned to spend by
now compared with what has
actually been spent

Earned
Value
Management

**EV**
the value of work done
to date at planned costs
– the 'earned value'

**AV**
the actual cost
of the work done
to date

**CV**
*cost variance*
the planned cost of the work that has
been done compared with the
actual cost of the work that has
been done

**Figure 19-2:**
EVM key
figures and
variances.

The variances are helpful to know what is going on, but also to give you a nudge to take project management action:

- ✔ **SV:** Is the work ahead of schedule, behind or on target?

- ✔ **CV:** Are things costing what was anticipated in the plan, or are they more or less expensive than predicted? Significant variance justifies some investigation with a view to altering the project budget up or down, or even reviewing project scope.

- ✔ **BV:** Is project spending happening when expected or has more or less been spent than predicted in the plan for this point? Significant variance in either direction may trigger a communication with organisational finance staff to review what is being spent in each financial year. It could be that things are costing exactly what was expected, but because the project is ahead of schedule you now forecast that some money that was due to be spent in the next financial year will now be spent in the current financial year.

# Working with EVM Ratios

Having got the six basic figures clear using the previous section, you can move on and get even more clever with the use of a couple of ratios to show how things are going. This can be really useful for forward projection 'what if' calculations. So, based on the information so far, what if the rest of the project behaves the same way?

There are two key ratios:

- **Schedule performance index (SPI):** The ratio of the budget for the work performed to the budget for the work planned. The SPI reflects the relative amount the project is ahead of or behind schedule, sometimes referred to as the project's *schedule efficiency*. You can use the SPI to date to project the schedule performance for the remainder of the task or even the project. So, if for the first few weeks of the project, the figures show that you are consistently doing work 10 per cent faster than planned, it's worth considering whether this is localised or will affect all the work still to be done and the whole project will end up delivering early.

- **Cost performance index (CPI):** The ratio of the approved budget for work performed to what you actually spent for the work. The CPI reflects the relative value of work done compared with the amount paid for it, sometimes referred to as the project's *cost efficiency*. You can use the CPI to date to project the cost performance for the remainder of the task. So, if everything so far has cost 5 per cent more than expected, it might be correct to say that the whole project will end up 5 per cent overspent. In turn, that might call for some re-planning or even de-scoping to bring the cost back down or just merely to warn the finance director that the project is likely to end up overspent by this amount.

If it does happen that your project is slightly overspending or overrunning, don't panic. There are often good reasons for that, such as the work is turning out to be more complicated than anyone expected. Projects are usually going into the unknown to some extent, so they rarely finish bang on target.

However, early warning of variance draws your attention to the problem so you can investigate. Are the teams performing at a level lower than you expected, for example, and that's why everything is taking longer than planned? Investigation may reveal that your part-time team members are coming under pressure from functional managers (see Chapter 11) to do more departmental work in order to meet annual targets, and so their work time on your project is getting both eroded and fragmented. Perhaps you should ask your Project Director to have a word with the functional managers and get the resource put back or, if the resource level can't be restored, to set change control going (see Chapter 14) to adjust the project for a new deadline in balance with the team resource actually available.

# Defining the Formulas of EVM Performance Descriptors

Having got the underlying principles of the EVM approach clear, the underlying formulas should make sense. Schedule and cost variances and performance indicators are defined mathematically as follows:

Schedule variance (SV) = Earned value (EV) – Planned value (PV)
Cost variance (CV) = Earned value (EV) – Actual cost (AC)
Budget variance (BV) = Actual cost (AC) – Planned value (PV)
Schedule performance index (SPI) = Earned value (EV) ÷ Planned value (PV)
Cost performance index (CPI) = Earned value (EV) ÷ Actual cost (AC)

Table 19-1 illustrates that a positive variance indicates something desirable (that is, you're either under budget or ahead of schedule) and a negative variance indicates something undesirable (you're either over budget or behind schedule).

**Table 19-1      Interpretations of Cost and Schedule Variances**

| Variance | Negative | Zero | Positive |
|---|---|---|---|
| Schedule | Behind schedule | On schedule | Ahead of schedule |
| Cost | Over budget | On budget | Under budget |
| Budget | Spend is less than expected for this point in time | Spend is in line with the expected cash flow | Spending greater than expected for this point in time |

Positive or negative cost or schedule variances indicate that your project performance isn't going exactly as you planned. After you determine that a variance exists, you need to figure out what's causing it so you can take corrective actions where necessary.

Possible reasons for positive or negative cost variances include the following:

✔ Your project requires more or less work to complete a task than you originally planned.

✔ Work outside the approved scope was performed.

✔ The people performing the work are more or less productive than planned.

✔ The actual unit costs of labour or materials are more or less than planned.

✔ Resources used on other projects were incorrectly charged to your project, or resources from your project were incorrectly charged to other projects.

✔ Actual organisation indirect costs are higher or lower than you originally planned. (See Chapter 8 for a discussion of indirect costs and how they can affect your project expenditures.)

Possible reasons for positive or negative schedule variances include the following:

✔ Work is running ahead of or behind schedule.

✔ The project requires more or less work than you originally planned.

✔ People performing the work are more or less productive than planned.

# Deciding What to Measure for EVM

When using the EVM technique, you have some choices on how to apply it. Earned Value is traditionally applied to project activities, and that's not least because most project management approaches are based on activity planning. However, after you've mastered product-based planning (explained in Chapter 5), you'll see that this fits well with EVM because you can use the products – deliverables – as budget blocks for planning and delivery. If that sounds high level, don't forget that if your project is anything more than small, you're going to break products down into more detail in stage or phase planning, and potentially to more detail still if team-level plans are needed. Indeed, part of the judgement on what level of planning you'll go to is based on control needs, and if EVM is one of your chosen controls then in turn that will have an influence on the plan.

It follows that you can apply EVM to particular parts of the work but then also to the project as a whole. If your project is fairly complex, you may consider using EVM to help monitor performance, although there's nothing wrong with trying it out first on a smaller project to get the feel of it. By providing cost and schedule performance assessments of both the total project and its major parts, EVM allows you to identify the likely problem areas so you can take the most effective corrective actions.

If you're basing EVM on progress with activities rather than on delivery of products, the key to a meaningful analysis lies in the accuracy of your estimates of earned value. To determine earned value, you must estimate:

✔ How much of a task you've completed to date

✔ How much of the task's total budget you planned to spend for the amount of work you've performed

If you assume that the amount of a task's total budget that should be spent to complete a portion of the task is directly proportional to the amount of the task completed, you should spend 60 per cent of the total task budget to complete 60 per cent of the task.

For tasks with modular components, like printing brochures or conducting telephone surveys, determining how much of a task you've completed is straightforward. However, if your task entails an integrated work or thought process with no easily divisible parts (such as designing a brochure), the best you can do is make an educated guess. That's a problem with progress monitoring (more on that in Chapter 14) but it transfers to EVM when you're looking to make the progress measures the basis for your EVM calculation.

To estimate the earned value in your project, you can use one of the following three approaches:

✔ **Per-cent-complete method:** Earned value is the product of the fraction representing the amount of an activity that has been completed and the total budget for the activity.

This method is potentially the most accurate if you correctly determine the fraction of the activity you have completed. However, because that estimate depends on your subjective judgement, this approach is also the most vulnerable to errors or misleading information such as project staff overstating what they have achieved.

✔ **Milestone method:** Earned value is 0 until you complete the activity, and it's 100 per cent of the total activity budget after you complete it.

The milestone method is the most conservative and the least accurate. You expect to spend some money while you're working on the task. However, this method doesn't allow you to declare earned value greater than £0 until you've completed the entire activity. Therefore, you'll always appear over budget while you perform the activity.

Valid as the last warning is, you can offset this by using key delivery points as major progress checkpoints, thereby taking into account that measures along the way aren't going to present perfect 'snapshot' data. In accepting this, you're no worse off than the inaccuracy in per cent complete, and you do have a steady stream of places (particularly if you're working with product delivery) where you can be very confident indeed on the figures.

✔ **50/50 method:** Earned value is 0 before you start the activity, 50 per cent of the total activity budget after you start it, and 100 per cent of the activity budget after you finish the activity.

The 50/50 method arguably gives a closer approximation to reality than the milestone method, because you can declare an earned value greater than £0 while you perform the task. However, this approximation can inadvertently mask overspending.

# Part VI
# The Part of Tens

'And what happens to the project leader
if the project goes wrong?'

## In this part . . .

Having hundreds of pages of detailed information to guide you through your project's ups and downs is nice. However, for some areas it's good to have a few handy tips in a concise form.

Just like every *For Dummies* book, this part gives you tidbits of interesting information that you can access as needed. There are ten tips for how to plan a project, ten for writing a convincing Business Case and then ten tips for how to be a better Project Manager.

# Chapter 20

# Ten Questions to Ask Yourself as You Plan Your Project

*In This Chapter*

▶ Clarifying your project's objective

▶ Describing deliverables, schedules and resources

▶ Addressing the uncertainties

*W*hen you begin a project, enthusiasm or organisational deadlines, or both, can make you want to jump in and start working on the detail immediately. However, you know you have the greatest chance of a successful outcome, including delivering the right thing, if you plan out your project before you start the actual work. Answer the ten questions in this chapter to be sure you've completely identified all the work your project will require.

## What Are the Objectives of Your Project?

A common cause of project problems to the point of failure is unclear objectives. It's easy enough for people to have very different ideas but use the same words so assume that everyone else agrees with them. You not only need to establish clear objectives, but also to get them agreed by the key players. You can do so by determining the following:

✔ Exactly what is the project being asked to deliver?

✔ What is the primary purpose of the project? Perhaps to speed up delivery to customers, comply with legal requirements, save money. The project can have more than one objective, of course, but the objectives should be compatible.

✔ Who'll benefit from the project?

✔ What would happen if the project wasn't run?

# Who Do You Need to Involve?

Knowing early on who you need to involve allows you to include the right people in your initial objective setting as well as plan for their participation at the appropriate stages in your project. Involving these people in a timely manner ensures that their input will be available when it's needed and lets them know you value and respect their contributions. Think about:

- **Budget holders:** People who hold the purse strings and can dictate the form of the project, and those who may not have budgetary control but have the organisational position or personal influence to block things.
- **Providers:** Those providing any staff resource that you need. For example, do you need IT staff input, which may be difficult if the IT department is mostly committed for the next two years!
- **Stakeholders:** People who have an interest in your project's results. You may need to resolve conflicting objectives.
- **Supporters:** People who can help your project succeed.

You can find more in Chapter 4 on identifying and managing project stakeholders.

# What Results Will You Produce?

Be clear on what the project is delivering in total, then in more detail as you get into project planning. Make sure that the key players agree the key deliverables or products. You may even produce a few Product Definitions when sketching out the project, because often people get a much clearer view of what the project is about when they understand what it will deliver.

Here are some tips:

- Think through what products you'll need to generate.
- Define those products carefully, involving others where necessary.
- Determine the sequence in which products need to be produced and the dependencies between them.

See Chapter 5 for much more discussion on project products.

# What Constraints Must You Satisfy?

Identify all information, processes and guidelines that may restrict your project activities and your performance. When you know your constraints, you can plan effectively to work within them if, for example, they are technical or time constraints, and to minimise their effects on your project if they relate to something like financial or staffing availability.

Identify whether any constraints can be challenged. For example, with a technical constraint, you may be able to challenge an instruction to use a certain type of machine if a new machine becomes available that's better and cheaper.

# What Assumptions Are You Making?

As soon as you begin thinking about your project, document all conscious assumptions you make about it, and think very hard so you can minimise the unconscious ones. After all, each of those assumptions can lead to one or more project risks that you may choose to plan for in advance. Continue adding to your list of assumptions as you develop the different parts of your Project Plan. Update your plans whenever an assumption changes or you find out its actual value. See Chapter 10 for a lot more on project risk.

# What Work Has to Be Done?

Identify all the activities required to produce your project's products so that you can assign responsibilities for them, develop schedules, estimate resource needs, give specific tasks to team members and monitor your project's performance. For each activity, specify the following:

- ✔ **The work to be done:** The processes and steps that each activity entails
- ✔ **Inputs:** All people, facilities, equipment, supplies, raw materials, funds and information necessary to perform each activity
- ✔ **Durations:** The number of work periods required to perform each activity

See Chapter 6 for information on activity planning.

# When Does Each Activity Start and End?

Develop a detailed schedule with clearly defined activities and frequent intermediate milestones – the products are perfect as milestones. Take the following into account when you create your schedule:

- ✔ **Duration:** The number of work periods required to perform each individual activity
- ✔ **External dependencies:** Such as on other projects

✔ **Interdependencies:** What you must finish before you can begin your activity

✔ **Resource availability:** When you need particular resources and when they're available (see the next section as well)

Chapter 6 contains more information on how to develop a project schedule.

# Who Will Perform the Project Work?

Knowing who will perform each task and how much effort they'll have to devote allows you to plan for their availability and more accurately estimate the overall project budget. Think about:

✔ The skills and knowledge needed to build each product

✔ The actual people needed on each activity and any specific roles they may have, such as team leaders and specialists

✔ The amount of time needed by each person

✔ The exact time when people will do their work if they will work less than full time on an activity

Consult with the people who'll perform the project tasks to develop this information. See Chapter 7 for help with estimating staffing requirements.

# What Other Resources Do You Need?

Identify all equipment, facilities, services, supplies and funds that you need to perform your project work. Specify how much of each resource you need and when. Chapter 8 has more on how to identify physical resources.

# What Can Go Wrong?

Don't be taken off guard. Identify risks and develop sensible plans to minimise their negative effects. See Chapter 10 for information on how to address project risks, and remember that some risk actions may be very simple, quick and cheap, but can work to prevent your project coming under unnecessary pressure.

Lisa Faulkner, winner of the TV cookery award *Celebrity MasterChef 2010*, said, just before the final, 'My food has to be fault-free today. It has to look good and taste good. And there are little things that could go wrong but I've got backup plans so that if they do go wrong I can turn them around into things that have gone right.' Good project advice!

# Chapter 21

# Ten Tips for Writing a Convincing Business Case

*A* project needs to be justified, not just done for the sake of it. You often need to set down that justification in the form of a Business Case, which, as the name suggests, explains the case for the project from a business perspective. It's easy to go off track in a Business Case so that managers in the organisation who have the authority to approve the project simply aren't convinced and so don't give the go-ahead. This chapter sets out ten tips to help you get the Business Case right first time.

## Starting with a Bang

Your project will normally have a number of benefits, and it can really help to start with the best one – start with a bang. That grabs the attention and gets people on side quickly. Don't exaggerate this benefit, but do let it have its full impact in the way that you write it. For example: 'This project will save £1 million in reduced wastage in the first three years of operation.' Notice that the £1 million figure is rather more impressive than saying £333,000 a year. If you think that sounds a bit like a sales pitch, you're right – don't shy away from that. You need to 'sell' the project idea in order to get the green light.

On the other hand, this is a business document, so although you should sell the idea, the Business Case should contain solid, evidenced business information and not be frothy sales talk.

If you're using a format in which the benefits aren't the first thing in the Business Case but something like a summary or a management overview is, use the opening of that to make the bang with the biggest benefit.

# Spelling out the Benefits Clearly

Spell out the benefits of the project in clear terms that those reading the document can relate to. You can find it all too easy to be convinced of the project yourself within the project perspective, where it all makes perfect sense, but fail to see things as people outside the project see them.

If your project is of any size beyond small, then with benefits you need to be particularly aware of the senior management perspective and, specifically, the financial management perspective. To a finance director and a managing director, a great deal of difference exists between a direct saving, a quantifiable benefit and a non-quantifiable benefit. Direct savings make directors sit up quickly and take notice, so be sure to point these out.

If you aren't sure of the difference between quantifiable and non-quantifiable benefits, have a look at Chapter 3 for an explanation.

# Pointing Out the Non-quantifiables

You should explain non-quantifiable benefits especially carefully and back up claims of these benefits and your estimates of their significance. Non-quantifiables can be extremely important in business terms, but as hinted in the previous section, senior managers tend to focus on the money; often they are less interested in the non-quantifiables. Where non-quantifiables are important, be sure to explain why.

# Being Prudent

Don't overstate or exaggerate benefits. Remember the financial principle of being prudent and erring on the safe side. If you make huge claims for the project that it can't deliver, it (and you) will be seen as a failure when those benefits don't materialise. If you slightly understate the benefits, you have a margin for error, but also if you slightly exceed them then your project (and you) will be seen as a big success.

Once again, you need to strike a balance with this. If you massively understate the benefits, then when your project delivers considerably more you'll be seen in a bad light for not having set down an accurate Business Case and not understanding the nature and impact of your project.

# Considering Three-point Estimating

Sometimes you just can't be sure of the benefits levels, or you're in difficulty because some enthusiastic manager has already told everyone that the project won't cost much, will take almost no time at all, and will deliver mind-boggling benefits. To deal with either scenario, you can set down three projections of each benefit: best case (the one the enthusiastic manager has been advancing), worst case and then the most likely case.

# Making Sure Benefits Aren't Features

Here's another dimension of thinking from the business or organisational viewpoint rather than the project one. If you have a technical interest in the project (you're a 'techie') you may be rather too focused on those technical interests rather than the business advantages. Having a 2-nanosecond transmission time through the outer core of the flange assembly may be incredible and the latest groundbreaking technology, but it's a technical feature not a business benefit. In all cases, think 'how does this benefit the business?'

It could well be that the technology represents substantial business benefit, but you must go further in your thinking and spell that benefit out. If the faster speed means that production costs will be reduced, then that becomes a business benefit and one which can be quantified and, later, measured and proved.

# Avoiding Benefits Contamination

Inspirandum coined the phrase *benefits contamination* to describe projects that claim benefits that are really due to something else outside the project.

Financial managers usually have a keen eye for benefits, and if they spot such contamination then it undermines your credibility and, along with it, the credibility of the whole Business Case. An organisational problem also exists. If you're claiming benefits that won't actually be delivered by the project, it could lead to the project being approved when actually that's not the right decision.

Take care to isolate benefits so that you can prove that they'll be from the project. Then those reading the Business Case can see that you've thought through the benefits carefully and that those benefits are real.

# Making Sure You Can Deliver Benefits

When setting down the benefits, make quite sure that they can be delivered. If you're showing savings from the sale of a building, are you absolutely sure that someone wants to buy it? If not, then there is no harm putting in the saving, but it should be qualified by stating your assumption that the building will be sold within a reasonable time. In turn, it would be helpful to back up the point with some stats on the average time taken to sell a building of that type in that locality at the moment.

# Supplying Evidence or Referencing It

Where you're claiming business benefits, you should back those claims up with evidence. However, if the evidence already exists, then you don't need to repeat it all in the Business Case; instead, you can reference it. So you can say, for example:

> As stated by Go-4-It Consultants in their market research report presented to directors last June, the new packaging options that will be delivered by this project are likely to boost sales by 5 per cent, which represents an annual profit increase of £XXX.

# Using Appendices

Don't hesitate to use appendices in the Business Case; you don't need to shove everything into the main body of the document. You may want to make use of appendices for two reasons:

- **Where you have an organisational standard:** If your organisation has a standard format for a submission to a finance committee, for example, the information on that format is probably a subset of what you need for a project Business Case. In that case, put the extra project-only information in appendices and don't submit them when you put the application to the finance committee.

- **Keeping the Business Case simple**: If the Business Case is to be seen by senior managers in particular, it helps enormously to keep it short and simple. The earlier section 'Making Sure You Can Deliver Benefits' made the point that if you claim a benefit, then there should be evidence that the level is realistic. However, it can make for a long read if you include the evidence in the main body. Instead, you can put the evidence into an appendix that readers can dip into if they want to. They'll thank you for that, and having happy managers doesn't do any harm at all to your prospects for getting the go-ahead.

# Chapter 22

# Ten Tips for Being a Better Project Manager

Successful project management depends not only on what you do, but also on how you do it. Your attitudes and behaviours towards people affect how they respond to you. Perhaps this whole chapter should have a large *Tip* icon on it because it offers ten tips that can help you successfully win people's support.

## Being a 'Why' Person

Look for the reasons behind requests and actions. Understanding *why* helps you make sure you respond appropriately to team members, senior managers and all other project stakeholders (which, in turn, increases people's motivation and buy-in). Always look for the reasons behind other people's requests and actions. People rarely do or think something without reason, and even if they're wrong, you need to understand where they're coming from.

## Being a 'Can Do' Person

Look at all problems as challenges, and do everything you can to find ways to overcome them. Be creative, flexible and tenacious. Keep working at the problem until you solve it. Pull in other people where you need to in order to crack the problem; that's teamwork. The UK military frequently uses the phrase 'we, not me', and that works for projects too.

# Thinking about the Big Picture

Keep events in perspective. Understand where you want to go and how your plan will get you there. Recognise and consciously think about the effect your actions have on current and future efforts, and don't become so focused on the fine detail that you miss something bigger that's right in your face.

Be specially careful if you're doing some of the work of the project as well as managing it, because then it's even easier to miss the big stuff because you're spending a lot of time focused on fine technicalities.

# Thinking in Detail

Be thorough. If you don't think through your project's issues, who will? The more clearly you describe your intended results, the more easily people can recognise the benefits associated with your project. And the more clearly you define your intended work, the more often people will ask important and insightful questions – *and* believe that they can perform the work successfully. Clarity leads to increased personal motivation and reduced chances of mistakes.

# Assuming Cautiously

Take the time to find out the facts; use assumptions only as a last resort. Where you've made assumptions, such as in planning, write them down so other people can see that a course of action is based on an assumption. With every assumption comes a risk that you're wrong. The fewer assumptions you make, the more confidence you can have in your plan. (Check out Chapter 10 for the detail on how to deal with risks and uncertainty.)

Keep in mind the old saying: 'Try not to *assume*, it can make an *ass* out of *u* and *me*.'

# Viewing People as Allies Not Adversaries

Focus on common goals not individual agendas. Making people feel comfortable encourages brainstorming, creative thinking and the willingness to try new ideas – all of which are essential to managing a successful project. But viewing and treating people as adversaries can put them on the defensive and even encourage them to become enemies.

Your positive approach must also include suppliers. Remember, suppliers working on your project are part of your project and so are part of the team. If they fail, you fail, so do all you can to keep them on side and to help them.

# Saying What You Mean, and Meaning What You Say

Communicate clearly. Be specific by letting people know exactly what you mean. Tell them what you want them to know, what you want them to do and what you'll do for them. You may think that being vague gives you more leeway but, in reality, being vague just increases the chances for misunderstandings and mistakes. Be absolutely honest, and when you say something, stick to it so people learn to trust you.

# Respecting Other People

Focus on people's strengths rather than their weaknesses. In each person on your team, find a quality that you can respect. People work harder and enjoy their work more when they're around others who appreciate them and their efforts. (See Chapter 13 for more helpful tidbits on respecting and encouraging other people.)

# Acknowledging Good Performance

Take time and trouble to acknowledge good performance. When someone does something good, tell the person, tell the person's boss, tell other team members and tell the person's peers that you appreciate the effort and its results. Recognising good performance confirms to a person the accuracy and value of her work. On the one hand, acknowledgement is a great motivator, but on the other hand, if someone's done something good, then they deserve recognition. When acknowledging a person's performance, be specific and timely – tell the person exactly what she did or produced that you appreciate, and do it promptly. (See Chapter 13 for more about acknowledging good performance.)

# Being a Manager and a Leader

Attend to people as well as to information, processes and systems. Create and share your vision and excitement with your team members, but don't forget to share a sense of order and efficiency too. Encourage people to strive for outstanding results, and do all you can to help them achieve those results. (See Chapter 13 for more information about management and leadership.)

# Index

• *U* •

• *V* •

• *W* •

# FOR DUMMIES®

## Making Everything Easier!™

# UK editions

## BUSINESS

Marketing Kit FOR DUMMIES
978-0-470-74490-1

Business Plans Kit FOR DUMMIES
978-0-470-74381-2

Consulting FOR DUMMIES
978-0-470-71382-2

## REFERENCE

British Politics FOR DUMMIES
978-0-470-68637-9

Football FOR DUMMIES
978-0-470-68837-3

Researching Your Family History Online FOR DUMMIES
978-0-470-74535-9

## HOBBIES

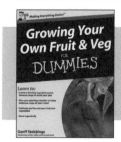

Growing Your Own Fruit & Veg FOR DUMMIES
978-0-470-69960-7

Allotment Gardening FOR DUMMIES
978-0-470-68641-6

Electronics FOR DUMMIES
978-0-470-68178-7

Anger Management For Dummies
978-0-470-68216-6

Boosting Self-Esteem For Dummies
978-0-470-74193-1

British Sign Language For Dummies
978-0-470-69477-0

Business NLP For Dummies
978-0-470-69757-3

Cricket For Dummies
978-0-470-03454-5

CVs For Dummies, 2nd Edition
978-0-470-74491-8

Divorce For Dummies, 2nd Edition
978-0-470-74128-3

Emotional Freedom Technique For Dummies
978-0-470-75876-2

Emotional Healing For Dummies
978-0-470-74764-3

English Grammar For Dummies
978-0-470-05752-0

Flirting For Dummies
978-0-470-74259-4

IBS For Dummies
978-0-470-51737-6

Improving Your Relationship For Dummies
978-0-470-68472-6

Lean Six Sigma For Dummies
978-0-470-75626-3

Life Coaching For Dummies, 2nd Edition
978-0-470-66554-1

# FOR DUMMIES®

## A world of resources to help you grow

## UK editions

### SELF-HELP

Cognitive Behavioural Therapy For Dummies
978-0-470-66541-1

Neuro-linguistic Programming For Dummies
Kate Burton
Romilla Ready
978-0-470-66543-5

Mindfulness For Dummies
Shamash Alidina
978-0-470-66086-7

Origami Kit For Dummies
978-0-470-75857-1

Overcoming Depression For Dummies
978-0-470-69430-5

Positive Psychology For Dummies
978-0-470-72136-0

PRINCE2 For Dummies, 2009 Edition
978-0-470-71025-8

Psychometric Tests For Dummies
978-0-470-75366-8

Raising Happy Children For Dummies
978-0-470-05978-4

Reading the Financial Pages For Dummies
978-0-470-71432-4

Sage 50 Accounts For Dummies
978-0-470-71558-1

Self-Hypnosis For Dummies
978-0-470-66073-7

Starting a Business For Dummies, 2nd Edition
978-0-470-51806-9

Study Skills For Dummies
978-0-470-74047-7

Teaching English as a Foreign Language For Dummies
978-0-470-74576-2

Teaching Skills For Dummies
978-0-470-74084-2

Time Management For Dummies
978-0-470-77765-7

Work-Life Balance For Dummies
978-0-470-71380-8

### STUDENTS

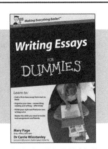

Philosophy For Dummies
Martin Cohen
978-0-470-68820-5

Student Cookbook For Dummies
Oliver Harrison
978-0-470-74711-7

Writing Essays For Dummies
Mary Page
Dr Carrie Winstanley
978-0-470-74290-7

### HISTORY

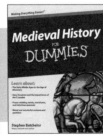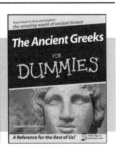

British History For Dummies
Dr Seán Lang
978-0-470-99468-9

Medieval History For Dummies
Stephen Batchelor
978-0-470-74783-4

The Ancient Greeks For Dummies
Stephen Batchelor
978-0-470-98787-2

**Available wherever books are sold. For more information or to order direct go to www.wiley.com or call +44 (0) 1243 843291**

FOR DUMMIES®

**The easy way to get more done and have more fun**

## LANGUAGES

978-0-470-68815-1
UK Edition

978-0-7645-5193-2

978-0-471-77270-5

## MUSIC

978-0-470-48133-2

978-0-470-66603-6
Lay-flat, UK Edition

978-0-470-66372-1
UK Edition

## SCIENCE & MATHS

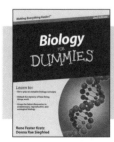

978-0-470-59875-7

978-0-470-55964-2

978-0-470-55174-5

Art For Dummies
978-0-7645-5104-8

Bass Guitar For Dummies, 2nd Edition
978-0-470-53961-3

Christianity For Dummies
978-0-7645-4482-8

Criminology For Dummies
978-0-470-39696-4

Forensics For Dummies
978-0-7645-5580-0

German For Dummies
978-0-7645-5195-6

Hobby Farming For Dummies
978-0-470-28172-7

Index Investing For Dummies
978-0-470-29406-2

Knitting For Dummies, 2nd Edition
978-0-470-28747-7

Music Theory For Dummies
978-0-7645-7838-0

Piano For Dummies, 2nd Edition
978-0-470-49644-2

Physics For Dummies
978-0-7645-5433-9

Schizophrenia For Dummies
978-0-470-25927-6

Sex For Dummies, 3rd Edition
978-0-470-04523-7

Sherlock Holmes For Dummies
978-0-470-48444-9

Solar Power Your Home
For Dummies, 2nd Edition
978-0-470-59678-4

The Koran For Dummies
978-0-7645-5581-7

Wine All-in-One For Dummies
978-0-470-47626-0

Yoga For Dummies, 2nd Edition
978-0-470-50202-0

# FOR DUMMIES®

## Helping you expand your horizons and achieve your potential

## COMPUTER BASICS

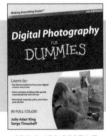

978-0-470-57829-2

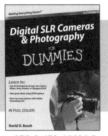

978-0-470-46542-4

978-0-470-49743-2

## DIGITAL PHOTOGRAPHY

978-0-470-25074-7

978-0-470-46606-3

978-0-470-59591-6

## MICROSOFT OFFICE 2010

978-0-470-48998-7

978-0-470-58302-9

978-0-470-48953-6

Access 2007 For Dummies
978-0-470-04612-8

Adobe Creative Suite 5 Design
Premium All-in-One For Dummies
978-0-470-60746-6

AutoCAD 2011 For Dummies
978-0-470-59539-8

C++ For Dummies, 6th Edition
978-0-470-31726-6

Computers For Seniors For Dummies,
2nd Edition
978-0-470-53483-0

Dreamweaver CS5 For Dummies
978-0-470-61076-3

Excel 2007 All-In-One Desk Reference
For Dummies
978-0-470-03738-6

Green IT For Dummies
978-0-470-38688-0

Macs For Dummies, 10th Edition
978-0-470-27817-8

Mac OS X Snow Leopard For Dummies
978-0-470-43543-4

Networking All-in-One Desk Reference
For Dummies, 3rd Edition
978-0-470-17915-4

Photoshop CS5 For Dummies
978-0-470-61078-7

Photoshop Elements 8 For Dummies
978-0-470-52967-6

Search Engine Optimization
For Dummies, 3rd Edition
978-0-470-26270-2

The Internet For Dummies,
12th Edition
978-0-470-56095-2

Visual Studio 2008 All-In-One Desk
Reference For Dummies
978-0-470-19108-8

Web Analytics For Dummies
978-0-470-09824-0